A Good Idea of Hell

Joseph G. Dawson III, *General Editor*

A Good Idea of HELL

Letters from a Chasseur à Pied

JOSHUA BROWN

Editor

Foreword by
LEONARD V. SMITH

Texas A&M University Press
College Station

Library of Congress Cataloging-in-Publication Data

Pellissier, Robert E. (Robert Edouard), 1882-1916.

A good idea of hell : letters from a chasseur à pied / Joshua Brown,
editor ; foreword by Leonard V. Smith.—1st. ed.

p. cm.—(Texas A&M University military history series ; 83)

Includes index.

ISBN 1-58544-210-0

1. Pellissier, Robert E. (Robert Edouard), 1882–1916—
Correspondence. 2. World War, 1914–1918—Personal narratives,
French. 3. France. Armée—Non commissioned officers—
Correspondence. 4. World War, 1914–1918—Campaigns—Western
Front—Personal narratives. I. Brown, Joshua, 1956– .
II. Title. III. Series.

D640.P384A3 2003

940.4'144'092—dc21

[B]   2002013492

CONTENTS

CONTENTS

MAPS AND ILLUSTRATIONS

Robert Pellissier in uniform of
the *chasseurs à pied*, September, 1914
frontispiece

FOREWORD

Letters, War Writing, and Robert Pellissier

LEONARD V. SMITH

Frederick B. Artz Professor of History, Oberlin College

If collections of letters have never been the most common or most celebrated form of published writings from the Great War, neither have they been exceptionally rare. In Jean Norton Cru's massive study of French combatants' testimonies published as *Témoins* (1929), he identified twenty-eight of some three hundred texts as collections of letters.[1] Norton Cru, like Robert Pellissier, was a native Protestant Frenchman who made his academic career as a professor of French in the United States, only to return to France to join the French Army in 1914. Like Pellissier, Norton Cru had the greatest respect for the written word, though in the case of the latter this led to a restricted view of the usefulness of published texts to historians. Norton Cru noted the specific conditions through which collections of letters found their way into print: "We must note that all these published letters are those of combatants killed in the war. Contrary to nearly all other war books, these collections do not depend on their authors for the preparation of the text for publication (the choice of letters, deletions, corrections of the text, annotation, etc.)."[2] Most often, families or friends undertake the publication of letters from the deceased, in part to memorialize the man killed and in part simply to bring a form of closure inherently lacking in the texts themselves. In the case of Robert Pellissier, Joshua Brown has followed this practice at a remove of three generations, for Pellissier was the brother of Brown's great-grandmother, Emélie Pellissier Alden, and his great-great-aunt, Adeline Pellissier. Adeline Pellissier printed the letters privately in the 1920s, presumably for circulation within the family. Brown has now made these letters available to a wider audience.

By definition, letters are written for a private rather than a public audience. They speak to another world, remote and specific, that readers today can only struggle to imagine—not just the terrible world of life and death in the trenches of the Great War but the particular, personal world of the Pellissier family. Why publish these letters now, so many years after the fact? The simple answer lies in their exceptional character. Pellissier himself provides us with a panorama of insights about the war—from the tiniest details of daily life to reflections on war aims and the meaning of the conflict in its broadest sense. He makes possible a unique kind of interrogation of French national identity, by musing on just what led a native Frenchman who had lived in the United States since his adolescence to return to France in its darkest hour and in the end to die for the country of his birth. The materials added by the Pellissier family in the original edition are almost as important as the letters themselves. His letters and the texts that frame them raise some of the trickiest, but also the most fascinating, issues of war writing, what Norton Cru called *témoignage*, meaning "witnessing" or "testimony."[3]

Published collections of letters follow a form, more or less invariably. The survivors who bring the letters into the public domain provide some kind of explanation that justifies their publication. In the case of the letters of Sgt. Henri Robert of the 123rd Infantry Regiment, the survivors sought to preserve the life of the deceased, at least in print. As Raoul Allier put it, "It seemed, to those to whom he was so dear, that his actions in this world should not cease at the moment when a stupid bullet put an end to his earthly existence."[4] The family of Ferdinand Belmont (of the 11th Bataillion de Chasseurs Alpins), which lost three of four sons in the war, sought to comfort other grieving families. Henry Bordeaux explained: "Because there have been so many other homes in France in this situation, these letters have been published."[5] Henri Volatier served in Pellissier's 5e Bataillion de Chasseurs à Pied at about the same time.[6] In the case of the letters of Volatier to his fiancée, a priest became the virtual coauthor of the published text, with a running commentary accompanying excerpts of the letters. G. Mouterde, S.J., made himself virtually a chaperone, carefully managing published relations between the couple in print, even after the death of Volatier. Mouterde encouraged a village priest who had been a spiritual counselor to the couple to collect the letters, toward a publication that would inspire Catholic patriotism. The village priest wrote to Mouterde: "You want to say to me that 'Henri Volatier no longer belongs only to you.' It is true that he

[Volatier] had been my friend for a long time, for fifteen years. Let us say then that he was aware of belonging to the Church and to France."[7]

The letters of Pellissier, of course, present a far less extreme case of coauthorship than those of his comrade.[8] It would appear that Adeline Pellissier undertook the original private publication. But she provided no introduction, though none necessarily would have been needed to justify publication, if the original audience was limited to friends and family. Yet Adeline Pellissier did supply the crucial documents that bring closure to the story— letters from the army chaplain that explain just how Robert Pellissier died, tributes from former colleagues, and an appeal from Stanford University for contributions to support an ambulance in France to be named in his honor. The proper introduction to the volume comes to us from today, from Pellissier's descendant Joshua Brown. At stake in part is a chapter in the story of the family and a description of the long-term traces of that family's mourning for Pellissier across generations. As Brown explains, Robert remained a revered, curiously alive figure in the family long after his death. Robert had become, in Brown's words, "an icon for all that was good and wise" in the eyes of his relatives. Robert's very name was pronounced in French rather than in English. The durability of his memory led Brown to undertake the republication of his letters, and this time publicly rather than privately.

There are many unusual aspects of the story of Robert Pellissier, and the ways Pellissier addresses them help explain why his letters belong in the public domain. One of the most unusual aspects is that he became a French soldier of the Great War at all. For Robert Pellissier was under no legal obligation whatsoever to join the French Army in August, 1914. Indeed, as someone who had moved to the United States at the age of fourteen, he had never done military service in France, the time-honored and protracted rite of initiation into French citizenship. Professionally, Pellissier had nothing to gain from returning to France and much to lose. He had finished his Ph.D. at Harvard University in 1913 and already had a promising position as assistant professor of French at Stanford University. Yet something about France and its great drama that began in August, 1914, touched Pellissier to the very core of his being. Among other things, the close connection in France between citizenship and military service made citizenship there a conspicuously male enterprise, more so than in the United States or Britain. Pellissier responded to the call of the outbreak of war in precisely the same, gendered terms as millions of his countrymen, none more so than those who, like Pellissier, were educated men of the middle class. As he wrote on August 25, 1914: "I see no way out which does not mean the giving up of the prerogatives and privileges which go with the name man synonymous with gentleman."

Pellissier's experience once at the front likewise disrupts in fascinating and important ways our predominant conceptions of fighting the Great War. Readers today are used to thinking of the "Western Front" in terms of the agricultural plains of Flanders, Picardy, and the Artois. In contrast, Pellissier served most of his war in the mountainous Vosges, in a tiny bit of Alsace reconquered from the Germans in the otherwise calamitous French offensive of 1914.[9] The French had planned to retake the "lost territories" of the Franco-Prussian War of 1870–71 by invading in rough terrain with very little support from artillery, with results that ought to have been foreseeable. The area in which Pellissier served, therefore, constituted a minute sliver of silver lining in a very dark cloud. His sector was as politically important as it was militarily problematic. Given the terrain and the poor results attained by the French in August, 1914, the Vosges was one of the least likely sectors for a major offensive. Yet this did not mean it lacked activity, quite the contrary. French and Germans battled each other across a wide spectrum of violent activity, from more or less ritualistic shelling to limited, tactical offensives, such as the attack at Steinbach in which Pellissier took part in December, 1914. Even "trench warfare," meaning what transpired in the trenches between pitched battles, had its unique character in the Vosges. Paradoxically, the Vosges was much colder in the winter than the northern part of the Western Front, and soldiers had to battle snow and ice, as well as mud, when the temperature rose. Supplies often had to be brought in by donkeys and mules. Serving in the Vosges meant fighting trench warfare in its most grinding and indecisive manner. It bears pointing out that Pellissier took part in only one "over the top," across relatively flat No Man's Land, in the Somme in August, 1916. And he fought there for only one day before his death. Pellissier's perspective of the war was formed from a particular kind of trench warfare rather than from pitched battle.

Pellissier's letters are truly exceptional in the level of detail they provide and in the range of subjects they cover. Everything interested him, to the great benefit of readers who want to know more about life and death in the Great War. We learn from him, for example, how cursory "training" was even after the near-disaster for the French of the first battles of the war. In his letter of October 28, 1914, he complained:

> Yesterday we played again that we were taking trenches. They always make us end by a bayonet charge for about fifty or a hundred yards. We

run all we can and yell like savages, but if they order the charge too soon
we get winded before we get to the trench.

One might have thought that the French would have known better, in the after-
math of the bloodiest month of the entire war. Clearly, serving in the trenches
itself would have to provide Pellissier's real training for the war.

There are any number of tiny, revealing details, such as a note left by a
German suggesting a tacit truce (undated, late January or early February, 1915)
and a horrifying story of a women from Thann whose house was fired upon
by the Germans. She found the head of one of her children in the garden
(April, 1916). Yet as with all good accounts of war, Pellissier includes lighter
but still illuminating moments. In early August, 1916, just a few weeks before
his death, he told a story of how men from his unit fed cats who crossed over
from the German lines. Most simply returned thereafter from whence they
came. According to Pellissier, they doubtless provided valuable intelligence
information to the Germans on their French hosts. "I have thought, since," he
concluded, "that we should have put them in irons right away." To disclose
many more such details here would be to deprive readers of the pleasure of
happening upon them in the text itself. His complete commitment to the French
war effort notwithstanding, Pellissier continued to feel his connection to the
United States. Indeed, he felt that the Old World had much to learn from the
New, as he wrote to his niece at Christmas, 1914: "One thing is certain—
Americans have fine traits which Europeans will get from them in the course
of time. A freedom from certain harmful traditions, your judgments are less
warped than those of Europeans when it comes to right and wrong in politics
particularly, it seems to me." But in most of the letters, he refers to the United
States as "your" country, rather than "ours." His letters were all written before
the entry of the United States into the war in April, 1917, across a time of considerable domestic controversy as to what role if any the United States should
play in Europe's Great War. Readers get an excellent sense of the fluidity of
the situation in the United States from Pellissier's letters. He clearly resents
pro-German propaganda, as well as support for Germany among millions of
German Americans. He remarks in jest in September, 1915, that "perhaps I will
be sent with reinforcements from France to take Milwaukee." But in most of
Pellissier's letters, he is glad that the United States has remained neutral and
seems to want the affairs of Europe to be resolved by Europeans themselves.
Yet his ambivalence between his two countries is never completely resolved.
He wrote before his return to the front in May, 1915, that "I will be fighting for

my two countries at once, even if your government manages to keep the lid on the part of the United States that is not pure Dutch."

Referring to the Germans as the "Dutch" (an anglicized version of *Deutsch*, the German word for "German") likewise suggests an unusually nuanced view of the enemy. The most common French term was *Boche*, clearly a racial epithet, much more so than the British *Jerry* or *Fritz* or even the German *Franzmann*. Pellissier certainly shows little patience for conservative French nationalism, whether in his comments on the writings of Maurice Barrés or on the somewhat bizarre assertion of French composer Camille Saint-Saëns that Richard Wagner had no musical talent. (In fact, Saint-Saëns's music owed a great deal to that of Wagner.) Pellissier clearly admired French émigré intellectual Romain Rolland, though he always stopped short of Rolland's rejection of the war in *Au-dessus de la Mêlée* (Above the Fray, 1915). The Germans, Pellissier thought, were from the beginning their own worst enemy. By committing atrocities in Belgium and especially burning the library at Louvain in 1914, he believed they had forever defeated themselves in the court of world opinion.[10] For himself, Pellissier came to consider the Germans both as the enemy and as human beings much like himself. They were, we are to conclude, good people behaving badly, as he wrote on March 6, 1916:

> If on a fine night when crossing the campus on my way back from Palo Alto, I should encounter a hold-up man, thrusting his revolver at me, I should do my best to smash his face, but once the deed was accomplished, I should be perfectly willing to have him taken at my expense to the Peninsular Hospital. It is the kind of feeling I have when fighting the Boches.

Throughout his letters, Pellissier emerges as a three-dimensional figure, with weaknesses as well as strengths. Like us all, he had his prejudices. A confirmed Protestant, he clearly considered himself spiritually superior to his Catholic compatriots. In April, 1915, he proudly rejected the "medals and other holy trinkets reminiscent of the Middle Ages." He did accept a medal of Joan of Arc (whom he mistakenly believed at that time to be a saint) because he considered her recent enough in sainthood to be theologically harmless. Just over three weeks before his death, on August 6, 1916, he expressed relief in overtly racist terms that the conflict between Mexico and the United States had concluded without war: "You can gain no glory fighting Greasers." Pellissier also had a healthy sense of self-preservation. He noted with refreshing frankness that he did not rush toward martyrdom in the trenches or toward suffering for its own sake. As early as June 23, 1915, Pellissier expressed his desire to leave the trenches, ideally to become a liaison officer with the British. He admitted on July 15, 1915, that "I don't see myself spending again any number of months staring at a loophole in the mud wall of a trench." In January, 1916, he expressed a whimsical desire to help defend the Suez Canal, not by that time under any real threat. By that point in the war, who could blame him?

Upon his death on August 28, 1916, the construction began of a new Robert Pellissier—the near-perfect, metaphysical hero who died in the name of a just cause. Pellissier himself initiated this process in his last letter, to Monsieur D—— and dated August 27. Short and moving, the letter is almost identical in form and content to countless other last letters written by French soldiers who died in the Great War.[11] Pellissier makes a sober assessment of his chances of survival: "It is perfectly possible that I may come out unscathed, but it is also possible that I will not." But in the critical next sentence Pellissier indicates how he wished to be remembered: "If I should not come back, you would tell him [his brother John] that to the last my thoughts were with him and with our family in America and also that I do not regret the choice I made in returning to France." In these few, emotional words, Pellissier connects the private and the public, his devotion to his family as well as to the country of his birth. He wants his survivors to make the same connection and so to confer meaning on his death.

The documents appended to the letters complete the construction of Pellissier after his death. Three letters, it would seem all from the same Protestant army chaplain, explain just how he died and so provide a literal conclusion to his story—a form of closure by definition lacking in Pellissier's letters. He died, we are told, heroically and selflessly. While there is no reason whatsoever to doubt the veracity of the claims made in these documents, they are likewise completely formulaic in the information they provide and how they praise the deceased. His battalion was being relieved, and Pellissier had been designated as the last man to depart, so as to assure the smooth transition between the units. While doing so, he was shot in the chest by a machine-gun bullet and died later that day. "During the recent encounters," wrote the Protestant chaplain, "he had shown that he had the qualities of a leader, and an absolute contempt of danger." His comrades "admired his intellect and his uprightness. He was a complete man." Less typically, Pellissier was awarded posthumously two very high honors, the Medaille Militaire and the Croix de Guerre avec Palme. The citation praised him as a "noncommissioned officer of remarkable bravery and fearlessness."

The obituaries appearing in the *Williston Bulletin*, the publication of the school where Pellissier had taught before Stanford, complete the construction of the larger-than-life figure who inhabited the youth of Joshua Brown. Adeline Pellissier, sister of Robert, wrote a detailed summary of his life. Herself an articulate academic, a professor of French at Smith College, Adeline Pellissier wrote the story almost of an apotheosis. "When I think of my brother's life," she wrote, "the picture which rises before me is that of a young horseman coming at full speed over hill and dale. He is neither dismayed nor halted by any obstacles; he clears them lightly and with a joyous shout. And at the end of his course, he meets death on the battlefield, bravely fighting for France." She praises his triumph over adversity, his difficult move to the United States after the death of his father, and his learning of English from scratch. She praises his combination of religious devotion and religious tolerance, his fine literary and artistic taste, his love of the land of his birth, and his impeccable moral character. A tribute from a former colleague from Williston speaks to Pellissier's academic talent: "His ambition was to excel. His standards for himself and for his pupils were high. He was a zealous worker for the first-best and exacted high grade work from his pupils." The deceased Pellissier, we are to infer, continues to do so, even now that his earthly life is finished.

In addition to creating a nearly flawless, metaphysical Pellissier who could continue to inspire the living, his survivors sought to create a practical trace of his presence by sponsoring an ambulance for the American Field Ambulance Service. According to a notice in the Stanford alumni magazine, the sum to be raised was considerable—sixteen hundred dollars. Yet the friends of Pellissier and of Stanford met the goal, an indication perhaps not just of admiration for Pellissier personally but also of the affirmation of support in the United States for the Allies in the months preceding the declaration of war in April, 1917. Indeed, we are told that funds were raised for a second ambulance in honor of Pellissier by Bridgewater Normal School in Massachusetts. In these ways, people who admired Pellissier sought to perpetuate his existence, in one way radically spiritual, in another radically material.

Jean Norton Cru had highly ambivalent views on the value of published collections of soldiers' letters. While he praised the immediacy of and lack of literary artifice in letters, he remained deeply suspicious of what amounted to the role of coauthorship on the part of the people who brought the letters into print: "This operation is performed by parents or friends, that is by non-combatants, who are ill-prepared to judge the value of the texts or the legitimacy of the opinions expressed in them. They are led to choose the most dignified extracts to appear in the collection, and are too inclined to omit that which does not conform with the heroic ideals of those who lived behind the lines."[12] We will never know whether Adeline Pellissier excised anything from this collection, though the wealth of opinions and diversity of details present in the letters suggest that this is unlikely. But whatever her degree of editorial intervention, I would disagree with Norton Cru's notion that the intervention of the living was ipso facto a "distortion" that undermines the value of the texts. For the letters and the admiring texts that surround them testify to different aspects of the life and death of the deceased. They tell us not just how the dead man lived his life but also how his survivors faced his death. Consequently, the letters, the documents provided by the survivors, and Brown's encounter with these texts so many years after they were written all have their own value as testimony of the vast human calamity that was the Great War.

ACKNOWLEDGMENTS

Special thanks are due to the following: John Keegan and Leonard Smith for their encouragement and advice; the staff at Texas A&M University Press for their assistance in putting the book in final form; Christine Larsen and all of the reference staff at Lilly Library, Earlham College, Richmond, Indiana, for their patience in locating materials for me; the reference staff at Morrisson-Reeves Public Library in Richmond, Indiana; Richard Teller, archivist at Williston Northampton School, Northampton, Massachusetts, who helped with many references to Williston in the letters; Patricia White, archives specialist at Stanford University Libraries, Stanford, California, who helped locate the names of several faculty members mentioned in the letters; the archives at Bridgewater State College, Bridgewater, Massachusetts, which provided class lists and names of faculty members; Ken Hoffman at Hampshire College, who helped with place names in the Berkshire hills of western Massachusetts; Omer Hadziselimovic at Indiana University East, who helped with many details about the Balkan front; Brian Sullivan, assistant reference archivist at Harvard University, Cambridge, Massachusetts, who located several faculty names; Wilma R. Straight, archivist at Wellesley College, who helped with faculty names; the reference staff at Dartmouth College, who helped locate material for several footnotes; Bob Ring, who helped with maps and detailed information on the Somme battlefield; Carol Sickman-Garner, for her meticulous proofreading and many helpful suggestions; and my wife, Joyce, who originally suggested this project and without whose constant encouragement I might never have finished it.

INTRODUCTION

JOSHUA BROWN

Robert Pellissier was born in France in 1882 and came to the United States as a boy of fourteen to live with his sister Emélie Pellissier Alden, who was my great-grandmother. He studied first at Bridgewater Normal School, then at Harvard, and then taught for several years at Williston Academy in Northampton, Massachusetts. After completing his Ph.D. at Harvard, he taught at Stanford from 1911 to 1914 as assistant professor of romance languages.

When World War I broke out, he returned to France and volunteered as an enlisted man in the elite *chasseurs à pied,* the troops who occupied the Vosges mountains of Alsace. He wrote letters to his family in Brooklyn; to his fiancée in Auburn, Massachusetts; and to friends and colleagues all across the United States.

Robert Pellissier's letters are factual, filled with comments on European and American politics, notes about wartime prices and social conditions, observations on the French character, and the ribald opinions of his fellow soldiers. The letters are interspersed with selections from his diary, which give his own unglossed, private version of events, in contrast to the more cheerful letters he sent home to his young nieces in Brooklyn.

Like many of his contemporaries, Robert Pellissier was shocked by the invasion of Belgium and by the destruction of Belgian and French cities by Germany in the opening days of the war. Volunteering, for him, was a moral imperative—not just a defense of French soil but a defense of European civilization. Along with most of the world, he hoped that the fighting would be over in a few weeks. He soon realized, however, that the conflict would turn into a bloody stalemate. He hated the senseless slaughter and the calculated cruelties of the new style of mechanized war. At the same time, he refused to give in to the propaganda caricatures of the Germans, and he distinguished clearly between German militarism and the mainstream of German culture.

In October, 1914, Robert Pellissier was stationed in the Vosges mountains of Alsace, overlooking the Rhine river valley. This area had been captured by the Germans during the Franco-Prussian War of 1870, and for over forty years the Germans had done their best to transform the local culture from French to German. The recapture of Alsace was a prime objective of French strategy before the war began.

The French tried to seize Alsace by pouring troops over the top of the Vosges and by invading up the valley from their base at Belfort toward Mulhausen. Although the Mulhausen campaign was a disaster, the Germans were unable to dislodge the French from the heights and the mountain passes. Holding onto the Vosges became a matter of national honor, as it was the only place where France was on the offensive.

Robert Pellissier was wounded in the shoulder in January, 1915, and was evacuated to a military hospital, where he stayed until May. His wound healed but left him unable to carry the heavy pack of a soldier, and so he applied for officer training. He spent the summer studying and entered the military academy at St.-Maixent in August, 1915. He was not commissioned as an officer—probably because of his age—but was made a sergeant at the end of the course and returned to the Vosges in January, 1916.

He was just in time for a battle, as the Germans tried to recapture the Hartmannweilerskopf, a mountain overlooking the Rhine valley. Although not as well-known today as major battles like Verdun and the Somme, the battle for the Hartmannweilerskopf was front-page news at the time. The constant bombardment made it impossible for the French troops to be relieved, and he stayed on the mountaintop for fifty-three days.

After a brief furlough in June, Robert Pellissier was moved slightly north, to the Munster/Colmar region of Alsace, where he spent five weeks. He was then transferred north again as part of the massive build-up of troops for the battle of the Somme, which began on July 1, 1916, with the attack of fifteen British and five French divisions against Germans who were dug into excellent defensive positions.

Robert Pellissier's unit was sent in on August 28, long after the battle had bogged down. The Somme lasted until November 13, 1916. By the time it ended, the British had suffered 400,000 dead and wounded; the French 200,000; and the Germans 450,000. This battle was surpassed only by Verdun, where 1,200,000 men on both sides were killed or wounded.

The original edition of the letters published by Robert Pellissier's sister Adeline was probably only a hundred copies or so—just enough for family and friends. Only a handful are still in existence. Most of the letters are long since lost; Adeline Pellissier presumably returned them to the original addressees or took them with her to Switzerland when she retired in the 1920s. I worked from my own copy of the original edition, now very battered and worn. I was also fortunate enough to find a few of the letters that he wrote to my grandmother, which she saved in a special box for more than fifty years after the war.

Many people have asked me why I undertook this project and why it has become so important to me. The short answer is simply that it is fascinating to rediscover the world that Robert Pellissier lived in. He was completely a man of his time—familiar with its events and its literature, analytical about its failings, dryly humorous about its incongruities. The world of 1914–18 was not just huge battles—it was the life that went on near the front, the events back home, the hopes and fears of daily living.

One kind of history writing eliminates details and uses broad brush strokes to sum up events. Another kind of history—the kind in this book—treasures details as a way of understanding the larger picture. In this second kind of history, the task is to learn about an era by studying people who are unknown and forgotten. Robert Pellissier's is the voice of an individual caught up in the biggest war the world had seen up to that time.

This book has also been an intensely personal project for me. When I was a little boy, I heard my grandmother and my great-aunt speak about "Uncle Robert" with reverence—his name always pronounced in the French way, *Roh-behr*, not the English or American *Rah-bert*. His pictures were in family albums. He was an icon for all that was good and wise and noble in their eyes. Some of their feelings might have been adolescent hero worship—though my grandmother was twenty-four when Robert Pellissier went to war—but there was still a hard core of fact that I never really grasped when I was a boy. I wanted to find out why he meant so much to my family, and this book is the answer.

A third reason—and one that is very relevant today—has to do with the nature of war and the way we respond to it. I grew up in the shadow of the wars of the twentieth century—World Wars I and II, Korea, Vietnam, the Cold War, and the endless regional struggles in different parts of the world. When I was a teenager, my father took me on a tour of the battlefield of

Verdun in France. Sixty years after the guns had fallen silent, Verdun still looked like the surface of the moon, with huge holes and craters blasted out of the earth, echoing and dripping fortresses, and unexploded ammunition in every field. We stood in the cemetery, and the line of grave markers reached out to the horizon. The enormous memorial building held the bones of over one hundred thousand unidentified soldiers. My father said very little about what we saw at Verdun—he didn't have to. The silence and scale of Verdun brought home the horror of war.

Robert Pellissier was not a pacifist, and he volunteered for the French Army, but he hated the insanity of war. His letters are a voice of reason in the midst of pointless orders and senseless, unending violence. He heaped scorn on the politicians and businessmen who jockeyed for power and profit during the war. He despised propaganda, and in his letters he tried to distinguish clearly and calmly among war hysteria, rumors, and hard fact. In his letters, he hoped for a world where nations would work together to prevent wars like the one he fought in.

In this new edition, I have divided the letters into chapters corresponding to the different periods of Robert Pelissier's service life. I have also added family photographs, a facsimile of one of the original letters, and a key to help identify many of the individuals to whom the letters were addressed. Maps have been added to orient the different events. At the back, there are appendices that include contemporary tributes from his sister and from colleagues and a chronology of events mentioned in the letters.

I have tried very carefully to keep Robert Pellissier's original spelling and punctuation throughout. Adeline Pellissier included a very few footnotes in the original edition, which assumes a good deal of fluency in French, a familiarity with the events and personalities of the day, and a wide-ranging acquaintance with French and classical literature. I have translated any words or phrases not in English inside square brackets [ ]. I have also tried to identify names and events and track down quotations, references, and allusions to authors when I could find them. This information appears in the notes at the end of the text.

It has been a moving, humbling, and enlightening experience to prepare *A Good Idea of Hell: Letters from a Chasseur à Pied* for today's readers. I hope that you will enjoy them as much as I have.

ABBREVIATIONS

Robert Pellisier corresponded with at least sixteen individuals in this collection of letters—possibly more. In the original edition, all of the proper names of the addressees were deleted and replaced by initials. All of the addressees were still living at the time and might have preferred to protect their privacy or their grief. I have deduced as many of the names as possible for today's readers, using family sources, class lists, news articles, and college catalogs.

B———	Beatrice Tower, his fianceé, probably living in Auburndale, Massachusetts. She never married and was still living when my parents were married in 1948; she sent them a wedding present.
A———	Adeline Pellissier, his sister, living in Northampton, Massachusetts; professor of French at Smith College
M———	Marie Alden Brown, my grandmother, Robert Pellissier's niece, living in Brooklyn, New York
L——— or L.A.	Louise Alden Kingman, my great-aunt, Robert Pellissier's niece, living in Brooklyn, New York
M———	Marguerite Alden Walker ("Peggy"), my great-aunt, Robert Pellissier's niece, living in Orange, Virginia

Edmund (also E.K.A.)	Edmund K. Alden, husband of Emélie Pellissier Alden, brother-in-law of Robert Pellissier, and my great-grandfather
Dr. J——	probably Professor Oliver Martin Johnson, a colleague at Stanford University; professor of Romanic languages from 1897 to 1932; head of the department from 1914 until his retirement in 1932
Allen B——	Allen Boyden, son of the principal at Bridgewater Normal School in Bridgewater, Massachusetts, which Robert Pellissier attended
Monsieur D—	Monsieur Dulac, family friend, living at Besançon
John	John Pellissier, Robert Pellissier's older brother, an officer in the engineer corps, living at Valence
F. P.	probably Ferdinand Pellissier, cousin
Miss H——	unknown friend from New England, perhaps at Williston Academy or Bridgewater Normal School
Mr. H——	Miss H——'s father
Mr. M——	either Sidney Nelson Morse, colleague at Williston Academy, or P. A. Martin, colleague at Stanford University
Mr. G——	possibly Professor Gabriel Henri Grojean, instructor in Romanic languages at Stanford University
Mr. W. V.	probably William Vinal, former classmate at Bridgewater Normal School
Mr. C——	possibly Sumner Cushing, a former classmate at Bridgewater Normal School, who later organized the purchase of an ambulance in Robert Pellissier's memory; living in Salem, Massachusetts
D. C.	person unknown
Mme. S——	person unknown

FAMILY MEMBERS (SEE APPENDIX A FOR MORE DETAILS)

Father	Marcel Pellissier, 1837–88
Mother	Sophie Emma Testuz Pellissier, 1840–? (died after 1896)
Siblings	John (officer in the engineer corps; see above)
	Louis Paul (at least one of the brothers, Louis or Paul, died when Robert Pellissier was a boy; the other may have died before the war, as Robert Pellissier only mentions his brother John)
	Adeline, 1864–1940 (professor at Smith College; see above)
	Emélie, 1868–1922, the editor's great-grandmother, married to Edmund K. Alden (see above)
	Helene Marie ("Marie"), 1876–1910

Map 1. Places in France mentioned in the letters

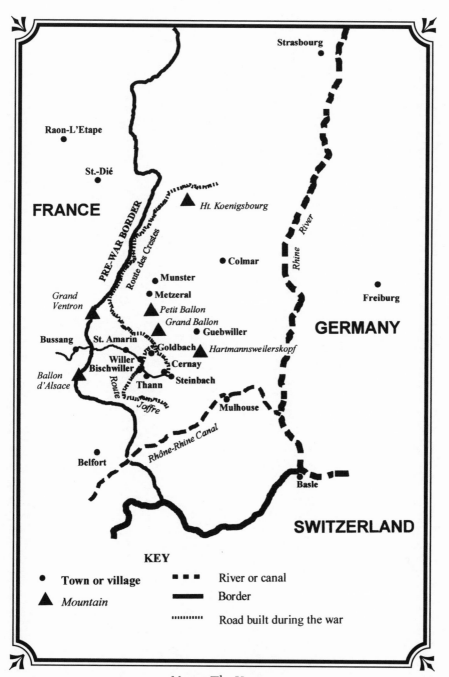

Map 2. The Vosges

A Good Idea of Hell

CHAPTER I

En Route

In a letter written the day before sailing

> *New York, August 25, 1914.*
>
> To B——:
> This is rather serious business. I don't know what use the Republic can make of me but "all men are needed" is the constant cry, so, by Jove, I see no way out which does not mean the giving up of the prerogatives and privileges which go with the name man synonymous with gentleman.

Translated from the diary

> *Sunday, August 30, 1914, on board* La France.
> Very quiet trip so far, neither pitching nor tossing during the first two days. Really a pleasure trip. Nobody worries and yet we heard on Friday that Roubaix, Lille and Valenciennes had been taken by the Germans, pretty hard blow. One of the ladies on board was weeping as if her heart would break.
> I got acquainted with a young Frenchman from Calais, a tulle weaver by trade; he had left Paterson, New Jersey, his brother having already joined the first army. Still under the grip of the emotion

of departure he said on the rst day "I should always have felt the pangs of remorse if I had staid away." Later during the trip he seemed quiet, contented, in good humor. He is about twenty-four years old, and had not done any military service having been excused on account of his prolonged stay in a foreign country. He introduced me to some of his friends who were third class passengers; three of them shirked military duty, but now they have enlisted so as to have their share in the dance. One is married and has three children, another one, twenty-one years old, very strongly built is the son of a saloon keeper. His parents did not wish him to go, but he went after considerable hesitation. The third one, a short red-haired man, with a goatee, was very bright and lively; he often came up to the second class. The two others got drunk on the first night, but he did not.

Wednesday. Great uproar in the canteen: a fellow, wearing spectacles and snarling his r's, was making an awful racket. He was a Parisian and was trying to be smart while being drunk. He attempted, without much success, to sing funny songs. On the following day he was in the lock-up for besides creating considerable disturbance on board he had made the mistake of embarking without a ticket. Nobody will ever know the reason why he came on board. He came to accompany some friends with whom he had just scraped an acquaintance and who did not want to come along, but who nevertheless took up a collection so that they might buy for him a third class ticket and thus free him from his cell. But people were not willing to have him in the third class. He knew too much. Besides beautiful songs, he could speak English, Spanish and German. They teased him considerably on account of his remarkable linguistic knowledge, but finally they relented. Another man named C—— is as much a Frenchman as I am. He has lived in the United States for ages and has forgotten a good deal of his French. He is the very type of the American business man, he speaks out clearly and firmly, wishes to have reserved for his special use the things of this earthly world, the good tangible things. His friends gave him a great banquet just before he left and of course he feels all the worse for it. You can see that he is in the habit of spending money freely like some of my American friends, but he does not do it quite so gracefully. He has enlisted in order to do his duty towards his family. At heart he is more American than French. Gestures, the lack of straight lines, put him in a state of exasperation. Above all he likes the correct Anglo-Saxon attitude. But after all he is very loyal and sincere. I understand perfectly well why one does prefer shoes of American make to the long spatula shaped shoes of our countrymen, a smooth shaven face to a thin beard, etc. These feelings I have shared many a time.

At the table, the saviour of the Parisian merry maker indulges in rather queer jokes. At his left a very lively little French woman who, although in my opinion she enjoyed the jokes of her neighbors a little too much, seemed to be a capable and kindly woman. Her husband, a sergeant, left her to take passage on the Sant' Anna, if I am not mistaken. She was going to meet him. Before starting he said to her "Well, my dear, my country first, my family next." She was peeved, but all the same she was proud of her man who is a sergeant.

Then there is also Mr. Le F., who was a cook at Sherry's, very nice fellow, good-looking, polite, very active and quick in his motions. "I may lose my life," he said, "but I don't care a rap." This remark he made with a feeling of deep conviction. His patriotism seems perfectly genuine and deep rooted.

With me in the cabin there was a Spaniard, he had just left Mexico where he had been through pretty hard experiences; he had to serve in turn under the federals and under Villa, in order to save his skin. Had many narrow escapes.

Tuesday, September 1st. Through the heavy mist we clearly caught a glimpse of the Lizzard [*sic*] and a little later we were saluted by an English cruiser; after having come very near us, she sailed off and while she disappeared through the mist, her crew shouted hurrah.[1] We saw fishing smacks in large numbers.

On the occasion of the last dinner, we had champagne, then the Marseillaise was sung and also the Chant du Départ. After this celebration I found it hard to sleep and besides at 2 A.M. my Spaniard turned on all the lights and began to smoke. Then he began the story of his life and the narration lasted til 3.30.

Wednesday, September 2d. When we reached Havre, the sea was perfectly smooth. We crossed Le Pérou crowded with Belgian soldiers, the ship being northbound. In the city we saw a good many English infantry and troops of English artillery men passed by singing.

In the harbor, a destroyer, several yachts turned into hospital boats. The hotels and the Navigation buildings were so many hospitals. The tramcars had women conductors.

A woman jumped into a car, then turned around to call back to some one in the crowd: "His lieutenant and second lieutenant have been killed—but he came out unscathed."

At military headquarters they put Admiral Charnier's stamp on my recruiting ticket. This ticket was to serve me as a passport. But at the station they refused to check my valise on its presentation. I lost my temper and bought a second-class ticket without asking for any reduction at all. That is why, instead of riding on the military train, I took the Paris express which, after crossing Dreux, reaches the station at the Invalides.

At Havre, I could not leave my valise at the station as the parcel's room was full. I went to the Hôtel de France, a most untidy place. While we were at dinner three gentlemen wearing sombreros entered the room shouting in English: "The Far West is coming—look out." Nobody paid the least attention to them. When I took the train, I was fortunate enough to find a seat in a second-class compartment, where I met again the cook from Sherry's; with him was one of the shirkers and a very mild man from Nice. There were also two comfortable looking business men who were going to Paris to remonstrate—"At Havre, two wagon loads of fish were being detained. Now, the ice is thawing, the fish will be spoilt." They were completely absorbed by their business—these two heavy-built civilians; wonder how much the war is going to cost them. And yet one of them has several nephews at the front—and one has just been killed—he was only twenty years old—killed in Belgium. "The old man has not yet dared tell the mother; she must be allowed to keep hoping a while longer"—for a few minutes he looked very much moved; then he resumed his conversation on business. Such was the attitude of Gargantua after the death of his wife.[2]

On the way, all the bridges were guarded—nothing happened until we reached Rouen—but after that we had to wait and wait. We crossed troop trains—and we caught up with trains filled with cattle or wheat. At one of the crossings, we saw an armored car mounted with a quick-firing gun. On a train transporting troops from Rouen to Besançon and beyond, I saw written on the sides with chalk: "Excursion train for Berlin." There were green branches around the car windows. A soldier called out to us, "We are going to cut off William's ears."[3]

Strong guards at all the bridges and tunnels. At the stopping places, which were numerous, there were only women and children to be seen. Almost everywhere the harvest had been gathered in, but on the Granville line people were still taking in hay. At one station a woman and child were selling pears; they went like hot-cakes. Those who were not quick enough to get some, felt their mouths water. At the next station, magnificent pears and in plenty. Two small boys are in charge of the supply. Impossible to buy one; they are all for the soldiers. But the boys are ready to do a good turn, so they fetch some cold water for the travellers.

The nearer we come to Paris the harder it is to proceed. We stop for one and a half hours between Saint-Cyr and Versailles. Cattle trains keep coming, trains full of cavalry horses and of war material disappear into the night. And then, there are trains full of Parisians who are skipping off. Poltroons? My fellow travellers become indignant; there is much fault-finding. As a matter of fact, the travellers are women and children who are very wise to get out. At Versailles crowds of "réservistes" are very much put out because there is no train to take them to Brittany, where they are expected to train the recruits. The 1914 class has just been called to the colors, so the train is full of young boys who are far from being sad. "O the fun of it!" "Just fancy, if I reach the barracks on time, by to-morrow I may don the uniform."

We reached the Invalides' station at about 10 o'clock. No taxi to be had. We had to foot it the whole way, carrying our valises—mild fun—Not a soul on the Place de la Concorde, but searchlights cross their streams of light above our heads—bombs having been dropped there the night before by a German aeroplane.

Towards the end I found a taxi, but there were no restaurants— finally I got two sardines at the station's restaurant,—that was all.

Rather trying but interesting day.

On the train people were talking mainly about German atrocities, murder of women and children. That is why the passengers did not seem to mind it very much if the turcos were acquiring the habit of cutting off the heads of their enemies.[4] Every passenger knew of someone who had heard that "So-and-so had seen a turco carrying the head of a German in his military bag." "Well, it serves them right. Why do the Germans murder our wounded soldiers?"

Thursday. Carrying my luggage, I reach the Lyons' station. Paris is almost empty. Two-thirds of the shops are closed on account of mobilization. The newspapers are reduced to one single sheet of the usual size. Nothing to read except the official announcement, stating in a few simple words the fact that the seat of government has been removed from Paris, without any other indication.[5] The nation is urged to remain calm, heroic, etc.—it could not possibly be quieter just now, although it is rumored that the Prussians have just entered the Compiègne forest. We are far from having as full news as in America; the situation is unchanged—nothing to say about the Northeast, nothing about the Vosges—the enemy is advancing slowly, south of the Belgian frontier. No details; to gain time means that in the end we shall get the upper hand. Place confidence in the government. The Prussians' advance does not mean anything. General Pau is in charge outside Paris; Galliéni inside.[6] As signs of a state of war, I notice the patrols and the statue of Strasbourg covered with wreathes [*sic*] of flowers and with flags. The city is as quiet as it is in the middle of August; it looks as deserted as on a public holiday, when everyone has gone to spend the day in the country—neither rolls nor crescents are to be had in the restaurants. The Latin Quarter empty, but in the Luxembourg garden, children are playing, as usual, and by the St. Michel bridge, a workingman is angling; some boys are doing the same. Madame F. is going to remain in Paris; she has seen a taube (she pronounces tob) and she is proud of it.[7] She tells me of a conversation she has had with a farmer from the North, now a refugee in Paris. He had spent four days in his neighbor's cellar, from which he could hear the shrieks of terror of the women and children ill-treated by the Prussians. When he came out, there were heaps of corpses on the street. People looking at them would say, "Ah! voilà le petit à un tel," "Voici la petite à un autre, la femme de celui-ci, la fille de celui-là" [Oh! There's the son of so-and-so, That's the little girl of someone else, the wife of another, the daughter of that one].

The train for Besançon leaves at 6.05.

At the Lyons' station, a regular mob. Women, children, baskets of all kinds and description. Whole families seated on the floor, munching crusts of bread, urchins howling, the women look harrassed [*sic*]—in the south-bound trains, there are more people than seats. It looks like New York, or rather, Ellis Island. One cannot leave Paris without a passport; it takes considerable time to get one, if one is dressed as a civilian.

A number of working people have all their belongings heaped on small push carts. No panic, but the awful lassitude of women and children who have been kept waiting for hours. To reach the train is hard enough, but to get into it is another proposition. The cars are jammed full.

At last my papers are vised—and loaded with valises I look everywhere for a seat. No such thing to be had. Every compartment is crowded. A woman, almost crushed to death with her two children, asks me if I am going to Besançon. Her husband is stationed there. Sergeant Carré of the Thirtieth. Please look him up. She had not heard from him for some time. Heaven knows if he is still alive? She is leaving for Savoy and she hopes I may see him.

After numberless attempts I give up the hope of finding a seat and climb into the baggage car with two soldiers in uniform and about a dozen of the Blues, class of 1914.[8] We are very comfortable in the baggage car—plenty of room, plenty of air, but when we reach the next station, they want to put in more trunks. The baggage-master loses his temper; he wants to make a clean sweep. We lose our temper; we shout—then everybody calms down, the trunks do not get in and nobody steps out. At Melun and at Fontainebleu [sic] the Blues leave the car. Only five or six passengers remain, and the baggage-master, now very much reconciled to the situation, listens to the conversation.

A chauffeur, an old wizened réserviste, tells what he knows—he knows a great deal. German shells do not burst, or at least only two out of ten. He knows a soldier who was struck by one falling on his arm, got a broken arm, that was all. Another had his knapsack put out of commission in the same way.

On the other hand, the German mitrailleuses [machine guns] are terrible, but fortunately our seventy-five is worse.[9] Turcos carrying the heads of Prussian soldiers in their bags? Now come, that is arrant nonsense, nonsense I say; a head never, but ears which have been cut off, that is a fact; that happens and not infrequently. The turcos have long knives; first they use the bayonet, then the knife; it is done before you have time to say Jack Robinson. And the English, they too have knives. He keeps on with this kind of conversation, but he sinks lower and lower in my estimation. At Montereau, where we wait fully an hour, he disappears. Conversation with the train conductor, the engineer and the chauffeur. They claim the service has been fair and, in spite of the exodus from Paris, it is still pretty good, but it is hard work. Yesterday, near Montereau a train jumped off the tracks, a train of wounded soldiers was thrown into a ditch—three killed—wounded re-wounded. It is heartrending. Of course, there was not a word of it in the papers. There is nothing worth reading in the papers. We have to take them as they are, but it is up to us to complain. After having spent four hours in the baggage car, I found a seat in a first-class car. Three passengers: a mother-in-law and her daughter had just left Champagne near Fontainbleu [sic], the general staff had been there, trenches were to be dug, houses and forest razed. At last I understand the reason why so many people are fleeing. They are the unfortunate inhabitants of the suburbs, who had to abandon their homes; in many cases they were given one hour to pack and go and they were strictly held to it. In most cases, they had to leave everything behind: furniture, linen, etc. One hears descriptions which are at once heartrending and comical: hens had to be given away, fruit and pigs to the French soldiers, of course, so as to keep these windfalls from the Germans.

In this train, no distinction is made between first, second and third classes. Passengers ride where they can. My friend, the great talker, whom I had lost sight of since Montereau, was there in this first class car, very comfortably settled, and he was telling all his stories over again; the shells which fail to burst, the ears, etc., etc. At last he leaves the car at Sens.

In the car with me there is also a concert hall singer who has traveled—she has seen the Cossaks at work, in them alone she trusts. Of course, she left Paris in the auto of a Colonel—for reference, see Roxane in Cyrano—she is very much annoyed, indeed, because she has to carry on her arm her field mouse coat which was at the dressmaker's to be remodelled and now it hangs together by pins only.[10] In addition to this trial, she has been sitting on the wine bottle hidden in her lunch basket. Of course, she felt something cool, she could not imagine what it could possibly be; now she understands, and we too understand. Her brother, who was to go to Nice, Marseilles, Bougie, Algiers on a very lucrative tour, is now sound asleep. He told us that his grief was generally keen, but that it did not last long. He evidently told the truth. One hour before we reach Dijon a large num-

ber of réservistes take the train. They had been sent home, then re-
called. Just now, everybody is called to the colors.

Friday. I reached Dijon about ten in the morning, as I had not slept
a wink during the night, as I had had hardly anything to eat and still
less to drink, I was all in. The town was overcrowded: immigrants,
refugees, soldiers. No room to be had at any hotel. As I did not feel
equal to continuing my trip without having had some rest, I tried to
find a room in a private house. It took time, but at least I found one
over a bakery; while the owner of the shop was preparing the room,
I went in search of a lunch place. The heat was unbearable. On my
way back from the restaurant, I noticed that the houses seemed to be
dancing up and down; I leaned against a wall and I reached the house
just in time to escape falling full length on the ground.

My room was on the fourth floor, I dropped on the bed and slept
like a log—half an hour later I woke up—the bed was black with
bedbugs—this sight made me feel as weak as a newborn babe, my
heart beating wildly. I threw the eiderdown on the floor and there I
tried to snatch a few minutes' rest, for now there were only fleas left
and one or two bedbugs.

On the streets some soldiers were marching by, and I said to myself: "Never in the world shall I be equal to this kind of life. I am a
fool." I placed four chairs in a row and, using my coat as a pillow, I
stretched myself full length on this couch, but the bedbugs were still
undaunted. Along the feet of the chairs they climbed as if they were
storming a position. And yet, I was able to get a little rest. I went out
and I spent a very unpleasant quarter of an hour in the park, which
is, nevertheless, a very pretty spot and has the general appearance of
all French parks between 5 and 6 P.M. I still felt shaky, alarmingly so.
A brilliant idea: I got a shave, a hair cut and a shampoo at a first-class
hairdresser. It gave me a chance to recline for a little while and the
parasites had a cruel time under a most generous alcohol shower. The
hairdresser was a very nice fellow. He noticed the condition I was in,
told me of a room I might secure, and, thanks to him, I had a night's
rest, which put me on my feet again. Very nice people—at Mme.
Louise (one franc a night) most cordial welcome. It would be hard to
find anywhere people who could have helped me out more graciously
than the hairdresser and his friends. On the other hand, the baker's
wife also had the best possible intentions.

I leave for Besançon at 12.39. A young woman and her son say goodbye to the father, who for several days has carried foodstuffs to the firing line. He has been through a good deal, but he does not boast about it; he is a fine man, not at all like the chauffeur. His wife casually drops the word danger; if he were younger, he would enjoy his new occupation; but, of course, he is forty-two. He added that up to this time the soldiers at the front had been well supplied with food stuffs. Two women, one of them coming from Choisy-le-Roi, have been obliged to leave their homes; one of them was courageous and, although she gave way to her feeling of discontent, she realized that there was nothing to be done. "Just think, our furniture which had come from Cochinchina, the mahogany commode which was price-less, but if a figure had to be given, it was certainly worth 4,000 francs, to say the least. And the house they had had such a hard time in build-ing, and now her husband had joined the army." The other woman was rather timid; she moaned and repeated, "We have been betrayed." Then, after lamenting considerably, she gave two pennies to the child of the other woman.

A fat traveling man is sure that the Germans are all in. He repeats it over and over again.

A wizened little old man, who has been traveling four nights without a ticket, tells of a great many happenings, putting on them his own interpretation. After leaving Chartres, he saw troops without number and navy guns sent northward to Verdun, most likely; all the money he has is seven francs. He fought in 1870 and he shows his deeply scarred hand; he also explains that in a battle he lost a tiny piece of the fattest part of his leg, without at first realizing the loss; only, the battle being over, he too felt a certain coolness, and he real-ized that the entire seat of his trousers was gone.

I reached Besançon by four, finding in town a tranquility almost depressing after the grand mixup of Dijon. I called at the recruiting office. The officers in charge expressed surprise that I should appear thirty-three days after mobilization had been called. I explained and they got over their surprise.

They gave me my matriculation and told me to go to barracks, but instead I stopped at the hotel and rested. On the public square, sometime during the evening, an account of the latest news was thrown upon a screen: "The Prussians have stopped their advance on Paris. They follow the edge of the Argonne forest, and they are shelling Maubeuge." That is all. People go home. I postpone to the next day the duty of becoming a chasseur à pied. I would have preferred to be a mounted chasseur, but I would have had to send in an application—bother—and after all, I was conscious that I could walk better than ride.

Sunday. After a good night's sleep at the Hôtel de Paris, I felt as if I had been made over. After sending for my valises I dressed as a gentleman and went to barracks. "Very simple matter, you belong to the Twelfth company." I was placed with the kids, of course, since I did not know anything about military art. The Twelfth company was stationed in another street; the réserviste who accompanied me was greatly impressed at the thought of my trip, although he had come from Paris and had been brought up in Pontarlier. He gave me some good advice and among other things, he suggested I put in an appearance at barracks only at 4 and then I might ask to have the money of my trip from San Francisco to New York refunded. When I reached the office, Sunday at 4 P.M. the captain roared at me—had been expecting me to report for hours—he was suspicious that I had taken more time than was necessary to come from San Francisco. The petty officers who were present told me not to mind the old boy. I was put in first section, fourth squad of Twelfth company. We were fifty in a schoolroom large enough to hold thirty. Straw very thin a strip all about the room, extending six feet from the wall; fortunately the windows were open. The food was served in big cans which were placed in the middle of the yard, which contained a fountain of undrinkable water, trickling over suspicious-looking algae.

Sunday to Thursday, September 10th. Fabulous amount of time spent in getting equipment. The captain had told the store to give me new trousers, new vest, old cape, later new tunique. Other things, overalls, towels, flannel belt, shirt in impossible condition as to solidity and dirt.

Drills so far stupid when not silly—We walk out three miles to a field and learn East and West, keep step, swing by fours. At times Swedish gymnastics, foolish games such as leap-frog, snap of the whip. I get out of them all I can. Petty officers are reserves and mean very well, but are tiresome with their constant nagging. So far all the work was petty beyond imagining. What was interesting was to hear the men talk who returned from the front. I spoke with a man who had been shot right through the neck, had walked some ten hours in that condition, had at last found an ambulance and been saved. The two scars were very small—one below the left angle of the jaw and the other on the opposite side, a little above the Adam's apple. This man's company had found itself in a position where it was fired on by German and French artillery. They failed to make the French see their error. These men who have come from the front are very still—they look listless; they are thin, but as a rule not pale. They are determined, but not enthusiastic; they seem all to have become fatalists. The horrible part to me is that so many of those who have been wounded are sent to the front as soon as they get well again.

One man is here who was captured near Mulhausen, then rescued. He testified to having been well treated by the Germans.

A 1902 soldier arrived here yesterday, dressed as a civilian; that is, he wore pajamas.[11] After a few days campaigning, he had fallen ill. He was sick in bed when the Germans entered the village where he had been left. Some German soldiers, discovering him, put the muzzles of their guns against his breast, saying: "blessé-achever" [he's wounded; finish him off], but he shouted in a shrill voice, "Not wounded, but ill." They left him alone. A few minutes later he jumped out of the window, remained for twelve hours in the garden, hidden among the raspberry bushes and by night he skipped off, walking across country. He was two weeks on the road.

All testify to the fact that the Germans cannot stand bayonet charges. They throw their guns and run. They are heavy and easy to kill. In every case they seem to have been three or four times more numerous than the French.

Here is a typical conversation which I heard not long ago. It shows the spirit of fairness which just now prevails among our soldiers. One said, "We should not take any prisoners." His comrades answered, "But they take prisoners and they treat them well; our turcos have murdered some prisoners. The Germans are like ourselves; some are good and some are bad." Generally discussions of this kind end by these words: "They are men, just as we are."

The Mulhausen campaign was a mistake—too great haste—rush without waiting for artillery, caused awful slaughter. One Bonneau, held responsible, was dismissed from service.[12] He seemed to have deliberately reckoned at the utter destruction of certain troops, particularly Forty-fifth chasseurs and some alpines. Meeting men of the former on the road, he exclaimed: "How does it happen that you fellows are alive? Couldn't you fight to the last man?" or words to that effect. The retort from the trooper was: "Why didn't you go yourself?"

The general complaint is that the Seventh corps has been used too much—that reserves have been sent to the front when vast portions of the regular army had not yet seen fire.

A corporal, who has just returned from the front, tells me that out of 1,600 men from the Fifth battalion, possibly six hundred are now at the front. The others are mostly wounded. "O, the daring of the officers! The commandant was walking back and forth, under fire, without trying in the least to protect himself. Too much daring," says the corporal, "the officers rush to their own destruction; they are swept away. Two captains only are left from the officers of the Fifth battalion. The death rate is also very high among lieutenants, for the very same reason—too much daring." The corporal is inclined to criticize the officers on account of their temerity. He is a tall, strong man, quiet of manner. The death rate, which is also very high among the Boches, is mostly due, he tells me, to the work of the "seventy-five." Today, Thursday, I saw the distribution of identification medals—tin with black cord.

Last night the order came for the last reserves of the battalion to leave for the front. In a very short time they were ready in every detail and with a three days' supply of food. The sack is frightfully heavy, though it is small and compact. They carry one hundred and twenty shells apiece. The whole outfit must weigh in the neighborhood of fifty pounds. During the night or early morning, some of the men sang and gave trumpet calls. While they were reviewed for the last time they joked with the lower officers. No excess of glee, however; as usual, they took their departure as a matter of course, but a serious matter, neither joy nor anything like distress. The normal feeling seemed to be earnest but moderate—in some cases, perfect indifference. Few, specially married men, were made pretty thoughtful, but that was all. The last thing they did was to write home. There was, therefore, nothing dramatic or even startling in these departures for the front—only intense activity: the coming in of cases of cartridges, distribution of tinned meat, loaves of bread, little sewed up bags filled with coffee, sugar, peas, respectively.

Sunday, 14th. Newspapers have been received containing the announcement of the victory of the Marne and of the beginning of a general retreat on the part of the Germans.[13] No details, nothing besides Joffre's proclamation.[14] The kids in barracks are more deeply interested in the dressing of their leathers and in the furbishing of their guns than in the news from the front. Absolute quiet reigns in town. No electric thrill. Everybody talks about commonplace or even silly things. The men from Mulhausen alone seem to see beyond the present instant. The attitude of the French I see around me might easily lead one to believe that a nation is like those animals whose make-up is so rudimentary that the health or the disease of one part of the body does not produce a corresponding state in the rest of their organism.

Several hundred thousand men have just been killed or are exposed to imminent death. Yet the thousands who remain are calm and follow their daily routine. I understand why a great patriotic drama is hardly ever immortalized through an artistic interpretation at the time it took place. Did the poets of the fifteenth century have any inkling of what Joan of Arc was to mean to posterity? Perspective is lacking. It is only later, much later, that people come to realize that the fate of a nation had depended on a certain event.

September 3, 1914.
Hôtel Terminus
Du Chemin de Fer de Lyon
19, Boulevard Diderot
Paris
To B———:

France is having a trying time, but it will be Germany's turn soon, though that is no consolation.

You would not know your Paris to-day. Two-thirds of stores closed "pour cause de mobilisation," few taxis, fewer horses, many army wagons and ambulances.

I leave for Besançon in a little while on a military train so I daresay I shall hear and see many interesting things and will not sleep much.

I wrote to you from New York. I don't have to tell you now that I could not very well hibernate in Stanford under the present circumstances. I have no regiment yet, but I have an army corps, the Seventh, and if I can keep my glasses straight I can do a terrible lot of damage to the Germans. I may also be put in infirmary work or in some clerical position. Indecision and uncertainty have their charm.

You and your people must have had a very hard time.[15] My sympathy and regard to your mother and your sisters.

The government left Paris to-day, but all is very quiet, except that the railroad stations are crowded.

Nearly every man, woman or child you meet has someone in the army, and so many say: my brother was killed, my nephew was killed at such a time and place, that one grows almost indifferent, but you can't help admire the courage of all the poor people. As for the soldiers, we met trains on our way from Havre yesterday; they had chalked on the cars, "Train de plaisir pour Berlin" [Pleasure train for Berlin], and men were shouting, "On va couper les oreilles à Guillaume!" [We will cut off William's ears!]

Goodbye. I hope your troubles will soon be over.

Hôtel Terminus, Paris
To Dr. J——:

I was very sorry to make trouble for you by leaving so suddenly, but I feel sure that you will feel as I did, that my staying in California this year would mean such moral misery that immediate traveling was imperative.

I have just reached Paris. I go on to Besançon to-night. Everything is quiet here, although the Government has gone to Bordeaux and many are leaving for the Provinces.

Please give my best regards to all.

Translated from the French

Written at the Café du Commerce
Besançon, September 13th, 1914.
To A——:

What do you think of my rash act?[16] I dare say you must have reached New York by this time and I feel rather uncomfortable at the thought that you may entertain an unfavorable opinion of me.

For the last week I have been sleeping on straw; I eat out of a tin dish and I am in perfect health. The drill is tiresome, but I had no illusions on this subject. I belong to a squad of men who are being trained for corporals. Should I belong to this squad for a few years I might become one myself. However, I would very much prefer to become again an Assistant Professor of Romance Languages. I hope that everything may be ended by December, and that I may spend Christmas with you all.

There are about fifty thousand men in Besançon, both infantry and cavalry, and I do believe that at the present time they are all gathered at this café, a fact which does not tend to make letter writing easy.

We are now thoroughly equipped. To-morrow we take to the field, creeping on our stomachs mostly, from one bush to another, in pursuit of imaginary Prussians, thank heaven! We will also practice shooting. If my eye-glasses will consent to remain on my nose, I shall cover myself with glory. It looks as if the Germans were being beaten quite thoroughly, but it costs us a high price. So many people are mourning for the loss of their friends. All this is very sad, but it tends to show the vitality of our race, which in my opinion is very far from deserving the reputation of decadence which so often has been imputed to it.

I really do not know what I am writing, but please do your best to understand. I am sleepy and it is so noisy here.

CHAPTER 2

Besançon

Besançon, September 22d, 1914.
To B———:

Hurrah! we are again in a state of communication. The letters you sent me at Stanford were forwarded and came two days ago. Your last letter, written when you received mine from New York was delivered yesterday. So I feel fine. That was a deuce of a stretch without any news from you. I feared for a while that it might continue *ad infinitum*. I had an idea that you must have gone back to the United States.

Life just now is more puerile than tragic. There is nothing stirring in military training. It's mainly monotonous drudgery. We get up at 5, drink a tin cupful of black coffee, eat a piece of bread and beat it off to a march or a drill or the shooting ranges and return at 10 or half-past. It's then we get our mail. At 1 P.M., we start drilling again and it goes on until 5 with 10 minutes rest each hour. At 5.30 we eat from our tin cans and from 6 to 8 we can go where we please. It's the time for correspondence. We don't feel like sitting up and we are always hungry. It's the most complete intellectual rest I have ever engaged in. The school in which we are quartered has to be vacated by the beginning of October, so we are going to be transferred to Pontarlier. We will be quartered in a factory out there, and we may get beds, though that is not certain, since the number of wounded is so great that beds are at a premium. It's a small matter, for after a few nights one sleeps on straw with absolute soundness.

You know where Pontarlier is. It is a few miles from La Ferrière, where I was born. I shall feel quite at home. It is up in the mountains I love best.

If the Germans are not cleaned out by the middle of October we shall be sent to the front, according to all probability. I am not worried in any way. I don't care to look for trouble, but if trouble comes my way it will not disturb me.

The news of the destruction of the Cathedral of Rheims came to-day.[1] The Germans must be crazy. Their actions are incredible. It's all up with their prestige as a civilized nation and whatever may be their efforts they will get whipped in the end.

I can't get excited about the battles. They seem incredible. This town is absolutely quiet. It's full of soldiers, but otherwise business goes on as if there were no war.

On the whole I am sorry for the German people. They are as good people as any, but their government is damnable. I believe firmly in the distinction made in *Le Temps*, I think, by Romain Rolland who speaks of the Germany of Wilhelm II and that of Goethe, and of the necessity for intelligent people to keep the two apart in their minds.[2]

I had a good letter from my brother. He is glad I came. He is with the *génie* [engineer corps] at Valence and will not have to go to the front.

One thing may keep me in barrack life to the end of things. Our battalion had a terrible time of it six weeks ago, and out of forty officers only three are in the service now. All the others are dead or else in hospitals. It may be that we will not be sent out for that reason, since the part of the country from which the battalion came has paid in full to the nation already.

We leave at 5.15 to-morrow morning to go off shooting, and I am fairly falling asleep now, so I will say good-night and write again soon.

La Ferrière-sous-Jougne, Doubs, birthplace of Robert Pellissier.

Café du Commerce
Besançon, September 26th, 1914.
To B——:

My corporal is now very friendly and my sergeant is getting tamer. Soon I think he will feed from the hand and want to be patted. The former is a locksmith, the latter a miller, and each I think looked askance at having a professor in their section. They are finding out that I know as much about my left and right hands as anybody and they are less rampageous in proportion. I broke my glasses but several new pairs are coming from Paris. It has handicapped me in shooting as I had to go to the range with my reading glasses and guess where the bull's eye might be. I did get six counts out of four bullets the other day, however; that meant two bull's eyes and at 250 meters. So I felt set up since I had no former practice with war guns. Now I am getting conceited.

The main amusement here for me, beside writing letters, is to make devastating raids on pastry-shops and cleaning them out of every kind of *petit gâteau* [little pastry].

This town is more quiet than London. Life goes on normally. People are hardened now. There is hardly a family which is not anxious about someone at the front; but the era of excitement is over. No one expects quick success, but all are confident of ultimate success. I think we may move out of here in three weeks or so. They may use us as *"troupes d'occupation"* [occupation or garrison troops] before they send us to the front. Whatever comes along I shall take cheerfully and calmly. I have a good dose of fatalism in me which may after all be a form of faith. At any rate all the people I care for [indecipherable] are back of me and, I repeat, it is a fine feeling.

Good luck, good night, and many, many thanks.

Besançon, October 2d, 1914.
To A———:

I am sending to you a photograph of me which was taken at the time of John's visit. You see I look very gentle for a warrior. Well one cannot at call look ferocious.

Nothing new here. We are waiting to be sent at the right moment to the right place. The only thing we know about the war is that the deadlock continues and that the Germans have just received as reinforcement five hundred thousand men. France may summon as many, whenever she may see fit to call them. Therefore, everything is all right.

Good news from Stanford. Several of my friends wrote me to express their good wishes and even their congratulations. I fancy the life of Frenchmen in the United States will be very different after the war. We will no longer be crushed by the fancied superiority of Northern races. We will have shown what we are in more than one way. Then, the Germans will have their turn "to eat humble pie." I even fear that many people deserving a better fate may have to suffer unjustly in consequence of the mean deeds of their government. I think it is a sad thing and it will be highly desirable for people to try to discriminate between the good and the bad Germans. In this respect I agree with Romain Rolland, although it is very difficult to stand by this opinion after the scandalous manifesto of the Prussian intellectuals—a manifesto which seems too clearly officially inspired to represent the opinion of superior men. Therefore, do not harbor too much of a grudge against your German colleagues and other honest people who are really to be pitied and will be still more to be pitied in the near future.

To-night I am going to dine in town, in a cabaret I know. On Sunday it depresses me to have to eat out of a tin dish. We are not supposed to eat in town but once in a while one is tempted to run a few risks. Good bye, my dear. If I write in pencil it is because there is no possibility of writing otherwise.

Café du Commerce
Besançon, October 8th, 1914.
To B——:

My three days' silence was due to the fact that my brother came to see me. We had a fine time together. I obtained first an 11 A.M. to 8 P.M. permission, then one from 6 to 10 P.M. The captain is a gentleman, and this morning, as my brother was on the esplanade, he told me in terrible tones, as befits a warrior, "Pick up your gun and walk with your brother!" And so I did, getting thus one more permission. My brother went off this morning, so my holiday is over. It was good to see him. The possibility of my going to the front hurts him much more than it does me.

I don't believe I'll be sent for some ten days yet, anyway. Drilling with regular soldiers very much more interesting than the same work with recruits. We are commanded by a very good lieutenant who has recently returned from the front and who is a cracker-jack; he makes us hop along over ploughed fields, into ditches and through bushes in a way fit to bewilder the Dutch.[3] To-day I must have destroyed thirty cents' worth of cabbages in the course of operations.

The fact that I am at last with older men, my brother's call and the getting rid of a beastly cold all tend to make me feel fine. Also we have been given a new lot of straw to-day. I went to the cart myself and pinched a bunch without asking anyone's advice so that I have a whole lot for to-night's nap. To-morrow I shall be more ready than ever to destroy vegetable gardens.

We have no definite news about the war. Fighting goes on in the Aisne Valley, that's all we know. We are simply getting ready to shove them out of our country.

My brother insisted on having my picture taken. I'll send you one when they are ready. That won't be for a fortnight or three weeks.

Besançon, October 12th, 1914.
To B——:

Here I am still, doing nothing and I have just received your letter in answer to the one in which I told you I was about to leave for the front. My not having gone does not mean much, as I am pretty sure to go before the month is over and perhaps before.

All the recruits with whom I was at first have been sent away to a small village and I remained with the regular reserves, nearly all of whom have already fought. We have also changed quarters and we are much more comfortable now. It's a fine schoolhouse, our room is flooded with sunshine every morning and we are not so many in one room. Also we are not worked very hard. I am writing you in the morning now, in the room. We drill or march only in the afternoon. The atmosphere is entirely different from what it was with the recruits. There is a feeling of comradeship among the men and the petty officers, which gives a fraternity atmosphere which is really pleasant.

Two weeks from to-day, the boys nineteen years old will be called in. That shows how much men are needed, and I am more satisfied every day that I did the right thing in coming over. I would have had a lifelong remorse if I had not.

As I am writing, the sergeant is going over the equipment of each man. I need a knapsack and a canteen and I don't care for government shirts. I am going to follow your advice and clothe myself in wool from chin to toe before I leave. Luckily I bought for the Sierra trip with my brother-in-law some fine outing shirts of very warm and heavy stuff, and they are coming in just right now. I say, "Hurrah for American shoes and outing shirts." Also, "Hurrah for Dr. Rasurel who sells fine excellent woolen clothes."

I am not learning much that is new these days. It's the same old thing. We run and lie down, get up and run, all the while keeping in mind some propitious looking bush or rock or wall or tree or hollow in the land about us.

Yesterday they made us shoot at silhouettes of men crouching. Pretty hard to get, especially as we had the sun in our eyes, and because they made us shoot with old type rifles, like your old Springfield rifle. I feel that a German lying down is pretty safe from my shots at 300 yards and conversely a German would have his trouble seeing me in similar position.

The weather is nice and crisp now. Just right for marches with a load. I fear the heat more than the cold.

From the diary

Now we are quartered in a different schoolhouse, on the fourth floor; it is cleaner, better lighted by day and by night. The food is better.

Everything would be satisfactory were it not that yesterday while taking a leap, the last one in the drill, I hurt my knee, bruising it badly; now it is swollen. The medical examiner having sent me to the infirmary. I witnessed the cleaning of a wound. I had to leave the ward and on reaching the corridor I fainted, falling at full length. The worst of it is that this accident has taken away my self-confidence—my knee, the rain, the straw, the remembrance of my mishap,—all these things depress me more than I can tell. What shall I do in the trenches?

October 18th, 1914.
To B——:
Just two words as it is getting late. This has been an uneventful day during which I watched my knee grow strong. The "major" gave me four days off duty this morning so as to recuperate completely. I feel that I shall be on firm foundations before that time elapses.

Sundays are foolish days in my new business. We just hang around all day until 5 P.M., when we light out. They might just as well give us the day, but they don't. Red tape I guess. No talk of leaving as yet. I am a humbug.

Had a fine dinner in a little dark, low-studded restaurant. It's amazing what good things, and in what quantity one can get in this town for two francs. I don't see how they do it. A meal like that would cost over a dollar in the United States.

Had a letter from my sister. All serene in the Connecticut Valley.[4] Also news from Stanford.

Do you like mice and rats? Some had a race across my prostrate body last night, then dashed across the next chasseur, and so on around the room. Lucky the chasseurs are not ladies, or else the company would have been routed.

My days off do not mean that I am free to go about as I please. It simply means that I don't have to drill or march. I must hang around the barracks all day just the same. A sad fate, but it might be lots worse.

It is twenty minutes of eight, so I must speed, or hobble, away as you may please to call it.

October 20th, 1914.
To B———:

I am writing this in a room where all the lame and shaky have been gathered. There is no furniture, so we all sit on the straw and do what we can. Fortunately I have a small box to write on. The other men are on their backs reading or squatting around a blanket playing cards.

No news in the newspapers. Reporters must have a great time trying to set in a new form the same old dispatches which don't mean anything anyway. Those confounded Germans are still in France, that's all that can be gathered, and Heaven only knows how long it will be before they are pushed out of Belgium. We are in it for a long time I think, unless something bursts inside Germany.

About one thousand men of line infantry left yesterday and a good deal of artillery went this morning. It seems to me that some men are being sent to the front when they have not fully recovered from wounds received at the beginning of the trouble. It's a pretty cruel business, whatever aspect of it one sees. It's amazing from what bullet wounds men recover, however, only two little bits of scars remaining to testify that the victim was shot right through the chest, the arm, the thigh, or even the foot, bones and all. We have dozens like that here. They don't seem to have suffered much either, at any time.

I have a task ahead. A chap wants me to compose a letter, meant for a man who is fooling with his girl! He is not certain that his literary training can cope with the emergency.

Besançon, October 21st, 1914.
To B———:

Another day gone by in laziness, though not unpleasantly. There was a "revue d'armes" [weapon inspection] at 10 A.M., so I spent most of the morning taking my rifle to pieces and polishing the hilt of my bayonet. In the afternoon, we took a stroll up a hill, which commands a view of the whole town. Besançon is very picturesquely situated. To-morrow I am going to drill in the morning. If my knee objects I shall cut the afternoon performance and complain to the surgeon the next day.

No talk of leaving for the front. Might just as well be in Stanford as far as warlike atmosphere is concerned, if it were not for the men who turn up from various hospitals in groups of two or three, nearly every day, and tell their experiences with or against "les Boches," that is, the Dutch. How Allemand ever gave Boche is hard to see. They do say "les Alleboches," though at times.[5]

Well, to-morrow I'll tell you whether or not I am again a walker. These last seven days I have felt like an inmate of an old ladies' home, which is no way for a warrior to feel. I feel as much like a warrior as I do like a millionaire, but time ripens one. I see how I might face some trouble, but I can't see for the life of me how I ever could damage anyone. It's lucky for the Republic they don't all feel as I do.

The government seems to be out of regulation army knapsacks, so they are giving us tyrolian rück-sacks, the kind tourists carry in the Alps—pear-shaped canvas bags much better and lighter than our regular square leather sacks, it seems to me. I am much rejoiced at that fact.

Hope to hear from you to-morrow and to hear good news.

Besançon, October 23d, 1914.
To B——:

I just ran at full speed to the photographer's as time is short to-night, and the old fool could not lay his silly hands on the pictures. I looked like Black Cloud himself. It caused renewed bustle through the shop, but did not bring out my photos. I left showered with promises that everything would be right to-morrow. So there we are. Photographers in this town believe in the "mañana" [tomorrow (Spanish)] idea.

Except for this mishap, this has been a pretty good day. We did fool drill stunts this morning, but this afternoon we took a fifteen-mile walk at a pretty fast rate and, as my knee stood it perfectly, I feel like a man to-night. I had a horrible panic for a while, fearing that I might be left in some infirmary while the others went away. Now there is no danger of that, though we don't know when we are going.

It was a superb trip we took this afternoon. We walked around one of the mountains which overlook Besançon. The country is beautiful just now with autumn foliage. The colors are not so vivid as they are in America (See America first!) but they are very delicate, especially the reds, and the fields are greener than they would be in New England.

It's fun to walk with a lot of Frenchmen and boys. I don't believe a yard is gone over without giving rise to some joke. They josh from start to finish. No man, woman, child, tree or bush or cow met on the way can escape from a jibe of some sort. They don't do it in a disagreeable spirit. It's simply to kill time and shorten miles.

You must know as well as I do that the Germans are holding like grim death in the North and that your race and my race are hammering at them and that the result is pretty nearly a deadlock. I think we are in it for a year at least, unless something bursts up inside Germany, which favor may God grant us.

I am pretty sleepy and muddled, so I think I shall say good night now—inasmuch as in addition, I must drop my brother a line, having at this minute received a note from him and money sent me by a Bridgewater friend as a war contribution!

October 28th, 1914.
To B——:

Another dismal and utterly useless day ahead. It's raining and we have nothing to do. The only thing to take up one's mind is the persistent rumor that two hundred men will go Monday next somewhere along the frontier of Alsace. Those who belong to the active army and those who have not gone to the front as yet, will be picked first. If this rumor is true, there is something to look forward to, but rumors come and go so often and are so contradictory that I give up believing in anything at all. You can't complain that I don't keep you informed since I tell you even the rumors. Yesterday we played again that we were taking trenches. They always make us end by a bayonet charge for about fifty or a hundred yards. We run all we can and yell like savages, but if they order the charge too soon we get winded before we get to the trench.

No news from anybody these days. The best time of the day is still from 5 to 8. We sneak off at 5 now, though the rule is 6. The place where I ate last night was full of territorials who are going to leave today. Some of them were pretty old and decrepit. It's a heartrending sight to my mind to see them in uniform. So many men by the time they are forty have seen their best days and are really beginning to be old men. Such troops, of course, are meant for occupation rather than for fighting and that is fortunate. No real war news. The same apparent stagnation coexistent with hard fighting.

This is an unenthusiastic letter to write you—but "que faire?" [what can one do?] This is real London weather. We can sympathize with each other. That of itself is a pretty good privilege.

Goodbye—good cheer and good luck.

Translated from the French

Besançon, October 29th, 1914.

To A——:

This day has been filled with noise and turmoil, a day of feverish activity, standing in pleasing contrast with the preceding ones. Tomorrow we start for the Vosges. Two hundred and fifteen of us are going to reinforce the Fifth battalion which is, of course, nobody knows where.

Don't worry. It is a departure; there is no denying the fact, but I have been expecting this day for a long while, and it is in view of this event that I have left America.

In connection with this trip, one thing pleases me. We are going to manouevre in the Vosges and later, God willing, in a country dear to two friends of my childhood, namely Erckmann and Chatrian. While looking at the map, these old names of Phalsbourg, Sarrebruck, le Donon brought back to my mind's eye several old books: *Le Blocus, Le Conscrit,* etc., etc.[6] Hence you see I am starting on a literary, military trip. Now, don't believe that I am starting in a mood of selfish light-heartedness. Far from it. Only there is a certain task to be accomplished, and this task cannot be accomplished if one gives way to emotions. That is why I say *au revoir* and be sure that my thoughts will constantly be with you. It is very possible that I may not always be able to write to you. Therefore, in case of prolonged silence, do not worry.

I say once more, *au revoir.*

Adeline Pellissier (1864–1940), Robert Pellissier's sister.
"A" in the letters.

[From the editor's family papers—not included in the original collection. The following letter was written to Pellissier's brother-in-law, Edmund K. Alden, the editor's great-grandfather, in Brooklyn.]

Café du Commerce, Besançon, October 30th, 1914.
Dear Edmund:

After two very dull, uninteresting weeks we have at last received orders to move out of Besançon. We don't know just where we are going but it's somewhere in the Vosges region in the neighborhood of St.-Dié at least to begin with. It is a splendid mountainous region. Some points overlook the Rhine valley and I have been told that the Bernese Alps can also be seen. At any rate, it is a fascinating region and I prefer it by much to Belgium and the northern plains.

We are leaving, 250 or 300 of us, to reinforce the 5th battalion. We have a good many days of peaceful traveling and tramping ahead of us.

I wish I could write to each one separately of my dear Brooklyn family but I have only a very short time ahead and besides it is not possible to write 5 separate letters and have them read intelligently. So please give my love to all—Emélie, Marguerite, Marie and Louise and tell them that I am keeping with each of you daily conversations and communions of thought.[7]

As soon as I can, I shall write again but it is quite certain that the mail will wax less regularly from now on.

Remember me too please to the Kingman family and to Alice and Allston.[8]

With much love to you and to the family,

Affectionately,
Robert Pellissier

P.S.—Keep writing as before. Letters are forwarded from the Dépôt.

October 30th, 1914.
To B——:

This time I think we are leaving. They are giving us all our things and we are to take the train sometime to-morrow afternoon or night. I don't know how soon we will be actually at the front. There may be several days of quiet yet. At any rate, feel sure that I am doing what

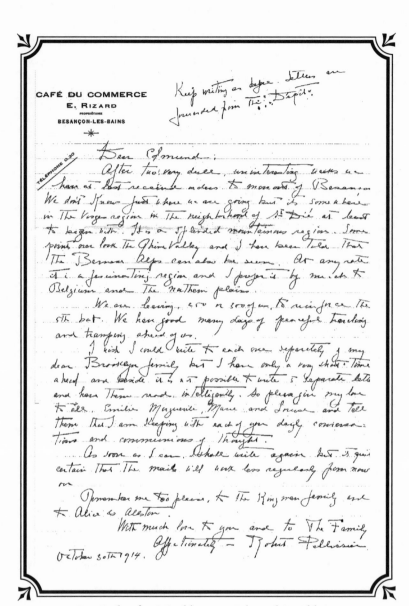

Facsimile of original letter to Edmund K. Alden.

I want to do, what I would be very unhappy not to do. If I had remained at Stanford, my life would have been utterly wretched.

Our correspondence will very likely be very irregular from now on.

Don't worry in any case. You should have good reason for worrying if I were not able to do what I want or if I had failed to try.

Bright hopes and best wishes.

P.S.—We are going somewhere in Alsace, but we don't know where exactly. I shall probably not be able to tell you, when I do know, or write more than postals. Mail, some of it at any rate, will be forwarded from here to wherever we will be.

It is better for one to go to Alsace than to Belgium at the present time, since the country is in much better condition. It is a fine country, too—forests and mountains.

CHAPTER 3

Vosges

November 1st, 1914.

To B———:

After riding all afternoon and all night we landed in a lovely valley of the Vosges. We have mountains all about and splendid forests. To-day the weather is perfect. In addition there are five fountains and lots of straw in this hamlet, two things making for happiness that were singularly lacking in Besançon.

The Dutch are a few miles from here hiding in trenches. We have dug some just in front of them and all a company has to do is to watch them over a day and a night twice a week. It's the most harmless form of war, purely observation, so don't spoil my fun by worrying. I am having a good time.

Will write more at length next time in a few days, as just now the wind is blowing in the back of my neck and I fear a *courant d'air* [draft] as much as any French private, which is saying a great deal.

Early this morning we went through villages and towns wrecked by the Germans—also saw numberless farms of which there remained but the walls.

November 17th, 1914.
To B———:

As for my life it has been somewhat strenuous. We went up the mountain to occupy the trenches four days and we remained eleven days instead and it was pretty hard work. We had three sets of earthworks about two hundred to three hundred yards from the German fortifications and they had to be occupied night and day of course. We were two companies and took turns every twenty-four hours. We would spend one night and one day in watchful waiting then fall back to some log-houses and spend one night there when we were lucky. When we were not lucky they would trot us to some outpost and we would spend another night on guard. There were times when we hardly slept for forty-eight hours. The last three days it rained and we were soaked and in mud for the period.

There was not much fighting, just scattered shots from one breastwork to the other. They killed two of our men and wounded two. We paid them back or better. I have now received the "baptism of fire" and feel quite like a man. I know the noise of bullets and shells. I can tell from the report whether the gun is French or German. The tough part of the business was that we could not remove our belts and cartridge boxes at any time next to the enemy, and trying to sleep with all those straps on and the weight of the cartridges is anything but a joke. So when we returned to the village yesterday and could sleep without equipment, on real straw it felt quite like heaven.

We probably won't go up there again for three weeks, so we have peaceful times ahead. We have an ass of a lieutenant who just came and he wants to "review" the inside of our sacks, so I must be off.

So far I have found war pretty good sport. To be sure I have not been near any place where there is artillery at work so I don't know much. Guns boom all the time to the North and South of us, but not where we are for it's too hilly for artillery right here.

Translated from the French

November 23d, 1914.
To A———:

I am sorry I have to write to you on such grayish paper, but *c'est la guerre* [that's war], and I am in the backwoods of the Vosges. We are kept as a reserve at about one mile from the trenches. They are not doing anything up there and consequently we are leading a peaceful life here. This little out of the way place reminds me of Domodossola, with its woodlands on all sides and its steep hills rising directly from the road, which is the main highway from Strasburg to Saint-Dié.[1] In my opinion, we have reached the final deadlock here. Possibly on the Belgian front things are different, but here nothing will take place.

We have been on a little expedition which lasted three days; we were to have a few days' rest after eleven days passed in the mud of the trenches, but the day after our return we were sent off to give support to a regiment of infantry which was to attack. We were five hundred and we crossed the mountain, Indian file, following the forest trail. When we reached the other valley, that is about ten in the morning, we prepared some coffee by the roadside; then, in little groups, we scattered over the fir grove for our artillery-men had begun bombarding the Germans, from where, I cannot tell, but the shells, whirring over our heads, were falling on the enemy with a tremendous crash. About two hours later rifle shooting began. Balls were whizzing through the branches. Of course, nobody was in sight and we were in perfect security hidden among our little fir trees. About two o'clock everything calmed down and we went down hill to strike the road which would lead us to the other slope where our friends the *pitous* [infantry] had their camp. Our two mitrailleuses packed on the back of horses followed us by trails which baffle all description and at four we reached the road on the hilltop. On the other side the fusillade still kept on; and from time to time, a wounded soldier on a stretcher passed us and we kept waiting, waiting. About five, they told us it was all over, we would not be needed because the Germans could not be dislodged without our losing a great many men and that the position was not worth such a loss, but, they said, we might be of help the next day, so we sped down hill and we spent an awful night in a saw-mill open from all sides to the winds—and what winds. However I have not yet seen anything which could in any way compare to what I saw in Rutland.[2]

On the next day by four-thirty we climbed up hill at full speed; this time we took our position above the road; we remained there the whole blessed day waiting, with cold feet. It was snowing a little and we had been allowed to kindle fires. Walking a short distance to the right we could see at our feet the small town of Senones, a part of

which is in the hands of the Germans, while the other is defended by
our marines. We could see the Germans walking along the streets.
The mitrailleuses were firing, but from too long a range to do them
any harm. We dared not bombard them because they make our peasants stand in front of them whenever the cannon is used. The whole
day was spent idling. Towards night they told us to go and come again
on the following day. This seemed rather trying and as we were getting ready to start, I kept thinking with some bitterness of the open
saw-mill. Fortunately the captain was not any more eager than I was
to spend another night in the saw-mill, and at full speed through the
dark he led us to Saint-Priel, ten kilometers from the crest of the hill.
There we found good straw, good roof, good cheese, good wine and
even good cream, with plenty of sugar in it and made even more de-
licious by being flavored with a few drops of brandy. But we had to
tear ourselves away at three thirty in the morning to go back to our
crest. Another day was spent at the disposal of the infantry colonel.
Again we froze, without fire this time, until twelve. Then we went
back to our quarters in wonderful weather. This is all we did during
these three days campaigning. You see this is not the great war, and
I believe the great war is really over. It was all right during the first
few months at least on this side, now it is a deadlock. In these mountains there is no chance, either for us or for them, to accomplish any
brilliant success. We are equally matched. It may be different in the
North. This last attack which was utterly insignificant, has nevertheless cost the lives of twenty fathers of families; besides fifty men
wounded. We have advanced fifty meters and broken some wire net-
ting. "The game is not worth the candle." I give you all these details
to show you that war is not very dangerous. The careless men are
those who run risks. As far as our fare is concerned we are wonder-
fully well supplied; never in all my life have I eaten such good things
and in such plenty. I am growing fat, it is a fact, and I sleep ten hours
at a stretch whenever there is no duty. Aunt Laure sent me packages
of woolen things and Madame Blancard sent me a wonderful woolen
scarf. Dulac, John's friend, is sending me some tobacco. I am living
on the fat of the land. I fervently hope that the Germans are not so
comfortable as we are. I must write letters of thanks for all these packages; that is why I must leave you, my dear. May I ask you to send my
letter to Brooklyn, it is not every day that I can write such a lengthy
epistle.[3]

Emélie Pellissier Alden (1868–1922), Robert Pellissier's sister.
Living in Brooklyn at the time of the letters.

November 23d, 1914.
To B——:

I am on friendly terms with the officers and I hold my own with the petty officers, so all is well.

My brother has sent me five cent stamps, so I can mail this directly. Stamps can't be bought out here at all. The Germans occupied this valley for three weeks. Just before they got kicked out, they burned all they could. At Raon, three miles from where we are camping, they burnt the city market among many other buildings, and as they were drunk, they never noticed that they were incidentally burning to death their own wounded soldiers together with our own. We can't shell many of their positions, because they put our farmers in front knowing that we won't fire on our own people. . . . Goodbye, good wishes of all kinds to you and your family.

November 25th, 1914.
To D. C.

Just returned from a week and a half stay behind earthworks in front of the Dutch.

Had one close shave; my sergeant was killed a yard from me as we were going out to pick up a fellow who was wounded. The hard part of that business is that you can't sleep much if any and you must lie down with all your traps and straps.

Don't expect to go again for two weeks. We live now on the fat of the land.
Good luck,
Bob.

Translated from the diary

We were in the 3d trench when Muller was killed. Salmon was not completely concealed from view. Roussel attracted Muller's attention to the fact. Muller told him to mind his business. Two minutes later Salmon was hit. Muller and I went to fetch him. To all appearances Salmon was dead, but one of his hands still preserved a rosy hue. Muller lifted him up, shook him, held to his lips my handglass, then began to roll him toward our trench which was thirty yards off. From behind a fir tree our sentinel called: "Look out!" A second later Muller was hit and he fell across Salmon, his back being turned towards me.

There was a death rattle, the gurgling of a hemorrhage, then he rolled over on one side and remained lifeless. After ascertaining that he was dead I went back to the trench. The ball, piercing his cranium, had come out through his mouth.

That night we slept under the telephone shed and on the next day we buried Salmon, but Muller's body was taken to Raon-l'Etape. The little cemetery contains half a dozen tombs, some of our men are buried there and some alpins. With nice and even pious care, the tombs have been decorated, green branches, white crosses, crosses made of moss, and all around the yard there is a hedge of pine trees. The tombs of the Germans are not far off, they are protected by a railing, but there are no crosses. The Germans have made a wire tangle over the body of one of our men, which they have left unburied.

A few days later our captain avenged Muller. He killed a German sentry and three out of four men who came to fetch him.

December 4th, 1914.
To B———:
Two American letters from you this week so I am again in a normal state. You must have received several of mine by this time as well as those slow moving pictures.

There has been nothing exciting of late and very little that was tiring. We spent from the 27th to the 1st of December in and about the trenches on our mountain top. We did not sleep much during that time, but the weather was good and during the whole time only three shots were fired by us. The infantry three miles to the right of us were attacked at night. I happened to be on duty behind a big pine tree in front of the trench at the time and had a chance to see and hear. For about forty-five minutes there was a rifle fire the like of which I had never heard, and on the crest opposite, the searchlight of the Dutch kept plying from left to right over the woods. It was very interesting. We thought that perhaps they might come on us and we were full of business, but nothing happened and by the time I was through my watch, the night was again perfectly still.

We did not suffer from either cold or rain this time as the trench in which we were is luxuriously appointed. Big rooms, with each a wide fireplace, have been cut into the hill and roofed over, also little holes have been dug in the side of the trenches and we can warm ourselves while watching. For that matter watching is easy. For thirty yards in front of the trenches there is a maze of barbed wire and of chicken wire which would puzzle a rabbit. Imagine what chances one or more fat Germans would have to get to us without being filled full of shot. They know it and stay still right where they are.

We are going up there again December 12th; we will come back here for Christmas and spend New Year's Day up there, that is if things continue as they have the last month, and there is every reason to believe they will. There are not serious battles on the front anywhere now. I am writing in the guard house. It is the quietest place around. My "escouade" [squad] is here on duty for twenty-four hours. Three of us at a time stand at the door and on the road to stop everybody and see the "laissez passer" [pass]. I was up two and a half hours this morning and I have nothing to do until night. They are playing French poker at the table where I am writing this. Lot of "gros sous" [large coins] floating about and much interest displayed.

I don't know how long this war is going to last, but I think we are in for it until Spring anyway. It's the laziest life I have ever led. I am great friends with the corporal who is a kid and with most of the sergeants. The lieutenant shakes hands with me each time he sees me and speaks English with me so you see I am living on easy street. If this reaches you about Christmas, A Merry Christmas to you.

December 7th, 1914.
To B———:

We have just spent three foolish days watching over a village that did not need watching. Hours and hours in the dripping woods from which arose white mists when the sun came out. No Germans for five or six miles at the nearest and no possible way for them to come near us, yet we had to watch as if the woods were full of them. This kind of boy scout work I do not like.

There must have been great fights in the East of us for the last three nights. Just about six there was the greatest amount of rifle and rapid-fire gun shooting I have ever heard. As before, searchlights work back and forth and back and forth in the sky. But these night attacks are mainly a bluff, at least out here in the mountains. They are very noisy, but neither side budges.

The monotony of those three days at Lajus was relieved by the clever combinations arranged between my kid corporal and myself and by means of which we managed to get once, hot chocolate, another time hot *café au lait* and three times, hot sugared wine. By such gastronomical trifles is life in the field relieved.

This war is going to last a long, long time, I fear. They are calling in more men, though there is not much fighting going on now.

December 11th, 1914.
To Miss H——:

When war broke out I came back to France to destroy the German Empire. After two months' training I have just spent five weeks or so at the front in the Vosges mountains. We had a set of four trenches to keep clear of Germans and we had no difficulty in accomplishing our task, as these gentlemen keep themselves in their holes, firing only on sentinels and isolated groups. They fired on me once, by gum! and missed me! Rainy nights in the trenches can be pretty mean, but on the whole I have not had a very hard time. Just now we are off duty, but likely to leave for Mulhausen and other contested territories about any day.

December 11th, 1914.
To B——:

We have left our positions all of a sudden being replaced by still more ancient troops. I conclude that our positions had no great strategic value since they entrusted them to plain ordinary line infantry. We are out of the danger zone, loafing about in a small village near St.-Dié. It seems that they are forming a new army of which we are going to be a part. Where it will be sent, is a great mystery. Some say we are going North, others in the Argonne region, others in Alsace. I think the last surmise is the correct one and that we will be sent to Mulhausen and neighborhood. There is a big lot of troops moving back and forth just now. I am glad to be out of the thickly wooded region. It's pretty wet at this time of the year and pretty dark.

We will be here a few days more; then we may move on to Epinal. This life is uncertainty itself, but that has its charm. Mail reaches us O.K. by the same address.

We are having regular Spring weather.

Translated from the French

December 16th, 1914.

To A——:

This very morning I received your Thanksgiving letter. For several days I have been without news because we returned this morning from a wonderful expedition. We had been released from our trenches in the Vosges and I from a little village three miles from Saint-Dié. Almost right away we were sent to Alsace by way of the neck of Bussang. We spent the night at Wesserling and the following morning we went directly to Saint-Amarin; there we took the mountain path on the left. At noon we were told that we would have to swoop down the opposite slope and take a village which lies at the foot of it. It was Steinbach. And we did it without difficulty. We came from two sides and we had our mitrailleuse in the middle. We came through the vineyards and the Germans fled. We were so few that they could easily have killed everyone of us. The inhabitants received us with wisdom. A woman called out to me: "We have been waiting for you a long time." Others were not saying anything, but one could see from their looks that they were more German than French. Mixed feelings.

While we were swooping down on the village, our captain was killed. With this exception, there were few casualties. About four o'clock the commandant came. He sent my company to the left. We dug trenches. During the night the Germans received about six trainfulls of reinforcements and we, nothing at all. As a natural result, the next day at daybreak they attacked us fiercely. My company took its stand on a crest still farther on the left and there we killed, killed all through the morning. We could see the Germans passing through the forest as they attempted to turn us. We were shooting at each other from a distance of fifty meters. About noon we had to withdraw. I thought we should take again the Saint-Amarin's path. No, indeed. Our officers brought us together down in the valley and then, by a big detour, we returned to take new positions, on the left, and of course we were attacked on the following day. We repulsed the attack but our positions were becoming untenable and on the fourth day, about 1 A.M., we quietly slipped away. Mountain trails, depth of night, hardly any sleep in three days and almost no food, this mountain trip was rather strenuous. At last we reached Thann and it is from there I am writing to you. I waved the *consigne* [orders or instructions] and I slept in a bed, in the house of an Alsatian family, who received me as a son and would not allow me to pay one cent. Now we are going to have a few days' rest. I shall try to write, so as to give you more particulars, but it is difficult. Now, I want you to know that this life suits me pretty well and I beg you not to be concerned about me. I enjoy meeting the Alsatians. They are so pleased to see us.

I must leave you now; love, much love to the family. I wish I could write to every one, but I cannot.

P.S.—There are a great many things I wish I could tell you, but how could I do it?

Military Hospital
To Miss H———:

Your newsy letter was given me, one morning in the trench. It was passed down from hand to hand to my place, and must have been surprised to find that it was destined to reach one of the men, all wrapped up in sheepskin and in a blanket and pretty generally plastered with red mud. I need not tell you that it was a genuine treat for me to hear from you and from all those about whom you wrote. It certainly was a rare thing to get Easthampton news, while in a nasty ditch in front of Steinbach, Alsace; so let me thank you very heartily for your kindness.

Well, to sum up operations, I was in Besançon (Caesar, Book I) eight weeks getting some training; then I was shipped with a detachment of about five hundred to a hamlet in the Vosges.[4] Said hamlet was eight miles from the trenches, which were 250 yards from the Germans. The six companies of our battalion would take turns two at a time, to occupy the trenches for a week or so at a time. There was no fighting to speak of, just sniping here and there, and very little of that. During the eight weeks, which we spent there, we did not lose ten men. The country is very rough and artillery could not come into play, hence easy times all around, except in rainy weather, or when the frost began to bite our toes. The mountains were beautiful, very heavily forested with evergreens, so heavily that while we could hear the Dutch talk and dig, we could seldom see them. This pleasant state of affairs changed, December 10th, when we were shipped at night, "for an unknown destination." In the morning we woke up a good many miles away on the Alsatian frontier, and by night we were in Wesserling, in the valley of the St.-Amarin, or of the Thann river. By morning we were on top of a mountain range north of the town of Weiler. There our captain told us calmly that we had come to take the town of Steinbach, which was somewhere on the edge of the Rhine valley; so we marched down forest trails and we were pretty full of thought. Cannon were booming down below us. Military balloons could be seen, swinging over the plain, and a "Taube," kept circling over us, making us take to the brush, every little while. At about 3 P.M., we suddenly came out of the woods into some vineyard and there was the village about six hundred yards away in the hollow. By that time we had been spotted, and shooting began. We scattered in along curved lines on the crest, leaving about six feet of space from one man to the next. We shot awhile. Then all got up, ran forward a few feet to lie still and shoot again. We had gone a hundred yards that way, [when] to our amazement, we heard our bugles sounding the charge. We still were the deuce of a way from the village, but there was nothing to do, but to get up and beat it down the vineyards, yelling like savages. At the foot of the slope there was a brook and we made for it. Men were falling here and there, some crawled away. Others were quite still. Our captain was killed just about then. His orderly told me that he was hit in the stomach, fell all in a heap, then sat up, braced himself, laughed and then fainted. He died a few moments later. By the time we had reached the brook and stretched in it and fired for a while on suspicious looking windows and roofs, the Germans had cleared out or hid in cellars. The fact is they had no idea that we would come over the mountain, and they were taken clear off their guard. We felt pretty fine, walking about the village, looking for prisoners, but before very long, the joke was on us. We were five companies and that was all, no way of getting reinforcements over the blamed mountain. It started to rain, and we were told to dig trenches about the village. We dug, but all night we heard trains, rumbling in the valley, coming from Mulhausen and Senheim. Their searchlights kept sweeping over us, and we lay flat in the mud each time. By morning we had sixteen companies of Germans on our hands and a lot of artillery. We were drenched to the skin, had had nothing to eat, and had not slept; still there was nothing to do, but to scrap it out, and all morning hour after hour, we lay in a wood and fired, and fired at Germans and more Germans, who kept coming, and all the time it poured great guns and still we had nothing to eat. By afternoon we had to retreat, so as not to be surrounded. I thought we were going back to where we came from, but instead of going down the opposite slope, turned to the right and by night, we were again over Steinbach only more to one side. We had one more night in the rain. We ate a few sardines and some hardtack. We learned we would attack next morning. The next morning it was found that we had lost too many men to attack. In the afternoon we were attacked, but we got out of that O.K. Still by 11 P.M. our commandant judged it was time to clear out, so we marched out quietly, one by one, found the trail as best we could in the dark. By 6 A.M. we were back to safety in the city of Thann, but needless to say that we were absolutely all in. We had hardly slept or eaten for three days and at times our clothes had frozen stiff on us. We had lost five hundred and twenty-five men, out of the fourteen hundred, so the whole thing could not be called a success. It would have been one if we had had five companies to reinforce us after we had taken the town. After that little expedition the powers that be saw fit to leave us alone for a few days, then they sent us to keep a mountain pass, Sudel, near the Guebwiller mountains, and we were there over Christmas and New Year's to the middle of January. It was cold. There was a lot of snow and a lot of work, but no danger. The Germans came only a few times and we called on them once or twice. We only lost one man and that was really an accident. While we were up there Steinbach was recaptured as you may have read in the papers. It had to be taken house by house, and to think that we had got hold of it a few weeks before, without any very serious losses. January 14 we came down from our mountain pass to sleep and wash, and January 18 we were ordered to occupy the new trenches, dug in front of the reconquered Steinbach, so up the range we went and down the other side, going over territory that was but too well known. We struck it rich again. It got cold and we could never light any fires for fear of artillery. Our cooks had to establish their kitchen a good mile back of the second line, and even then they were bombarded. Two were killed while trying to bring us our dinner. I staid up there only nine days, because I got hit as I told you above, but my poor friends remained three weeks on duty and were bombarded practically every day. They repulsed three attacks, lost their machine guns twice, and won them back each time by counter attacking at night, and each time gathering a respectable number of prisoners. On the whole we suffered mainly from exposure. There were hundreds of our men, who had to be sent away, because of frozen toes, frozen feet or bron-

chitis. The whole region around Steinbach is now hideous. The town
is deserted and completely wrecked. The fields and vineyards all about
are honeycombed with pits, made by the explosion of shells. The trees
in the orchards are covered with a thick coating of red earth. Before
the trenches in front of barbed wire tangles there are horrible sights.
If anything on earth can give a good idea of Hell, it is the region between Steinbach and Uffholz. If this is not the last European war it is
because all of us Europeans are stark mad. It is pitiful to ride through
the country now. One sees only women and children and old men. All
wars are bad, that's certain, but as they go and so far as we are concerned, this one is certainly a fairly honorable one. France has at least
as much right to exist as Germany.

Translated from the diary

At Lajus the old lady told me that German soldiers had a hang-
dog look in the presence of their officers; they remained bare-headed,
dared not call their souls their own. Their commanding officer was
heard saying, "Why this war? Why this war?" He paid twelve cents
when he was asked six, etc. The soldiers took to shooting the poul-
try promiscuously and he had them shot in order to save the fowls.
And yet two "castles" owned by Germans, one at Selles, the other the
hideous structures at the end of La Trouche, were both filled with
supplies for the German troops.

We left La Trouche on December 10th; we went down to La
Pêcherie where we were nicely quartered in a hay loft. We were expecting to spend some time there, but twenty-four hours after our arrival, the quartermasters were hurrying about—we ate at 4 P.M.,
started at 6 and, after waiting for hours in the rain at Saint-Michel-sur-
Meurthe, we rode in a baggage car; as we were forty in one car we
could not all get seated at once. On arrival, rain in torrents, we ate a
few sardines, then marched towards the frontier. When we reached
Wesserling we were all in; we were lame and completely bespattered
with mud. It was not the length of the trip that told on us, but rather
the lack of sleep and of food. My section being on duty Goujon
treated us to a mess of sweetbreads. The mayor and his daughter
thinking that we might be allowed to be quartered in private houses,
had beds ready for us. Kindly French people they were, and we found
in this town a much more cordial welcome than in the Vosges.

As sentries we were requested to watch the church steeple! What nonsense—a man was said to be in the church under pretense of mending the furnace—likely at 9 P.M.!

The old servant of the priest discovered me behind the church. I told her to go in. What do you think she wanted to do? She was planning to go all over the village in search of the officers which were to spend the night at the parsonage. She wanted to hurry them up, for the priest had gone to bed and she, not feeling very well, wished also to retire.

Translated from the diary

How the Night Was Spent Near Steinbach
Rain in torrents and thick mud. We placed our afghans under the tent-flaps and we settled for the night as best we could. Suddenly, from the valley flashes of light shone brilliantly, passing over the forest, they crept slowly towards us and finally rested right above our heads. We huddled together in the mud, but we had to go through the same ordeal over and over again. Sometimes, when we least expected, the light would go out suddenly, and at the very moment we tried to lift ourselves out of the mud, the lights shone again brightly. Thus we might have been very easily spotted. Well, it was an awful night. Again and again I rose and walked about. The men, singly or in groups, with their heads and shoulders shrouded in tent-flaps, formed ghostly masses. We could not stack our guns because the flashing bayonets would have been too easily detected; they were lying in the mud of the trenches useless and in many cases entirely unavailable. The time spent in our last stopping place was most trying; we were all discouraged, we thought we would have to attack immediately and our strength failed us; no food, no sleep, no officers—exhausting marches and as far as we could see no definite purpose. Gras, the lieu-tenant, had been asked to take command, and I had been appointed agent de liaison pro tem.

Tuesday morning Gras asked me to find out how many cartridges were still to be had; then I fetched for our new commandant his horse and while we were standing around him thoroughly disheartened, he gave us our supply of cartridges.

Suddenly on the road we saw coming at a triple gallop a tall man on a large horse, it was the head major who roared from afar, "The attack is to be postponed. Captain de la Baume is strictly forbidden to attack!" We all heaved a sigh of relief. Meanwhile the horse wanted to go straight on; his master wanted him to go up-hill. Finally the spurs had to be used to make the reluctant beast mind. What a man, that head major!

I spent the whole morning waiting for orders from the lieutenant; he did not give any. Wednesday about midnight our cook awakened us. Take your knapsacks. An attack is no longer possible. An hour later our section stood at the edge of the forest, we met the others at the crossroads a little farther on, some men were missing, one or two here and there, forgotten sentries or smart fellows who had found comfortable places where they could sleep soundly and who at the last minute could not be found by their corporals. We started, it was pitch dark, one man only, at the head of our single file, carried a lantern; the others had to flounder in the dark. It is the hardest trip I have ever taken, the damp afghan weighed tons. I felt the pangs of an empty stomach; at most we had had two hours of sleep and the nights had been preceded by the most exhausting days. Very steep path, rolling stones at every step. I kept hitting against the tin dish of the man who walked ahead of me. When I felt too weak, I ate a piece of bully beef, but I was awfully thirsty, for my flask had been left on the top of the hill at the time of the sudden surprise. I saw stars and sparks dancing before my eyes; occasionally I would catch a glimpse of another man's gun. It was a regular retreat. The one thing which kept up our courage was the certainty that we were not going to attack on the following day. Finally we heard that we were going to Thann. At last the lights of Mulhausen grew dimmer and dimmer; we were on our way towards the reconquered part of Alsace. About 8 A.M. we found quarters in a factory between Bishwiller and Thann.

December 23d, 1914.
To B——:

Since our fight at Steinbach, we had three days of rest between Thann and Bishviller [*sic*] in eastern Alsace; then we were trotted up to this little mountain village, or hamlet, rather, to spend the night. The next day we walked up a few miles to the height of land and took charge of the *avant-postes* [advance posts] along the crest. I guess we are distinctly mountain troops, for we are always kept on ridges. This time we were at an altitude of about 4,000 feet, like Kearsarge in N.H. The alpine troops had built fine log-houses, with stoves and all we had to do was sentinel work six hours in twenty-four to keep spies, scouts and patrol in a respectful state of mind. Nothing at all happened at my post and I enjoyed the scenery. There are just a few inches of snow—the clingy kind which remains like furry-muffs about the twigs. Before us we had the Rhine Valley with the hills of the Black Forest in the distance. To the right the serrated outline of the Bernese Alps and, I think, of that old friend of you and me, the Jungfrau. Who would have thought last year that I would see these mountains from that point of view and under such circumstances?

We expected to stay up there five days and five nights, but we were replaced without warning this afternoon by alpine troops. We have only come down to the nearest hamlet and expect to go back there in a day or two. We don't know what's going on in the rest of the world. I have not seen an up-to-date paper for a deuce of a while, but one thing is sure. We hold the crests and mountain tops of Alsace all the way, and if we wanted to bombard their cities as they bombarded ours, nothing would be easier. Our guns, great big eight-inch, long distance guns, are trained on the valley and something will happen one of these days; only we don't fire on civilians the way they do. I don't believe they feel very easy in their minds, as at night we constantly hear trains rumbling along near Mulhausen and they can only be troop trains.

This is not a cold winter, but nevertheless night watches are pretty chilly at this altitude, so our benevolent government has given us sheepskins (not Ph.D. diplomas) with the wool on. There is a hole for the head and strings to tie to the body. With these contraptions on, we must look like Biblical characters looking for grasshoppers to feed.[5] It keeps us warm O.K.

I will write again Christmas day if they leave us here in peace.

Translated from the diary

Spies at Thann have been forwarding information by means of bottles thrown into the river. If at Steinbach our artillery did not give us support in time it was because the telephone wire had been cut down by a German officer—disguised as a woman, they say.

The small, isolated farms in the mountains are held more or less in suspicion. Here in Goldbach part of the population is evidently hostile. They are bringing up here barbed wire and planks in large quantities; the village is full of mules. One would think they are intending to build fortified camps on all the crests. To-night is Christmas eve, 1914.

Christmas, 1914.
To His Niece, L.A.

Pardon this dingy looking paper. Supplies will get mussed up. I received your letter the day before Christmas, and Marie's and Peg's the day after; your mother's with yours, so had a fine celebration. I thank you all you dear ones, from the depths of my heart, for your greeting and also for the gold which I can't use now, but which will come in very handy next time we reach a town.

We celebrated Christmas eve with the help of the government which being paternal, gave us green peas, *boudin* [blood sausage] and first-class white wine in addition to the usual stuff, but we were kept on the jump all day because of a possible attack in the back hills; an attack which did not materialize, fortunately. The main interest now comes from the fact that we have hit it rich in getting quarters. We (our squad), twelve men and a corporal known as the "Cabo," are with a lovely Alsatian family or rather the women of the family, for the three men are with the German army somewhere. We sleep on brand-new hay. I mean hay that has not been slept on before; we roam at will through the kitchen and the sitting room; we can buy milk and butter and get our clothes washed at ridiculous prices; we can always get next to a roaring fire. It is mighty good, only it may not last long, because in two days we will receive reinforcements, to make up for what we lost in our last expedition, and then we will be off again to guard the crests. Since Christmas afternoon, heavy guns and small guns have been roaring in a way defying description down the valley in the direction of Mulhausen. We don't know what has happened yet, but there certainly has been some fighting. Yesterday, two German headsergeants were brought in. One of them was the only survivor of his section (sixty men). They had attacked the alpine troops in the morning and practically the whole company had been cleared out. One of these men made a pretty fine appearance. Everybody admired him for his bearing, and our captain saluted him graciously, but he seemed to see no one at all. He was very different from the fat bald-headed German whom we corralled when we took the village two weeks ago; also different from a skinny officer whom our adjutant caught in the brush near said village. The prisoners we get now tell us that they have just come from Dixmude to Alsace. I don't see any quick termination to this war. Our troops are piling in rapidly and we have a lot of heavy pieces, but the Dutch are not what you might call inactive, and it's raining so that the valley must be a regular swamp. I have an idea that they are going to keep us in the mountains as the line infantry make terrible work of it as soon as they leave the level country. In the house where we are, there are a dozen artillerymen hailing from Nice and neighborhood. They add to our enjoyment of life. They have the real southern accent; at night they play the *Merry Widow*, *Sousa's March*, *Sous les Ponts de Paris* and other classic music on their "flageolets," a kind of flute with very few holes. For that matter, there are some of these gentlemen quartered elsewhere in the hamlet and if you step out of the house at night you can hear these flageolets all over the neighborhood. At the same time the guns are booming in the valley. There was another musical contrast Sunday. We were on duty—that is, our company spent all day on the village square in case something should happen. I was seated on the wall which is about the graveyard and the guns in the valley made a sort of bass to the music which accompanied the celebration of the mass within the little church. Men become religious in war time. On Christmas day our officers went to mass in state and style. Yesterday I had some fun watching various kinds of "chasseurs" and dragoons and muleteers and artillery men sneaking into the church, coming by the back way and progressing cautiously and somewhat sheepishly towards the church, opening the door stealthily and entering crab fashion. Bold bad boys in ordinary times and weather, but made meek by the events.

Great surprise to write this. I moved to the next cottage. The girl in the house was born in Buffalo, N.Y. Came to Alsace when seven months old, knowledge of English limited, but the mother remembers hard times during the Cleveland administration. She remained in the United States two years only.

I wish we might spend the winter together in Europe; perhaps some day we will. Nothing like keeping up hope. I think I know what you mean when you say that Europe helped you understanding

America. One thing is certain—Americans have fine traits which Europeans will get from them in course of time. A freedom from certain harmful traditions, your judgments are less warped than those of Europeans when it comes to right and wrong in politics particularly it seems to me. I am messing this up, not having thought it out enough. Will report later. Give my love to all. I will keep the family posted on all excitement as much as small facilities will allow. I hear from John quite often. He keeps me supplied with tobacco, chocolate and sardines in a way that would do credit to the administration of the Republic. Good bye, Youngest, and best wishes.

Goldbach, December 25th, 1914.
To B——:

This is Christmas night and the first one of its kind for me, as for many others. We are still at Goldbach, a few miles from Thann. We are apparently waiting for things to happen. Troops and more troops keep coming up and taking positions along the mountain side. It's mainly artillery and mountain infantry.

All day long they kept telling us to be ready to leave at any minute, so we were kept in suspense, but nothing happened until 4 this afternoon, when my *escouade* was told to go to the guardhouse for the night and do the police duty of the town. I have just been relieved from the post at the end of the town and I am writing at the guardhouse, which is simply a schoolhouse converted in warlike fashion. I am seated at the desk, my natural place. Last night being Christmas eve, we celebrated a little. The government treated us to green peas, blood sausages, a superior kind of white wine and sweet crackers. That well meant mess was distributed in addition to the usual "feed." I partook of it and as a result have been a physical wreck all day nearly, in spite of the fact that I managed to get a feather bed to sleep on last night.

The people of this town seem to be sharply divided in their opinions. They either like or dislike us. At the house and barn where we were day before yesterday, they hated the sight of us. They tried to keep us from sleeping on their hay; they would not let our cooks into their kitchen, and we did not get a look inside the house. In addition they made faces at us when they went or came. Fortunately we were made to move to another place after twenty-four hours, and we were very well received in our new quarters. Our cooks were given freedom of the kitchen range, and all of us were let into the lower rooms in which we could sit down, warm ourselves and write. There are only women in the house. The grandmother remembers having been French before 1870.[6] She still speaks broken French. She has some of your sister's principles about smoking in the house. As it was getting pretty thick with smoke in the sitting room she asked us to quit, and we did very promptly as she was a dear old lady. But she was filled with remorse after her request and she trotted over to a sort of bureau, pulled out a little black box from a drawer and passed it around—it was snuff! All who partook sneezed with a will. It was she who got me a feather bed in her grandson's house. I hope I shall be able to say goodbye to her before we leave. If it hadn't been for this fool guardhouse business, I could have spent another night in regal luxury.

I wish I knew where we are going next. This is a life of great geographical instability.

Sometime ago my brother shipped me a lot of chocolate, cigarette tobacco and canned goods, which reached me to-day, so that I had a Christmas tree of my own.

I was going to forget to tell you that the old lady at the house took me in an inner room last night and showed me what they had prepared for the children. It was a little barn made out of pink paper. Inside, together with lighted candles, were the Christ child in the manger, the ox and the ass to the left and right, the Wise Men all about. She told me that the war might stop soon after Christmas, because already once before in history just at that time of the year, Jesus had taken time by the foot and made him change his course.

People out here are very religious. Also to my amazement, our officers seem to be religiously inclined. They all went to mass this morning. I don't know whether it's because they really want to or because they want to show unity of sentiment with the reconquered people of Alsace. Religion and politics usually go hand in hand in the army.

I only have four cents' worth of stamps left. I hope the United States mail will be merciful.

January 7th, 1915.
To B——:

Our life is so taken up with trifles; we get into a real house so seldom that writing is still very difficult. I am worried about you. It's a long time since I have had a letter. I am wondering whether something is the matter or whether it's simply the mail service. We have had piles of snow, then a two days' rain and the result on mountain roads is wonderful. Our mules lie down *et ne veulent plus rien savoir* [and don't want to know anything more]. I don't know when we shall be in a village again. We are living in log houses up in the mountains. Every other day we sleep in a farm house. If the weather were not so damnable, it would be pretty good fun, but this is not real winter weather,—more like New England in March, late March, with some snow but more mud and a most damnable wind.

The Dutch keep themselves in the valley bottoms. Hope they stay there.

January 11th, 1915.
To B——:

I have received your New Year's letter and was much relieved as I had begun to fear that you were sick.

Nothing new. We still live much like lumbermen in snow and rain and are none the worse for it. There has not been much fighting in the hills. Too much snow. The town which I helped capture on December 13th and which was recaptured by the Dutch is ours again. This is a rotten war. Neither side can lick the other, I think.

Will write again if I get to a town in a few days as is rumored.

January 14th, 1915.
To B——:

We are at last in a little town after a month spent either in a diminutive hamlet or out in the woods. This business of seeing that no Dutch come over a mountain pass is no joke when the weather is bad. What made things worse was the fact that the officer commanding the company is very young (he replaced our regular captain who was killed last month) and he was scared blue of not holding that pass and so made our work twice as hard as was needed. Every other day we were on guard every third hour for twenty-four hours and mainly during raging snow storms. Fortunately it was never very cold. There was no shooting to speak of. We were shelled once or twice but no one was hurt.

Now we are going to be allowed to sleep a day or two; then we will go off to some other place, no one knows where. Such is life in the army, alternations of boredom with excessive excitement.

I wish I knew what percentage of my letters reach you—you mention mainly cards received and so does my family. There must be piles of writings from my pen stored up somewhere.

This town saintamarin, which I write in one word to fool the censorship, is very friendly to us.[7] The old barber who fixed me up this morning has one son in the German army; the other one is with us, and the father mourns for the fate of his German son. There are tragedies of this kind all over Alsace.

I don't see the end of this war at all. Both sides are determined to win out and after tremendous efforts either side may have won one-quarter or one-half mile of territory! It costs at times the lives of several hundred men to win an advance of fifty yards! Those people in the United States who clamor for armament can't begin to know what they are doing or with what kind of pernicious fire they are playing. I am told that the Hearst papers are campaigning in favor of Germany vs. the Allies.[8] It's not wonderful that this master opportunist should have snatched up such a dandy cause. I don't believe that he can swing popular opinion. Americans love force, but they despise treason and sneakiness. I don't believe the Germans will recover from their nasty actions just because Hearst talks in their favor.

I shall write again as soon as I know what is doing. I shan't seal this letter, hoping that it may go more easily.

January 14th, 1915.

To A——:

We have just spent three weeks on the mountain. The weather was detestable. We are very happy to be in a little town. O, the delight of having one's hair cut, the joy of shaving. We wash our hands many times a day. Up there, we could wash only once every three days and sometimes not even so often. Civilization has its advantages. We are going to be sent somewhere else, I don't know where; uncertainty belongs to military life, but what surprises me is that the conditions which in ordinary life would develop pleurisy, pneumonia, rheumatism and a thousand fatal diseases, do not even cause a cold when we are soldiering. It is really puzzling.

I am glad you heard Brieux.[9] I have read about ten of his plays. I always liked him because of his virility. He stands in fine contrast with a good many of our modern writers who are altogether too supple. From a moral standpoint I hate flabbiness. I am more of a Huguenot than most people think.[10]

Up there, the Germans would shoot at us, using little mountain cannon of Austrian make. All they could do was to nick off the edge of some rocks, make holes in the snow and bring down some branches from the trees. Again and again they sent patrols which went down double-quick. We also went patrolling in their direction and we came back quite rapidly. Patrolling is fun of a mild type. One starts through the forest, rifle in hand, going from one tree to the next like Gustave Aymard's heroes.[11] You think all the time that you are going to meet a Boche face to face. Most of the time you do not see anything at all or you exchange shots from idiotic distances. One day, one of the Blues, a boy twenty years old, came down like a gust of wind—German patrol thirty meters off! Another man and I went to investigate. It was a picket fence which, piercing through the snow, simulated pointed helmets. On the other hand a man from the Vosges told us he could see magpies; and by gum the Germans were there.[12]

January 28th, 1915.
To A———:

I am now at the bottom of a valley enjoying profound peace after a week filled with whizzing of shells and reports of guns. Fortunately there has been on both sides more noise than mischief, but as far as noise was concerned I assure you it was a success. One day I counted in eleven minutes, eighty-two shells bursting close by us. Henceforth, Fourth of July celebration will not make any impression on me. We spent as much as seventy-two hours at a stretch in open trenches, at different intervals; we came out of these trenches as red devils, for the earth is of the same shade as the soil which forms Mount Tom, or rather, Titan's pier.[13] Fortunately the winter is very mild. There is a little snow, but the cold does not compare with Northampton weather, and yet some poor fellows manage to get their feet frozen, or rather, frostbitten, and in consequence of this they suffer cruel pains, but they have also the advantage of spending a few peaceful days in the infirmary. Well it is a wretched business and I hope this war will close by the end of the summer. In my opinion there is no possibility of a complete victory either for them or for us. The nations will have to come to their senses! But to know that our country did not wish to go to war is for me a great source of strength and courage.

January 28th, 1915.

To B——:

We have had a most strenuous week just where the foothills merge into the plains. We could not light any fires at any time for fear of being discovered by the artillery, and as they did not know otherwise than in a general way about our location, they just rained shells on the whole neighborhood. We spent two days in shelters—trenches covered with heavy beams, and two days in open trenches. The main trouble was in going from one to the other over open spaces. We made the trips at such convenient times as 2 A.M., etc. In one case I counted eighty shells which exploded near us during a walk of eleven minutes—and yet no one was hurt!

Now I am at rest in a little town on the other side of the mountains. I don't know when we shall go back to the shell region. More troops are piling in, but so far as I can see the war is as much of a deadlock as ever; either side is strong enough to check the other but not strong enough to lick it.

What with the snow and the shells (not egg shells) the mail is upset so our correspondence is bound to be again one sided for a time.

I have seen some amazing things this last week. I can't write about them now, but I shall tell you all about them. The French are a pretty brave race, believe me, and the only real darn fools in the lot are those who write novels about them. If I ever get back to Stanford I shall give a course on the French novel with a view to rehabilitating the race. I am putting all manners of curious and interesting facts in my diary, which one hundred years from now should be worth millions of dollars from an historical standpoint.

We have been very fortunate in the weather—it snows a little, but never gets very cold; nothing like New England winters. I don't believe the thermometer ever got below twenty-five degrees Fahrenheit this past week. It thaws in day time and if you could see us when we come out of the trenches you would not think we were human beings, being actually plastered with mud from head to toe.

Well, goodbye for the present. Write as often as you can and keep up our cause in the United States.

Weiler, February 1, 1915.
To B——:

Your last letter (January 6th) came right after I had written to you on coming down from the trenches for a rest.

These days I am leading a perfectly animal life. It is so good to be able to warm oneself "à volonté" [at will; any time one wants to], to eat warm things, and to sleep twelve hours at a lick after nine days in and about trenches and under a shower of shot averaging from 1,000 to 1,500 shells a day.

We had a scare the day after I reached here. I was asleep when I thought I heard the too-well known hissing of a shell. When I woke up fully they were bringing in two men, one hurt in the foot, the other in the side. In addition a woman had been killed as she was coming out of her front door and an "alpin" also killed behind the house. That shell came from the other side of the range. It had gone nearly ten miles to do the mischief. We expected a regular bombardment, but that was all, and that was enough. That's the most disgusting thing about war, the killing of civilians.

We with uniforms expect trouble, but who can become reconciled to a state of affairs that kills blindly? A German aero flew over Thann yesterday, threw a bomb casually and killed women and children. The more I see of war, the less I respect it. It is fundamentally inane. That does not mean that I regret that France pitched in. Quite to the contrary. It was high time for her to do so.

Only it's idiotic to allow the development of conditions which gradually bring on war. I do hope that your country will be able to check the wave of militarism which the Republicans, I believe, are trying to set going. If you start fooling with that kind of nonsense you are sure to develop a wrong kind of patriotism and end up in bloodshed.

Well, good-bye for to-day. Keep up good courage.

Weiler, February 5, 1915.
To Mr. G——:

My poor battalion had again a devil of a time. We took up trenches between Steinbach and Uffholz. The same are so placed that the Boches can bombard them abundantly from the plain with guns mounted on auto trucks and therefore not to be spotted by our artillery. The result has been that they have repeatedly demolished part of

our trenches then attacked those parts and captured them by dusk. We
have counter-attacked after dark and recaptured them with the bayonet. The sum total of the fighting being o = o since we regained what
we had lost and nothing more. Bloody and idiotic, but pretty necessary from our standpoint at least since we must hold the foothills at
any cost.

There is something ridiculous in the contrast between the amount
of steel thrown, of air displaced, of dirt thrown up and actual harm
done. Some days ago we received about 3,000 or 4,000 big shells,
"marmites" which dig in the earth holes big enough to bury a horse
and our losses could be counted on the fingers of two hands.[14]

Translated from the French

Weiler, February 6, 1915.
To A———:
I have been worried by your last letter because I saw that you
were too anxious about me. I hasten to tell you that at the present time
I am in complete security and, in all probability, this state of things
will last through February and perhaps even beyond that time.

To-day my poor battalion is completing its third week of first line
service, three weeks in the trenches between Steinbach and Uffholz,
and our men are in a state of health which is far from satisfactory.
Almost all of them, having had their feet more or less frozen, suffer
cruel pains. It will be absolutely necessary to let this poor battalion
rest for a while, because, having remained too long in a sitting position, the men are no longer able to stand on their feet.

I am in very good health because I remained only nine days over
there. We went up on the 18th of January and on the 23d, during the
night, I received on the left shoulder a *slap* which made it permissible
for me to enter the infirmary three days later, and ever since then I
have been here sleeping and eating copiously.

I had fully made up my mind not to mention to you the *slap* but
John writes me that you complain I am gilding the pill for you. *Pero
hombre!* [But man! (Spanish)] it is a libel and henceforth I will not fail
to report even a cold.

My battalion covered itself with glory. It was mentioned in the
order of the day, both before and after I went away. The Boches bombarded us daily with unheard of violence, then as we were greatly

outnumbered by them, they attacked us three times in succession. The first time we lost a small part of a trench, and it was on that occasion, while on sentinel duty that I was hit. On all other occasions the Boches were driven back with such losses and in such confusion that had we had a battalion to support us we could have taken Cernay and made a clean sweep of it all. It seems that the prisoners we took were completely demoralized. In connection with this encounter they tell a story worthy of Corneille.[15] The captain of the sixth company wounded, stretched full length on the ground, was giving orders the best he could. Being in great need of reinforcement, he sent word to the commandant who had not one man to spare. The commandant answered: As reinforcement here I am! And without wasting time he jumped into the trench, revolver in hand. Great enthusiasm. Everybody followed him and those of the poor Germans who did not fall dead, run like rabbits. And what do you think was the net result of a furious bombardment which lasted nearly two weeks and which was followed by three attacks? We kept all our positions. It seems little, but in fact we accomplished a great deal, for the Germans, through the valley, receive all the troops they need and they concentrate their forces as they please. On our side, in the gorges and on the crests, it is very difficult for us to receive any reinforcement, because behind us we have a mountain range crossed only by mule trails.[16] Of course I did not *see* the commandant when he made his hit, but the story is absolutely true, I know it for a fact.

Aunt Marie and Aunt Pauline have just sent me another package. That explains why my knapsack is full of dates, figs, quinces and Suchard chocolate. At the same time John has been sending me some nougat from Montélimar and I am daily looking for some chocolate from Dulac. I fully expect after my wound is healed that I will have to prolong my stay in the hospital on account of gastric troubles.

Good-bye, my dear, do not worry until the middle of March and even then don't.

February 7, 1915.
To Mr. G——:

For the last ten days I have been in the infirmary, and I have a sneaking hope that I may be shipped to a hospital one of these days, although my general health is excellent. My trouble is a flesh wound of no particular consequence, except for the fact that it is very well placed, right under the cartridge belt strap (left) and the knapsack strap. I can't be made to carry anything for some three weeks anyway, and as the infirmary is very full, I am hoping that they may send me away to make room for others.

My battalion had a devil of a time the second half of January. We went up the range and down the other side to take up the trenches about Steinbach and Uffholz.

Hardly had we reached our positions than the Dutch began to give signs of unusual activity. They began to bombard, and they kept it up day after day. The first forty-eight hours my company was held on reserve and all we could do was to sit in covered trenches and listen to the shells burst in our neighborhood. It was quite a stunt to get out at all as fragments came buzzing along at any time. Although the explosions took place near the regular trenches quite a distance from us we could not have any fires because of the danger of being spotted, and it was freezing pretty hard. Another thing, we could not lie down. The covered ditches being too narrow, we slept with our knees to our chin. The third and fourth days we relieved the company in the first line trenches. The one we occupied made me think of Dante's *Inferno*, the part assigned to Brunetto Latini, who runs madly on a sandy plain under a rain of fire.[17] The trench was in yellow mud. In the front of it in the mud there were poor fellows stretched out in their last sleep, fifteen or twenty of them. In addition many humps over the field, all being hastily made graves. The trench was German originally. It had been stormed by the 252nd regiment and turned around to face the German front. The slaughter had been terrible. To our back and to the right was the village of Steinbach, or rather the ghost of the village. My company took it December 13th. It was retaken by the Dutch. Soon after that, taken away from them by line infantry, every house riddled with shot. Few roofs and many black walls, the steeple showing the light right through in a dozen places. To our left was the road of access, and perhaps the most striking element in the picture, every square yard ploughed up by exploded shells. There the earth was red, just as it is near Holyoke. Well, the trees, fruit trees and the vineyards were all red from the amount of dirt kicked up by shells. While on duty we were bombarded reasonably well, but no one was hurt. One of those big shells exploding is a great sight. The dirt is kicked up as high as a three-story house. A hole big enough to bury a horse is dug up. Stones fly in all directions, and also fragments of metal weighing pounds. Yet they do little harm considering the noise and the fuss. If they fall on a group of ten or twenty men, they will clean them all out, but they may fall ten yards away, and do no harm. It stands to reason that soldiers do not stand in groups under bombardment. The fifth day and the sixth we were to be in the second line, they made us build an artillery shelter in the back woods. All went serenely until about 4 P.M. There was just the regular number of shells, two or three every five minutes, but at four, by gum, things began to hum, and we received orders to move to the front P.D.Q. My section started up, I pulled out my watch and started to count. It took us eleven minutes to get to our second line position and in that time we received in front and in back to the right and left eighty-two shells. The noise and the stuff kicked up and the branches cut made an "ensemble" impossible to describe, yet no one was hurt. Our adjutant turned once to shout a command and got his mouth full of dirt. That was all. To me our escaping scot free was a real miracle. Well, the bombardment stopped and before we had time to get to the first line the Dutch had grabbed hold of a bit of trench. All we could do was to dig one right back and so we did. It was pitch dark by that time and as I am not much good at digging, I asked to be put on sentry duty to see that no "Boche" sneaked up to those who were working. Four of us went about twenty yards forward, sat down and listened. Our artillery had set fire to three houses in the plain. The red smoke was all we could see, but we could hear our men digging and the Germans digging. We were about eighty yards from them, suddenly things started up again. I don't know who did the starting or why, but we were caught between two perfectly fiendish fusillades. Our light artillery fired over our heads, dangerously close to our pates. The Dutch fired bombs with their trench bombs and their hand grenades. Some kind of fragment finally hit me on the shoulder so I stopped firing and took to cover behind a big log. The other sentinels crept up also and we waited for the storm to slacken. I was not in any pain so I did not go to the field hospital. By morning our trench was ready for occupancy. We spent three days and three nights in it. Once in a while there would be fits of furious firing, with little or no harm done. Once we were ordered to put on our sacks. I found I could not stand mine, so retreated and came here where I am now. Since I have been here the Germans attacked twice, and got theirs richly each time. The first time was on the Kaiser's birthday and they came up by fours, shouting drunk and got cleaned out. The second time they came in hordes, rushed two trenches and pinched a rapid fire gun, whereupon our commander came along, drew his revolver and my friends charged with him, kicked the Dutch out of the trenches, got hold of the machine gun and made a lot of prisoners. I have been told that the ground in front of the trenches is gray with German uniforms. One of our captains wept when he saw the slaughter of the Germans, for young men are young men, even when they are Germans. These slaughters take place at dusk or at night. Such is war, Tim! It does not seem credible that we are in the twentieth century. Things like that happen every day, from Switzerland to the Atlantic. Neither side advances but both sides lose heavily, the Germans more because they attack nearly always in close formation, whereas we scatter and run up individually. I am hoping to be off duty through February. War may be a stimulating occupation, but these hours when there is no good reason why any one second should not be your last are pretty trying, though it is astonishing how rapidly one gets used to danger, and takes it as a matter of course.

From the diary

After I was wounded I remained in the hole perhaps ten minutes. My shoulder did not hurt, though I knew it was bleeding. As soon as the firing died out, I crawled out and went back to the section, told V—— that I wanted to find a nurse and I started for the road. I had not gone five minutes when I ran into an officer—the commandant— who asked where under the sun I was going. I told him I was slightly hurt and wanted my wound dressed. He told me that all medical attendance was way back, where we had slept in the woods the first night and that if I was only slightly hurt the best thing for me was to get back to my section. A man with his foot shot through was wailing by the roadside. The officer's attitude piqued me. Rather than argue or beg I turned back rather angry. I took the wrong road and stumbled on the adjutant who was dozing away in a log-house. He made me come in and sit down. Later Coutil came in. He had a slight wound in the face, from an explosive rifle ball. The Germans certainly use two kinds of shot. Some whiz and hiss as they go by, just as ours do. Others are heard only as they hit something near one, when an unmistakable explosion takes place. One such (dum dum?) exploded right over my head, in day time, cutting a twig at the same instant. And yet, Captain Beaugier says that bullets hitting the trunk of a tree make exactly the noise of a small shell exploding and that the explosive bullet is a myth. I spent wretched hours in that hovel waiting for daybreak. I could not lie down. I sat hunched up. When I went back to the section the trench was well under way. There were no rocks at all, soft red earth, and in a few hours more we had a good trench in which one could stand while firing. That must have been the morning of the 24th of January.

We spent the whole day seated. There was little artillery fire. They could not fire any marmites at us without endangering their own trench, for the two trenches were less than one hundred yards apart. Rifle shots were frequent. We were resting, after a fashion.

The next day was dull except in the afternoon when the Germans got a gun way to the left which sent a few marmites back of us and pretty near—pebbles and "flies" falling near us.

Then the rumor started that we were to attack. We were in worse shape than ever and that piece of news was received mournfully. Then we were told for a fact it was the fourth company which was to attack and that we were to remain in our trench ready to back it up. At about quarter of four, we heard a rush back of us and a section came to us on the run, they jumped into the ditch and sat with us. Later we got out and lay flat on the ground to give plenty of room to the new comers who were to attack. A little while before their arrival D—— had returned with orders to send a man forward in our wires, with a wirecutter and a shield. He was to cut three paths in the tangle for the attacking party to pass out towards the Germans. Lots were drawn between the ninth and tenth squad. The ninth drew the short end. B—— was appointed. He did not hesitate a second. Quickly, without a word he lifted the heavy shield over the embankment, threw the cutters over then jumped into the danger zone, setting to work immediately. For this he was proposed for a corporalship the next day.

This attack seemed inane to all, as the trenches lost were badly placed, not connecting with the others, whereas the one we had constructed only ninety meters back abutted exactly with the left and right lines of defense. I understand that the commandant and captain attacked under protest being compelled to do so against their judgment by the colonel. About four the signal was given for the attack. With fixed bayonets, without the sack they jumped over the embankment shouting. It was a fine sight. Those men knew for a fact that only a few would ever come back. The majority never hesitated a moment to rush forward. One or two did not start at all, remained among us. I could see one standing in front. He had an axe and was cutting wire. He stood fearless in full view of the enemy.

The firing became intense. The alpine batteries had showered us with shells, then our machine guns had swept the woods. The rifle fire was intense from then on. Some time after dark the wounded began to come in. Laurent jumped over to get a man whose arm was broken. A corporal with his leg broken was also lifted over. They told us that the attack had failed. Only about twenty reached the trench. A few jumped in. All were shot through the head sooner or later and at very close range. Some claimed to have heard the Germans shout later in the night "Chasseurs kaput bravement" [Chasseurs died bravely]. Some eighty men perished in this affair. Useless sacrifice, but as fine a display of gallantry as one might hope to see under any flag. When they dashed over the embankment, I could not hold back my tears. They were so cool, so determined and yet they knew they could not succeed—no fanaticism, they were obeying orders that bade them look Death right in the face. "Theirs not to reason why."[18]

The man with a wound in the arm moaned a good deal asking why the bearers did not come, etc., etc. Suddenly he discovered that one of our section was from his home town. He forgot his troubles, became less dramatic and finally gathered courage to get out under our own steam and power.

The corporal much more badly hurt, said little but that in a firm voice and to the point. Bourrinet arranged a shelter with a tent flap. One of his section who is now in this room with me, at Weiler infirmary, comforted him. He himself had just escaped death. I can still hear him say to the corporal, "Wait, little one, we are going little one," as tenderly as a mother. He had carried the corporal from the wires to the ditch; he was a farmer, most gentle, a ladies' man in his rural way.

Finally they carried away the corporal, no easy matter, for the Germans were sending an occasional "marmite" on the road leading to the relief station. The rest of the night was uneventful as also the following day. It thawed and we lived in liquid mud. I went as sentry for six hours at night, in the machine gun shelter. I stood behind a shield. I fell asleep over and over again for a second at a time being awakened by the knocking of my knees against the wall as I collapsed. I was relieved at midnight, dug a nice long sloping seat in the back of the trench, threw my afghan over my head and slept until daybreak, not bothering to look out when spasmodic outbreaks of wild firing took place. By morning I decided to have the wound in my shoulder examined. I started up and reached the field-hospital without trouble. I found Meunier who dressed my wound and assured me that I was amply entitled to rest at Weiler's infirmary. He gave me some hot coffee, emptied my cartridge boxes and gave me a pass.

CHAPTER 4

~

Wounded

Bussang, France, February 10, 1915.

To B———:

I am in France again.[1] Have a job as interpreter with the British ambulance which does the Alsace-France service. It came about by my being hit very slightly in the shoulder January 23d. On my way towards the infirmary, I ran into our English friends and they went to the head surgeon and asked that I be retained! So I have a sinecure for three weeks, probably, and will get a vacation after that. Shall spend a week with my brother. Talk about luck! Ye gods. Will send details soon. With enthusiasm. Will send address later—don't know it yet.

Bussang, Vosges, February 11, 1915.

To B———:

This is a great world, but particularly so in war time. I am in this confounded town with nothing to do and no way of receiving mail because I am in hopes of getting out one of these days and it would not pay to have letters follow me. My mail is mixed up enough as it is.

We had great excitement at the infirmary to-day, as Poincaré, the President of the Republic, came to visit the plant.[2] Such sweepings, derangings and arrangings of cots, blacking of shoes, etc., one never had seen in the Vosges before. He came with the president of the cabinet and a handful of generals, took a circular look and beat it, to the relief of all. I have been told that he was going as far as Thann. If I had known that, I would have told him to watch out as it is a bad place for presidents just now. There is a lot of shooting in that direction as I know from experience.

The snow is rapidly disappearing from the hills and there is none at all in the plains. It is fortunate enough for the suffering of the soldiers keeping mountain passes has been horrible. It would break your heart to see in the infirmaries a regular line-up of poor fellows walking on all fours. They put their knees in shoes and drag themselves along. They are in such pain that they can't sleep for days and days— their poor feet hurt so. I was in luck to get my cut at the time I did. It probably saved me from having frozen feet like the rest of them.

My poor battalion had a heroic time of it after my departure. Decimated as they were, they repulsed three attacks and made a lot of prisoners. Twice the Germans pinched our machine guns and twice my people charged with fixed bayonets and got the guns back again together with a lot of German officers and men. For a decadent race, the French are doing well, but good Heavens, what a futile and a criminal thing war is. No one who has not seen it can realize how wicked it is. Only an ass or a bandit can talk about the necessity or the beauty of war.

I had a talk with an Alpine soldier this morning who is here with frozen toes. He had some great yarns to tell about German tricks. One day his company saw five German soldiers standing on the battlement of the trenches in full view! They started shouting that they were tired of the war and that they wanted to surrender, that the Alpines had better come right on and get them—Kamarade, Franzoze [comrade, Frenchman], etc. My Alpine friends suspected treachery and answered nothing; but as the Germans kept shouting and gesticulating for them to come out, they fired on the men who tumbled back into their trench; then all became clear, for right back of the gesticulating rascals was a machine gun and if the Alpines had come out of their hiding place not one would have come back to tell the tale. Another time the Dutch tried to reinforce a company by having the reinforcement disguised as stretcher and Red Cross men. They are pretty brave in their knavery. They came once before our trenches at night and shouted (two of them) "En avant! à la baïonnette!" [Forward! with bayonets!] hoping to make us come out at the moment they had chosen, but their accent gave them away and they were killed for their pains. No Frenchman is going to charge when he hears "païonette."

I am beginning to believe that this war can not end by force of arms. The two sides are too evenly matched, or rather, with this war in trenches, he who attacks is lost. One man back of any kind of an earth work is good for ten or twenty men coming at him.

Translated from the diary

One great day at the temporary hospital, as there were rumors of a visit from President Poincaré on an inspection tour. Much sweeping and dusting. Sheets for the cots put in an appearance—only as there were not enough to go around, we each took one, folded it in two and let it go at that. The surgeon in charge, a very nervous, fidgety white-haired man, dashed in and out like a little rat—to see about the sheets, then about the sweeping, then about the attitude we were to strike when his Nibbs would come in, then he came to tell us to take off our caps—after discussion—Should soldiers be bareheaded? A sergeant who remembered his "theory" ruled that soldiers without arms, could be bareheaded and not lose their dignity. Poincaré accompanied by Millerand and staff came in.[3] The President had a curious costume intended to strike exactly half way between the "bourgeois" and the military. Fatigue cap of seal or other fur, putties, the rest quite "bourgeois." He looked grumpy and said nothing at all but looked all around. Millerand looked a good deal like a very solid business man. Our surgeon scarcely could keep from jumping out of his skin—he stood like a hundred yard dash runner—hardly touched the floor at all.

That surgeon was a fine man. He took the best care of us. He managed to get me out of Bussang quietly, putting me on the next list, feeling pretty sure that the pudding head of a head physician had forgotten having named me as interpreter in chief. I went to our surgeon when I saw that a new batch of wounded men were to be sent off and asked him in the name of God to put me on the list and he answered in his nervous way, in a whisper—"But, it is done, it is done." I thanked him heartily and beat it exulting. A new major came to take charge of the hospital at the time of our departure—an ass that one, a perfect specimen of the type. Made us form in line outside the buildings, under a pelting rain, kept us there for half an hour and acted like a cheap sergeant.

We were all in the train by 2 P.M., and left the station about four.

We passed through Tillot and Cornimont to Gray, the last station of the army zone. Great anxiety, as all those who were told to leave the train, to Gray included, were to return to the front directly while those who went out of the zone must first go to the "dépôt" and what was even more desirable had a right to a seven days' furlough.

It was only late in the day that we found we were going to Lyons and it was only at Lyons that we were informed that our train would proceed by the right bank of the Rhône to Anonay.

There was nothing lugubrious about this train of wounded, but on the contrary it was an almost joyful return, a return after months of privations, to happy life, a life of more than plenty, a life in which we were sure to have always something to eat and good things, too, where we could always keep warm, sleep in a warm place, sleep as long as we pleased—wash ourselves and bathe—it was a journey which was bringing us back to normal life—a journey which was taking us directly to a place where we would be able to have all the things of which we had been deprived for months.

While crossing the "département" of Haute-Saône, after leaving the rather austere scenery of the Vosges which was too much like Alsace to be entirely reassuring, a feeling of infinite peace came over me. At early dawn after wiping off the mist on the car window, I was able to see well cultivated fields and lines of slender trees by peaceful streams, comfortable looking houses and pretty cottages. Everywhere peace profound, an air of prosperity, the whole country appearing as a beautiful garden, small towns which in earlier days might have appeared lifeless to me now seemed to have a most restful atmosphere— everywhere security and order. What a contrast with Alsace and with its roads constantly crowded with lines of heavy wagons, where cavalry and infantry men cover miles and miles in order to find the most elementary necessaries of life and return driving before them wheelbarrows or pushing baby carriages full of packages. The sad roads of Alsace with their endless trains of refugees—driven from Thann or from Goldbach—poor old men, poor old women, wretched bundles of clothes piled up on shaky carts—here and there a stubborn cow who does not want to walk any further, a calf which lies down and refuses to get up again, pigs carried in bags, and always on the faces of the people the same expression of lassitude, discouragement; and when you spoke to them they answered with the whining accent of the land: Yes, the Germans are bombarding, we had to go—for the tauben which flew over the villages dropped bombs. And even greater was the contrast with the Vosges and their destroyed cities, Raon-l'Etape, for instance, and the surrounding country with its burnt down farm houses. The scenery, in the "département" of Haute-Saône and later in Bresse, so sweetly peaceful, was to the aching heart as a healing balm, and the rather ignoble life of the front in general and specially in the trenches, seemed now to assume the highest dignity, for it was thanks to our life in the mud that the rest of France was sound.

From the Fourteenth of February 14 to the Seventeenth of May, at the Hospital in Givors

The surgeon in chief was Dr. Cornillon who was at one time surgeon for the Boleo Mining Co., in Lower California. A splendid man, an excellent surgeon, a man full of tact and kindliness. After a time his wife joined him. She is the daughter of a Franco-Mexican magnate of great wealth. The lady very simple and kindly—timid, homesick for the Mexican plateau. Cornillon was just before the war surgeon of the French hospital in Mexico City.

The assistant physician was Dr. Charmeau from Thonon and Lyons—efficient and irresistibly funny in his irreverence—his conversation one streak of slang of the most amazing character and complexity. With all that very keen and watchful—his boyishness somewhat of a mask.

All the sisters were of St. Vincent de Paul order—very good nurses, but sorrowing because of lack of work. They dreamed only of [the] possibility of complete self-sacrifice to men chopped all to pieces. The "petits blessés" [slightly wounded] did not fulfill their requirements. I told them that their attitude was sinful, but that next time I should try to return to the hospital in a more creditable shape, surgically speaking. I argued that they yearned for illicit pleasures—they expressed admiration for my ability as a theologian.

One sister took her task so much to heart that she was a perfect pest—spending all her time in straightening out bed spreads and picking up cigarette tops—known as the "adjupette" [little adjutant (?); diminutive].

Ladies from the town came to help the sisters. One was particularly kind—Madame Piguet,—every time she went to Lyons, she brought back newspapers for me. *The London Times* and the *New York Herald*. *The Daily Telegraph*, etc.

Before my arrival at Givors a negro from Sénégal was in treatment—arm badly torn by bullets. When he left the hospital he was given a convalescence leave of two months. The poor fellow did not know where to go—had no alternative—it was the "dépôt de convalescents" for him, a poor place at best—under strict military rule and with beans and "boeuf nature" [plain beef, without seasoning] as fare. Mme. Piguet took him into her house and he spent all his vacation at Givors. I saw him at Mme. Piguet's table. He acted like a very good boy—"à table jusqu'au menton" [his chin on the table]—never took up spoon or fork until everybody else had done so, thus averting many social errors. Brahim was very polite and unobtrusive, very different from a Kabyle soldier—Sidi, as they are all called—who blew into the hospital in a spectacular fashion, arms, back and abdomen wounded.[4] First conversation to the assembled multitude, "I brave, I killed many Boches. I eaten Boche's ears when still hot, very good with sugar." The chap very rapidly grew unpopular—he bragged and boasted—"I brave" in the operation room. He never said a word when his wounds were dressed, but made fun of those who could not help but groan with pain. He lost caste when he made amorous remarks to the sisters and Red Cross nurses, but the climax was when he tried slyly to pat Mrs. Cornillon's cheek. Charmeau said to him, "Look out, Sidi, she is the wife of the great boss"—"Je m'en fous" [I don't give a damn], said Sidi. He was finally taken to a hospital for Africans. Cornillon took him there in a car. Sidi felt injured, did not want to go. Cornillon—always kindly—tried to make him forget his grievances by making him admire the scenery, but Sidi would not be fooled. His last words were—"No comrades here! No comrades here."

At the hospital we had twice calls from prominent ecclesiastics—once an old priest, another time the Cardinal of Lyons. Each time, to avoid embarrassing situations, the abbé and Lady Superior warned the gentlemen in question of the presence of a Protestant in the ward. In the room with me was Masson, a Parisian lawyer, who naturally was more impressive looking than I, and the distinguished visitors, glancing around the room, guessed him to be the heretical professor—and went to him with outstretched hands and words of flattering conciliation. Tableau—as Masson was a fervent Roman Catholic.

Translated from the French

Givors [undated]
To A——:

After a few days, I gave up my job as an interpreter for the English ambulance men at Bussang, because I thought it lacked the official stamp. The commandant who gave it to me had been sent somewhere else and I was afraid that after my wound was healed his successor might send me back to the front without giving me a few days' leave of absence. That is why, when I had a chance, I asked to be taken farther back into France. I have had a wonderful trip on a sanitary train. We were admirably treated all through. This service is very well organized. Bouillon, hot and cold meats, coffee, tea, milk, cigarettes, bread, cheese, chocolate, regular meals and pique-nique, all along the road or rather at every station. We did not know whither we were bound. After having passed through Epinal and Gray, we felt more at ease, for we knew that now we were far beyond the fighting zone and in the region of leaves of absence, with the accompanying prospect of a return to the company via the dépôt. I feel sure now that I shall be able to visit our brother and that I can soon after call at the Dulacs on returning to Besançon.

We reached Lyons yesterday at about 3 o'clock, twenty-four hours after leaving Bussang. I came near being sent to a hospital in Lyons, but as I wished to be as near our brother as possible, I quickly climbed back into the train and I succeeded in protracting my trip as far as the town of Givors, Rhône. From here it must take about four hours to reach Valence on the train. They say the service is good. Therefore I may expect to see our brother within a short time. I should not be surprised if on returning to my battalion I should find that it has been relieved from the first line trenches where it has been on duty for two full months. It has suffered too much to be in any condition to do any hard fighting. The first company, for instance, has lost all its officers with the exception of the captain, a second lieutenant and a sergeant. Therefore it is barely possible I may only return to Alsace when you and I some fine day will take a reconnoitering trip over my battlefields. Life indeed is a strange adventure. Here am I close to a city with which so many family recollections are connected.

This hospital is fine. It used to be an asylum for old people and has been turned into a hospital because of the present emergency. The head surgeon came from Mexico where he was in charge of the French hospital. I wonder if our brother knows him. Anyhow he is a very capable physician. He knows the United States and asked me if I had met So and so, naming doctors in New York and San Francisco.

Au revoir.

Givors, Rhône, February 18, 1915.
To M———:

I have been remorseful these many days at not having written to you sooner. My recent travels are my excuse. Your last letter was particularly a joy. What do you know about pigs and the manufacture of the various kinds of "delicatessen"? You are a versatile young woman and the South may well bow before the North. Could V——— go to Marshfield and make brown bread that would be countenanced by the Baker boys?[5] I have great doubts. I have been in this hospital three days. Yesterday there should have been a letter from Valence for me. There was not any at 9 A.M. and I was peevish, but at 9.15 I happened to look up from the table at which I was writing and in the door stood my brother in the flesh. That was much better than a letter. I had told him with solemnity in all my letters that my cut was nothing at all and that my precious health had never been better. He had not believed me and had taken a night trip to this place fully expecting to find me in skillfully sewed up fragments. We went out together right away, had an immense smoke and talk, then a dinner during which I amazed him by the quality of my appetite. He will be here again Saturday. By the first of March I expect to be kicked out of here, but as a compensation I shall get an eight-day furlough which I shall spend at Valence naturally. The chances are that when I return to my battalion it will not be as near the front as it has been since the middle of December for the simple reason that it is practically without officers and that the men who have not had the good fortune of being slightly hurt, or of getting bronchitis or frozen feet are pretty nearly exhausted after weeks of squatting in trenches under artillery fire of the most damnable intensity at times, and constantly on the lookout for attacks from the Rhine valley. I only had nine days of it, this last session, and felt that it was quite enough. My comrades came down only after three full weeks of this kind of life and I believe that after a few days' rest near St.-Amarin they went up again. Those who claim that the French are an impatient race without endurance don't know what they are talking about.

The trip back to peaceful parts was very interesting. English ambulances took us out of Alsace back to the French border at Bussang. Had quite a talk with the Chilly Boy who drove my car and who was full of solicitude for his hosts.

At Bussang we saw Poincaré and Millerand who happened to be on a glad hand and inspection tour, but the really interesting part of the trip was from there to Lyons. We were about twenty carloads of "wounded" of various degrees of respectability. Some like myself cheerful to see the people who watched the train go by. They were nearly all women and old men. Some of the women were crying. At the stations, specially in the Vosges, they would run up the to the cars and ask breathlessly, "Do you know So and so who is at the Fifth, or the Fifteenth or the Twenty-eighth?" Sometimes we knew the man and could give good news. It's certainly the women and the middle-aged and old men who have to bear the greatest suffering these days.

Now I am living on the fat of the land, for the land, in spite of everything, is still fat. As far as food and fuel go, you could never tell that the country was at war.

Soeur Jeanne, Monsieur l'Abbé, Monsieur l'Econome, [Sister (nurse) Jeanne, the priest, the almoner] minister to my needs—physical needs only, as I have already told them that being a Protestant, I could not very well be expected to go to mass. We are taken care of admirably. The surgeon in charge of the hospital is a wonderful man in every way.

Give your husband my most cordial greetings and keep up a lively anti-German agitation in the whole of Virginia.[6]

Givors, Rhône [undated].
Dear Mr. M——:

Thank you for your good letter, which came to me in Alsace at the infirmary, where I was nursing a lame shoulder. I am now in France doing the same thing, but in a week or ten days I expect to be fit for service again. But before going back to the front—to the meat shop, as we say here—I shall have a week to myself, and shall spend it with my brother, who is in the engineer corps very near here.

The story of the Kilkenny cats certainly gives a good idea of the war in its present stage.[7] Men in trenches take pops at each other through loopholes, while waiting for the artillery to demolish the mud walls of the other side. Whenever this is done successfully, there are attacks, usually followed by counter-attacks, and when a few hundred men have been killed on one side or the other, quiet reigns again, and as a rule the relative positions of the opponents have suffered very little change. More Germans are apt to fall than Frenchmen for the simple reason that they attack in close formations, in long columns, four men from left to right marching elbow to elbow. All we have to do is to keep cool and fire into the moving mass. We on the other hand, attack as individuals scattered on a very wide front. Each man runs, and then lies down, gets up and runs again, taking advantage of every rock or tree, trunk or depression in the ground. When the barbed wire entanglements are reached, however, the slaughter on the two sides is about equal. To get over a fence you must show yourself. And the fences in question are very complex, the wires standing chin high and extending back ten, fifteen, or twenty feet in a hopeless tangle. Sometimes there are two or three sets of wires; wires running so close to the ground that the dead leaves cover them up and you are tripped up before you see them; wires so arranged as to lead into a labyrinth of other wires, etc. You can neither jump over nor crawl under, and unless the artillery fire has been very accurate, when a body of troops reaches these wires it is all up with them. In the vast majority of cases he who attacks is lost.

Still a day is coming when the deadlock will be broken. Enormous forces will be concentrated on one point and the barrier broken. One thing I saw clearly on my trip from Alsace to France, namely, that our trenches are being held by a comparatively small number of men who have not left the front since the beginning of the war, while the various "dépôts" of the country are filled with fresh troops. I believe there are more soldiers in these recruiting camps than at the front. Some fine day those who are in the trenches now are going to step aside and let the fresh troops go by them to find out whether or not the artillery has properly plowed up the wire regions, and on that day it will have been plowed up in fine style.

In the Vosges the wild boars are plentiful, and many have had their hides pierced by watchful sentinels who at night took their nosing about in the dry leaves and their snorting for signs of an approaching German patrol. Yet, there are times when both sides get tired of shooting and not a gunshot is heard for days. In the Vosges there was a saw-mill which stood between the two lines at the bottom of a gorge. Scouting parties from both sides were sent there from time to time to see what was going on. One day our men found a piece of paper nailed in a conspicuous place. On it was written in Germanized French: "You leave us alone and we will leave you alone."

Givors, Rhône, France [undated].
Dear Friend [original addressee unknown]:

The winter, fortunately for us, has been very mild, and only wounded men, who could not be picked up, have perished from cold; but, nevertheless, it has been pretty tough. We have spent some damnable nights in the mud—with drenched or frozen clothing. Many men have had their feet partly frozen, and have suffered frightful pains as a result.

To answer your questions: Usually back of the trenches, sometimes a few hundred yards, sometimes a mile or two, there are shelters, whether log houses or dugouts, covered over with logs and earth. If a company has charge of a certain length of trenches, it is divided into two shifts. One is on duty in the trench while the other remains behind to rest, but always ready to move up at a second's notice. The guns are stacked in front of the shelters, and the men must never take off any part of their equipment. The men in the trenches are not permitted to sleep, even if they stay on duty twenty-four or forty-eight hours. But, of course, they will sometimes doze off. In some trenches they can lie down. Often they can only sit up. But whether lying or sitting, they must have their guns close by them, and whether in the trenches or in the shelters they have only the bare earth to sit or lie on. Everything is so damp that it is better to have no straw, for vermin soon develops in wet straw. One gets used to that kind of life. I have seen men so tired out that they slept soundly in snow or in puddles of water.

Weeks may go by without a shot being fired. On the other hand trenches may be bombarded by artillery fire day after day and attacked over and over again. Or you may have to attack yourself, and then you are sure that a good many men are going to get killed or maimed.

In mountainous regions, such as the part of Alsace where we were last, all supplies have to be brought in on the backs of mules over pretty bad trails. It takes a train of about eighty mules to supply a day's food for a regiment. This part of the service is admirably organized. In spite of bad weather and deep snow, we have received our food very regularly. Once in a while we have been a day or two without eating, but that was due, not to lack of food, but to inability to cook it. In such cases the smoke from the cooks' fires gave our positions away, and shells fell thick and fast in our kitchens, driving the best-intentioned cooks to cover.

In the first line trenches the food is usually cold. It may have to be cooked a mile or two back from the firing line, and it can be brought only late at night or before sunrise. The men who drive the mules have a hard time of it. They have to travel over the trails at night, because all day the Germans fire shells on the roads back of the line to prevent any one from coming up with reinforcements or food. Our artillery, of course, does the same thing to them.

German shells make a tremendous noise when they explode and kick up an incredible amount of dirt; yet unless they fall on a group of men they do comparatively little harm. One week they fired an average of 3,000 shells a day on the trench where I was, but they killed only about a dozen men. Such weeks, however, are pretty trying, as you may imagine. The shells explode in front of you, behind you and on either side of you, and you keep wondering whether the next one will not drop right on you. Fragments of shell and pieces of rock fly all around, branches are chopped off right over your head. It is no fake at all, and it is a veritable miracle that so few are killed.

After all, it is the rifle fire and the machine guns which do most damage. The day before I left the front I saw eighty men start on with a rush to capture a stretch of trenches. Twenty came back. The others were nearly all shot through the head. May peace come soon.

Givors, Rhône, February 24th, 1914.
To Mr. D. C.———:

For a whole month I have been doing nothing but loaf and travel. I received a superficial cut in the shoulder from a shell fragment on the night of January 23d and 24th. It became impossible for me to carry the equipment necessary in the business. So I stepped out of the trench, shook hands all around and made for the field hospital a mile and a half back of the firing line. They dressed up my cut and I proceeded to walk to the infirmary eight miles away, on the other side of a mountain range. It was a great feeling of relief to get out of the range of shells, as I thought. Up in the trenches, near Steinbach (Alsace), we had been bombarded mildly or furiously every blessed day for a week and a half. Besides we had slept very little, eaten

mainly cold stuff and had not once been able to warm our toes by a
fire as any smoke at all gave the Dutch a clue to our position. I slept
like a brute for twelve hours, ate a lot and felt fine, but the very next
day I was aroused from my nap by a too-familiar hissing and whis-
tling sound followed by a grand general blowing up. Those damned
Germans had seen fit to heave a few shells, casually like, over the
mountain on the town. Fortunately only two shells exploded. Four
soldiers were hurt, one woman and two children killed. One of those
two shells fell right side of the infirmary.

After such a good beginning, we thought that the town was
going to be bombarded every day, but such was not the case. An aeroplane did come four or five times and dropped bombs but that does
not amount to much as these projectiles very often fall in ploughed
fields, in rivers, in snowbanks, etc. It seems to be very difficult to aim
from an aero. Of course bombs that fall on soft ground don't explode.

If the Germans don't give in, and it's idiotic to hope that they
will, there's going to be a tremendous loss of life during the next
phase of the war. Well, anyway, we shall be fighting side by side with
the troops from Ireland. If you had only taught me a little Irish in the
old days I might be able, next spring, to get on the right side of your
compatriots. I have already met some Englishmen. The ambulances
which carry wounded men out of Alsace have English chauffeurs. I
had a great talk with one of them. He was full of business, hoping
fervently that within a brief space of time the whole German race
could be erased off the planet. While waiting for that happy event he
and his car worked night and day. Each trip he would begin operations
by giving cigarettes to all the men in his car. As he could speak very
little French he proceeded mainly by gracious gestures and play of the
features that would have delighted our old and much abused teacher,
Auntie H——.

If you feel like writing send your letter to Valence as my where-
abouts may be uncertain for some time to come.

Translated from the French

Givors, March 1, 1915.
To A——:

In one of your letters you spoke of the fellows who entered the
church so stealthily at Goldbach. Just fancy, the reverend priest had

to be shot. This holy man had a small telephone in the church hidden under a flagstone. Whenever something interesting came up, he hastened to impart the news to the German artillerymen, and for one thing he told them where our batteries were laid in Goldbach. I am not romancing after the fashion of Gaboriau.[8] This man was caught in the act, red-handed. He was driven to the wall and shot. It was discovered later that he was a German officer of the reserve and that he had the right to wear the uniform, when he chose, and that the German uniform and the priestly garb were equally becoming to him.

I also wish to set you right in connection with washing facilities in the trenches. I wish you could have seen your own brother after he had been eleven days in the trenches without even having had a chance to use a towel once! We had spent three days without having had anything to drink, washing was simply out of the question. When we are lucky enough to use snow for that purpose, we deem ourselves fortunate. War is unclean.

Translated from the French

Givors, March 8, 1915.
To A———:

Your two last letters reached me yesterday. Of course I enjoyed them very much, and the clippings, too. This poor Kuno Francke makes the most of his subject; the first part of his article is inspired by the circumstances; the second is quite strong.[9] I feel sincerely sorry for the honest Boches and I dare say there are many of them scattered among the crowd of rascals and the numberless hosts of visionary brutes.

Our Easthampton friend sent me the letter written by one of the Williams College instructors.[10] He was not in the Vosges but in the Argonne forest and it is very possible that he may have had trouble in finding an opportunity for washing himself. Our positions on the Sudel and on Hartmannweilerkopf [*sic*] are on the very crests. The brooks spring far below. We cannot leave our positions for the sake of washing our faces. But it is unusual that by hook or by crook he who wishes to wash cannot have a chance every second, third or fourth day. And yet there are some specially trying times when it is almost impossible to be relieved from duty, therefore everything is possible. Sometimes we are so tossed about and ill-treated to such an extent by unforeseen contingencies which bring to us in quick succession hunger, thirst, sleepiness, dirt, prolongations of duty at times when we should be relieved, attacks at times when we would have a right to snatch a few moments of sleep that neither *Lazarillo de Tórmes* nor *Gil Blas* ever experienced anything like it.[11] The time comes when one does not count on anything except on the present moment. The nearest future seems to be full of uncertainty. We live from one minute to the next, all our interest centers on the present fleeting instant.

On Christmas day I was not at Thann but at Goldbach, the last village before one reaches the neck of Sudel. I gave as few geographical indications as I could so as not to have my letters suppressed. I believe the censor is not very strict when over-sea correspondence is concerned, for all my letters from the front seemed to have reached you.

Now, of course, I am indulging in a life of utter peacefulness. In the morning soup and clear coffee. Between 8 and 9 a walk and a smoke in the yard, from 10 to 12 reading of newspapers and books sent by our cousin, then letter writing. From 1 to 4 a walk in the environs of Givors to one of the high-perched villages from which one sees in the distances the Cévennes mountains and a beautiful extent of plain on the banks of the river up and down the Rhône valley. We spend half an hour in the best village inn and we drink a cup of coffee or a glass of light wine. The peasants ask us for no end of war stories and most of the time the innkeepers refuse to take any money from us and when we go they slip into our pockets: cigarettes, cookies, etc. After we return to Givors, reading and letter writing till supper time. This is how the weeks glide away.

Givors, March 10th, 1915.
To L———:
  You will see by the enclosed picture that I am growing fat, a calamity which I cannot combat at present. There is no telling when I shall be able to combat it, as my stay at Givors is prolonging itself scandalously. The last time I was dressed (two days ago) I took a good look at my "wound" with the aid of a looking-glass and saw that the muscle had grown back into perfect shape, but there was not the slightest appearance of skin on it. I judge from this that I shall be here until the last part of March, so that it is perfectly possible that my

battalion will be without my service as late at May 1st. What that body will do without me is difficult to say. Yet it is very true that it got on nicely before my arrival. My corporal wrote me a fine letter; my sergeant sent me a postal. That last surprised me a great deal, because circumstances compelled me, the night before I left the front, and between the hours of 1 and 2 A.M., to give that gentleman a great call-down and he was so peeved that he had to make a visible effort to extend to me his right hand when I took my departure some hours later.

My friends have gone up to Steinbach again, after a two weeks' rest at Saint-Amarin. They are in for it this trip for a thirty days' stay. As we are having a cold snap and as the snowfall in the Vosges has been very heavy, they will have a devil of a time, *si j'ose m'exprimer ainsi* [if I can put it that way; if you'll pardon my saying so].

It makes me feel cheap to be here by a radiator while they are "getting thin" out in the elements. And yet it would be a lie to say that I am filled with a fanatical desire to return to Steinbach or even Weiler, where the infirmary was. Tauben flew over that town every day and dropped bombs between 10 and 11 A.M. You would have thought that mothers would have locked up their children in the cellars, but nothing of the kind. Boys and girls were all over the place, faces turned skyward, fingers pointed eagerly towards the machine. The women, who were forever washing clothes in the river, never gave up this occupation until after a bomb had exploded somewhere nearby. Givors is on the railroad. We watch the trains go by. Many of them are made up exclusively of reservoir cars. They come full from the South and come empty from the front, all of which tends to prove the old saying that the French are fond of light wine. Will you believe that in a German school geography I read the exact statement which your father used to quote—the French are fond of dancing and light wine!

On the main line, trains go by headed for Marseilles, with all kinds of military supplies. A whole division of colonial infantry has already left for Turkey. Some heavy artillery and one regiment also left Lyons for those parts. Something is going to happen to the valorous Turk.[12]

You delighted my brother with your plan of a United States of Europe. He has long cherished that idea. So have I. Some such arrangement would be a partial compensation for this European slaughter. Some great good is bound to come out of it, because there is no doubt that the man in the street and the woman, his better half, are thinking now as they never thought before, and if anything can make people really think, make the masses think, who as a rule prefer to be led, why good is bound to result.

Ferdinand has sent me a lot of books.[13] Two more just arrived from Valence. My mail comes very well. What more to desire, I say? Every afternoon we go upon the hill and have a *café noir* or a glass of wine at some inn.

Givors, March, 1915.
To B———:

Here at Givors, nothing new. Life goes on with perfect regularity. I read and write in the morning, range the hills in the afternoon and talk it over after supper. Also I eat faithfully three times a day.

It makes me blush with shame when I get letters from those who still think I am in those confounded trenches. I don't believe I'll see them again before the middle of April or even the first of May. My shoulder does not bother me at all, but it simply has to be dressed. It is still raw and skinless in part.

The war seems to be as beastly as ever, though we seem to push ahead a little in Champagne. It is still too early for a definite forward movement with a lot of troops concentrated at one spot. Good many regiments are being shipped to Turkey in view of operations about Constantinople. The front is thus still expanding. The feeling of the people about here is that it is getting pretty wearisome, but that we are bound to win in the end.

I was glad to find a new note in the newspapers to-day, to the effect that it was silly for us to talk so much about the good intentions of our neutral neighbors, and about the bright day when they would join their forces to ours, etc., etc., and that we would do very much better in minding our own affairs, counting on no one but ourselves. That's the right attitude. Those politicians who keep looking for more allies make me tired.

This pen, as you see, is infernal. I can't go on with it—it scratches and spits like an angry cat, giving a very false idea of my character.

Your aunt had a great scheme. To wit, that all French teachers return to the United States to combat the German-American propaganda. I was to be one of the first ones to be sent back. A luminous idea, indeed, but before anyone had time to impart it to the war sec-

retary, I learned that G—— was doing precisely the thing and that
the Paris Chamber of Commerce, together with the most prominent
literary, political and business men of France were helping him out in
his task. Now isn't that mean?

Givors, March 16th, 1915.
To B——:

Nothing new here. I may clear out of the hospital at the end of
the month; my cut is getting very small and has stopped kicking up
any row. I feel strong and nimble. Down with the Germans! We are
sending more troops to Turkey.

By the way, young lady, whom do you take me for? I am not a
biffin or a *pitou* or a *pousse-caillou*. I am a *chasseur*. In other words I
hold in horror and abominate red trousers, and consider it one of the
fine things in life to say hard and haughty things about the slow moving head of line infantry. My trousers are of a very dark blue with a
quarter or eighth inch stripe of canary yellow, by gum, running on the
seam to the legging. I am a *chasse-bi*, alias a *vitrier* or a *diable bleu*—
no reference to delirium tremens.[14]

These last days I have been growing intellectual. I read and give
English lessons to the assistant surgeon, a kid twenty-one or twenty-
two, who has difficulty with the "th" and the rapid locating of the
tonic accent in "geography" and "institute." He wants to know why,
just like an ordinary Stanford student.

The war drags on as usual. There is no way of telling about the
end. I may write to Stanford to tell them to elect a man, since I can
give them no assurance of returning in time to take up work in September. If war should stop, say in November, I would be without a
job and should have to ask your cousin to let me currycomb Reggie
and do odd jobs around and about the formal garden. Break the news
to her gently.

Still I have the firm hope that something decisive will be done
during April and May. We have plenty of fresh troops; we have
more heavy guns now than the Dutch; we still have a clear conscience and, figuratively speaking, clean hands. Will we keep that
purity if we ever get into Germany? I fondly hope so, but some of
the men will be pretty hard to hold; those, who are many, who come
from the northern departments, and whose families were slaughtered last August.

So far I have seen no atrocities or traces of atrocities committed by our men. One chap in our battalion did commit an outrage. When we took Steinbach, the Dutch prisoners were lined up against a house. I have been told that one of our men, a farmer about thirty-eight years old, stepped in front of the line and as he went snapped the pointed helmets of the Dutch so as to see their faces better. He would throw the helmet on the ground dramatically, and say, looking at his victims, "Bon Dieu! qu'ils sont laids, Bon Dieu! qu'ils sont laids!" [Good God! How homely they are!] and so on down the line. Let us pray that the Wolff Agency may never hear of this.[15]

Givors, Rhône, March 17th, 1915.
To Miss H———:

Your first letter came in the trenches, the second when I was still in the infirmary in a town visited daily by bomb-dropping aeroplanes and subjected once in a while to long distance shelling. The other two were given me at the hospital itself, in the heart of France, thank Heaven! Some of the news certainly startled me. What! O——— in the ministry? That's the best yet. However, he did well not to stay in Germany. If France had had as poor a cause to fight for as our across-the-Rhine friends, I would not have come back.

Yes, I could without difficulty, after reading your letter, see the Westhampton group of houses, with the steep hill in the back, the church on the right. I know those old roads pretty well. I think I could find my way from the top of Turkey Hill to the Montague's at night and in a blizzard without difficulty. You must know at least as well as we do that nothing in particular is happening at the front. Mean little fights for the reconquering of a few hundred yards of territory, good many men killed on both sides and not much change in the situation. Troops are piling into northbound trains all the time. There must be a tremendous concentration of forces somewhere, but where no one knows, of course. New regiments are being formed to be sent to Turkey. Men coming out of the hospitals are often put into such bodies. It would be a joke if I winded up matters by going to Constantinople. My cut is healing rapidly now and I dare say that I'll be out of here by April 3d, so that by April 8th, after a week off with my brother, I ought to be back at the Dépôt. I may leave for the front a month later or the day after my arrival at Besançon, no one can tell. Life will begin again to be delightfully indefinite.

I was interested to learn that the fame of the *chasseurs alpins* had travelled across the ocean. I am a *chasseur à pied* for the present, but the *alpins* are our brothers and we are united by our common scorn of the regular line infantry. There is no worse insult in the battalion than to say—you walk or shoot like a *pitou*, which is slang for infantry of the regular brand. The alpine troops are a fine body of men, all picked from the mountainous parts of France. Instead of remaining in barracks during peace time, they spend nearly six months of the year camping and marching in the Alps. They have a fine gun; cannon I mean. It's very small, sixty-five mill. It can be taken to pieces in a jiffy and three men can carry the parts. It shoots six miles or seven. The shell does a lot of damage. When the gun is in battery in the snow or in the woods no aero can see it. If its location is ever found out, the artillery-men just take it to pieces; that is, for a mile or two and start shooting again. It can shoot with startling rapidity, because when once trained it stays put no matter how often it is fired. Fortunately the Germans have nothing like it. For mountain artillery, they had to borrow guns from Austria and they were not much good either. Some of the *alpins* are trained "skiers." These last months they would go about in white overalls and jumpers so that they could not be distinguished even when in close formation. Alsace—the little bit we have of it—is held entirely by alpine troops and by chasseurs à pied.

With your interest in animals, you would have been pleased to see our mules. All food and drink and ammunition had to come over the mountains on mule back. It takes about eighty mules to keep a regiment fed and supplied with cartridges. It's a great sight to see those everlasting lines of mules along the mountain trails. They go over anything and at any time of day or night. The convoys are usually started so as to reach the danger zone between sunset and sunrise. The business of the mule driver is no sinecure. A good many get killed with their mules because the Germans know where the trails are and they drop an occasional shell here and there at any time of day or night. It's all guess work, of course, but some shells are bound to hit some one some time. On the return trip the mules are made to carry the wounded who can't walk. There are two ways of getting the poor fellows over the mountain. The first is by means of a kind of saddle shaped like a chair, or rather there are two such chairs, one on each side of the mule and the men sit up in them. For those who can't sit up there are little two-wheel affairs resembling the trucks used in

railroad stations to carry trunks, and these are very light and have
rubber-tired wheels like bicycles. They are known jokingly as "baby
carriages."[16] They can ride over any place good enough for a mule to
find a footing and that's about anywhere on earth. A third and less formal way to leave the front if you are all in, is to hang on with one
hand to the tail of a mule. They don't object and never kick when on
such duty. I tried it when I came up, but the mule walked too fast and
I had to let go. We are having splendid weather now, but the first of
the month was very cold. As a result of that "snap" we have just received at the hospital ten *alpins* afflicted with frozen feet. One of the
poor fellows will probably have to lose both feet and he is only
twenty-two years old. The next calamity will doubtless be epidemics
of all kinds and of typhoid in particular. If this is not the last European war, it will be because all Europeans are crazy.

Translated from the French

Givors, March 22d, 1915.
To A——:
    The countries where war is not waged have no history and the
Rhône valley is extremely peaceful.
    I laughed till I cried when I heard of your skirmish with the
German widow; she always worked on my nerves. She used to
bother me to death, wanting me all the time to go to her house to
play bridge. I can't tell you how hard it was to get rid of her. Therefore, I am delighted that you expressed to her our views. Sooner or
later there is a day of reckoning for everyone in this world. I cannot yet tell you when war will be over, but as a large majority of Europeans are living in the same uncertainty, I do not feel in the least
humiliated by my ignorance.
    The Germans are doing their best to spread terror among Pari-
sians.[17] On the other hand, I have a sad thing to tell you. There came
yesterday to our hospital, straight from the front a Senegalese sharp-
shooter, a peculiar looking negro, with pointed cranium, who began
right away with confidences. "I broken arm, but soon will go back to
kill Boches. I already eaten seven Boche's ears. Boche's ears very
good; melt in the mouth like sugar—I always carry Boche's ears in
my bag." I believe if we had a few gentlemen of this type on the front
we would lose forever our moral superiority over our dear neighbors

and invaders. Don't be scared, however, as you know my digestive organs are rather delicate. I shall not disgrace my family in this way.

Givors, March 23, 1915.
To B——:

Both yours of March (3–5) came yesterday. At last immensely relieved at the thought that you know that I never wore red trousers. By the way red trousers are a thing of the past, not since very long. All uniforms are now an uncertain kind of light grayish blue which is really very inconspicuous. We, the chasseurs, keep our canary yellow "liseret" [piping]. Ye gods, what color harmonies.

No, chasseurs are only human and they can't be always on the run like college girls. Only they average many more miles a day than line infantry. The "pitous" don't go much over eighteen miles a day. We are supposed to go as much as thirty with the whole load. When going through a city we hit up a sharp, snappy gait which is supposed to be smart and which has given rise to the saying that we always run. As soon as we get out on country roads we go more leisurely. Can't write more having no note paper. This is a middle of the week note to say that I shall leave here only May 10th and will not see the Boches before June 1st.

Translated from the French

Givors [undated].
To Mr. G——:

Yesterday I received two letters from you. I was highly pleased, as usually when so favored, but I must admit that the list of books I must read in order to escape intellectual starvation made my head swim and my ears buzz.

What you say concerning your own impressions about Alsace is extremely interesting to me. I cannot tell you how often I said to myself when I was on the Sudel, getting an occasional glimpse from behind a fir tree at the lesser chains of the Black Forest, "It is almost the same view one has from Black Mountain, when facing Mount Hamilton." And drawing a more extensive parallel, I felt rather disgusted at the thought of the untold miseries and of the huge sacrifices in human lives which were made in order to recover a stretch of Alsatian territory that could easily be included between Red Wood City and San Jose! Evidently the gains should not be reckoned in kilometers, what should be taken into account is the number of inhabitants and the homes (*les feux et les âmes*). Did you also notice that the harvested wheatfields, scorched by sun take on all the shades of the Stanford "brown hills?"

Yes, indeed, I realize that with the exception of a few bombardments, I have seen so far nothing but outpost fights. Steinbach was nothing but a surprise attack well carried out and poorly supported. In Alsace, it has been for months guerrilla warfare. We had just enough soldiers to hold the trenches and support our artillery. There were no forces behind us and often we felt uncomfortable at the thought of what would happen were our lines to be pierced at such and such a place. I do believe that a similar state of things prevails all along the frontier and yet I am told that the dépôts are overcrowded. Life in the trenches tires the men out and takes all the vim out of them; therefore, it is very wise to leave on the front a thin line of men until the time when the troops who are resting will march forward to the final offensive. Even some regiments belonging to the regular army have not yet been at the front. My cousin, F. P., who belongs to the Belfort division has just started for Alsace. I do not think that one needs fear a return of acute nationalism in France. We shall have to be modest for victory will have been too long delayed and the glory will have to be shared with too many allies. There will be a renewed surge of confidence in the destinies of our race, but nothing more. The open letters of our intellectuals and the declaration of faith of our grammar school teachers seem to indicate a state of mind which must be very much in accordance with your wishes. France, of course, but humanity and civilization are placed above France, a point of view which widely differs from that of our neighbors.

The more I think about your trilemma, the less I understand it. Time spent in meditation is not altogether wasted, even when one does not reach the desired conclusion. It seems to me I have succeeded in analyzing, in a measure, the feeling which the reading of your authors invariably awakens in me.[18] Your trilemma might be reduced to a question of good or bad faith. Does freethinking necessarily destroy good faith in relations existing between men? When he shows his sympathy for the lowly, which is the best side of his nature, what does Anatole France ask for?[19] Is it not simply that the boss or the wealthy man be fair in his dealings with the working man or with the poor? In his opinion, this need of absolute confidence is an axiom. Then why does he not admit that the same fairness is the basis of sexual relations? When he stands up for the poor, he demands justice, integrity. Should one mention to him justice and integrity in his relations to women, his tone changes entirely; a while ago he was kind of compassionate; now he becomes ironical, subtle, slippery. It is because he is weak in this respect. He can only be just when his physical appetites are not concerned, but as soon as his sexual selfishness gets the upper hand he becomes a very poor specimen of human nature. It does not seem to me that this weakness is necessarily the result of freethinking. Did Berthelot, Claude Bernard, Pasteur have a lesser amount of intellectual freedom than Anatole France?[20] Did they for this reason become fast men in private life and did they officially preach loose morals?

Anatole France, Bourget and Barrès are men of morbid temperament.[21] In support of their weakness they place all the resources of a skillful dialectic which used in favor of a good cause might do much good and people come to think that it is freedom of thought which has created such a temperament while as a matter of fact it is their temperament which has given a twist to their minds. As soon as these fellows speak of sexual problems, they show an extraordinary weakness and this very weakness leads them directly to a lack of uprightness. You must be just in your dealings with the poor and lowly. Very well, and what about women? That is an entirely different question. Never mind the women. Why? Have you any right to take such a stand? Well, I should lose too much if I cared. Of course, they have not the courage to express their thoughts. All they do is to repeat, "I don't care a rap." They are no longer willing to be fair-minded in their reasonings. I always felt that these writers were in no way the leaders of French thought. From a moral viewpoint, they are the wretched descendants, the last heirs of a long line of fast *esthètes,* which have for a common ancestor Chateaubriand, as he appears in the *Génie du Christianisme.*[22] These people cannot teach anything to the young men of modern France. As leaders of the new generation, they have made a dismal failure. Barrès specially, who at one time had high pretensions in this respect. Young men turned to other writers like R. Rolland and Brieux, who were not obliged to display so much art in defense of temperamental weakness.

Barrès disgusts me more than I can tell. His leading articles in the *Echo de Paris* are frequently masterpieces of hypocrisy. I am sending you a letter from an American (possibly an Irishman) which Barrès thought worth his while to translate and bring before the French public. Now, the time is really not well chosen to stir up in an underhanded religious animosity. Do you really think the Americans are deeply grieved because the French government severed relations with Rome!

Yes, the poor Alsatians show great courage in receiving us as they do. I was told that our hosts, in Steinbach, were shot when the Germans retook the town. One hears of so many atrocities that one's heart sinks. Near Chambéry there are seven hundred French women refugees from the invaded departments; two hundred of them are to become mothers as a result of German violence last August. What shall we do with these infant Boches that are coming?

Givors, March 30th, 1915.
To B———:

Still leading the Lotus Eating Life and waiting for May (the month, no girl in the case) to come along. If your cousin could send me Reggie, I would get all the fat off his ribs and make him look like an English hunter. The country here is very hilly, an ideal resort for horses afflicted with obesity.

So you have fallen to studying birds. You don't know the call of the white throated sparrow, alias, the Peabody bird, because you belong to the seashore tribes and have a very insufficient initiation in mountain and wood lore. You can know only sophisticated and superficial suburban birds. I suspect that the red-nosed wood-pecker who is now making such a social splurge in Auburndale gives informal and formal teas, hence his sudden rise and popularity.

There must be something wrong with international mails these days. No information at all about my war muffler; also I know that a whole lot of cigarettes that were sent me by Dr. A———, a Brooklyn–Palo Alto friend, have been returned to the sender. I call that a scandal. Please thank your cousin. If the socks "get across," I shall show them all around, as a tangible proof of America's friendship for us. Perhaps I'll be able to wear them on a Sierra trip next Christmas. I would prefer this to another winter campaign.

Things are as dull gray as usual around here. Nothing much on the front except the usual slaughters, a few hundred men in Alsace, a few more in Argonne, and the same farther west, and about once or twice a week people throw up their hands in horror when a battleship is lost. Tremendous loss of life; they don't realize that every time a trench is taken or lost, the lives sacrificed are more numerous than in the sinking of a battleship.

No self-respecting attack is ever pulled through with a loss inferior to four or five hundred. The *alpins*, who were on our left, the first time they attacked the Hartmannweiler-Kopf [*sic*] lost two thousand men in about an hour. The papers didn't even bother to mention it. What must the English have lost at Neuve-Chapelle, if they admitted that 530 officers were killed or wounded.[23]

To my mind, this war is the deathblow to armies and to settlements of international questions by force. It's the bankruptcy of arms, and may they go out of business once for all. I don't believe this war will end by great victories for either side. Starvation of civilians and lack of funds and general disgust at the whole business will bring peace.

Hospital life is pretty dull, so please don't give up writing. This is the religious-military-hospital. . . . One sister has tried to convert me and to make me wear a kind of medal with a flaming heart on it. I was so very polite that she saw that she had fallen on a street-lamp-gas-jet—from the neo-French—*tomber sur un bec de gaz*—meaning to get in wrong. She is a fine lady, however; takes a motherly interest in all the badly wounded who come in, but being a nun, she has religious aims, which is natural enough. She has a good sense of humor, so that even if I stay here four more weeks, we may not come to blows. Still you will sympathize with me in my homesick feeling for lay American hospitals.

This is all the news that's fit to write about, I believe, so I will say good-bye.

Remember me to your families. Tell your Mississippi brother to go back to California right away, before he gets malaria in his swamps. The fish is not worth the ague.

Givors, March 31st, 1915.
To A——:

The St. Vincent de Paul sisters are nursing us. One of them has made a feeble attempt to convert me. She asked me if I believe in God. I almost fell backwards. I said I did—which is the truth—but in my own way. After this she confronted me with the problem of Christ's divinity. She received a courteous but negative answer. Not yet satisfied she asked me what I thought about the Sacred Heart? I acknowledged my complete ignorance on the subject, giving her to understand at the same time that further discussion would scarcely change my deplorable attitude. Finally she said, "It is a great pity. I had put aside a medal representing the Sacred Heart. A Carmelite monk gave it to me. I cherished the hope you would wear it."

I fled. Just fancy! Can you see your brother going back to the front with the clink of amulets about him! In spite of all this the said sister is a very kind woman who gives herself up entirely to her work; she is a constant blessing to those who are seriously ill. When I find the Catholic faith so deep-rooted, it seems to me that some kind of a magician has carried me back to the Middle Ages. After this conversation I felt as if I had been dreaming. Au revoir, my dear, I do not say anything about the war, for there is nothing to be said. The same uncertainty still prevails. When will the great offensive take place? Will there be one? Of what will it avail us? "Zat is se queshtion?" said the Major, who is studying English under my guidance.

Givors, April 7th, 1915.
Dear B———:

Three days late in my correspondence! With the good will displayed by German submarines, when will you get this precious document? Having not much to say the matter has no great importance. Life at Givors is at least as regular and respectable as at Auburndale. I wish I had horses to exercise. Cabby must be a new dog. The one I met, Angel's contemporary, was Boulot or Boolo. What have you done with him? Has he, too, tried to race with B. & A. expresses?[24]

My brother was here two days, Easter and *le lundi de Pâques* [Easter Monday], which as you know is a great holiday. We had a great banquet with champagne. I did not get any as I was out with my brother, but I heard great stories about it. When I returned, Sunday night, there was a little package on my bed. There was chocolate in it, and a cigar case full of cigars; also a small box with a medal—Joan of Arc on one side—flags and crosses on the other. Joan of Arc as you may remember (even though you are unbaptized) is a Saint of France.[25] As the region about here is quite firmly catholic, people from time to time try to give us medals and other holy trinkets reminiscent of the Middle Ages. So far I had skillfully escaped having to accept any. This one I shall keep because it is quite artistic in design and because Joan is such a recent, up-to-date Saint that she must be quite harmless.

It's no wonder that the United States keep a sharp lookout concerning their navigation rights. I think that, throughout the whole business, your country has kept to a very wise and very just policy. Whatever may be true of Wilson along business lines, he has won for himself the respect and admiration of the belligerents.

April 12th, 1915.
To B———:

Your letter via Besançon came via Valence to Givors. I am wondering why you don't get word from me regularly. Perhaps the sailing of mail boats is purposely irregular in view of the submarine activities of the Dutch.

Nothing new here. I may leave the hospital April 26th. If I am put off again, it will be until May 10th. No one can say but that I am giving the war a fair chance to change its nature and even come to an end. If Austria gave in, that would be a great blessing. This is a period of great uncertainty and expectancy. Something seems to be accomplished near Verdun, but ye gods! it's slow and costly work. G——— (Houston, Texas) tells me that American papers pay attention only to what is going on on the British front. Please tell American journalists that the total front is 630 miles long. The English take care of thirty-four miles, the Belgians defend twenty miles, and we are holding the remaining 576 miles, which is nothing at all side of what the Russians are doing, but is pretty good just the same.

The victims of the great war at this hospital are getting along so well that every evening they give terrible concerts. Two violins, two accordions, one mouth harmonica and a tin flute are brought into play. A certain censorship is exercised over the performance by *le Sidi*, a Kabyl, from a regiment of Spahis.[26] He hardly knows any French, but has definite ideas on the kind of music he wants to hear. His speeches are limited to *"Y'a bon"* [It's good] or *"Y'a pas bon"* [It's no good]. He is a terrible rascal, to my mind. He looks like a hyena, and I should tremble for France's fair name if many like him ever penetrated into Germany and got away from their officers.

Life at Givors is certainly as regular and uneventful as it is at
Auburndale. There are birds but no horses. There are dogs, however.
All the town dogs are interested in us. They sneak into the court of
the hospital when we come in and go out with us on walks. Turc does
not come along, being too dignified. He is a huge Dane (not pure) and
his business is to keep cats out of the way of the sisters. Kiki, a doubtful mixture in which the spaniel predominates, used to be the most
faithful, but we lost him in the hills one day or in the streets of Givors,
where attractions of all kinds fairly swarm and tend to divert the
minds of patriotic dogs from higher things.

I don't believe that your mother will be surprised about your garden. I'll bet a twenty-five cent cigar—Romeo and Juliet variety—
which to my mind is the last word of high life and dissipation—that
you will plant some of the seeds upside down and will not plant the
rest at all—and that when the few seeds planted will have struggled
up into planthood, you will find that you have a straggling lot of
réseda, potato plants and dandelions, all mixed up.[27] Them's my
prophecy.

I don't say that you will not fill all the oil barrels in the garage
with rabbits. Why don't you go into rabbit raising for money? A
friend of ours did it. The skins sold very well. In six months he only
lost 20,000 francs.

My family write me of their plans for the Summer. They have
rented a cottage in the Pocono Hills—somewhere in New York
state—a fine lake, sleeping porches, etc., etc. They invite me over. If
this ——— war only could come to an end! If I ever get on the ship
for New York I'll carry on so that I'll have to be put in irons for an
hour, at least until I am normally seasick.

April 13th, 1915.
To Miss H——:

Your letter of March 29th came this noon. Sorry to hear that the
Red Cross is having internal scraps—but I dare say that the pro-
allies are having it all their own way, because in this region we have
just received bales and bales of clothing and woolen things from
America. In those cases, when there are notes and addresses put in by
the senders, the men have been told that they could and ought to send
a word of thanks. That is an unusual permission, because as a rule
correspondence with foreigners is not encouraged. It has been proved

that a certain tobacco firm—Swiss—sent our men cigarettes and a few kind words simply in the hope of locating troops on our front, hoping that some would say in their reply, just to what corps they belonged and where they were. The firm, of course, was German disguised as Swiss. Well, it is certainly fine to receive these tangible proofs of America's sympathy—as it was also fine to see a whole section of Ford cars taking our wounded back to safety—American cars run by American college men. Did you know that twelve of them have received the "war cross," which is given for some specific deed of bravery? When I saw them last, they had to go over a certain hair-pin curve which was shelled conscientiously every day by the Germans.

I have had a streak of good luck or rather I think I have. I am pretty sure of going off to a camp near here for a sort of three weeks' course in military arts and sciences. As the battalion is about ready to go back to the hills, that means that I am going to get out of at least three weeks in the trenches and as April is a wet month, the matter is not to be sneezed at. Besides I'll be perhaps higher up in the hierarchy when I come out. You know I am beginning to have difficulty in spelling out English words. It is nearly two years since I have heard your tongue and I suppose I am forgetting it a little.

Well, the Germans have not yet taken Verdun and I don't believe they will, and if they did they wouldn't have won the war for all that. There is hope that the English put in a good lick before long—and the Russians likewise. Nobody wants to see another winter's campaign.

Givors, April 17th, 1915.
To Mr. W. V.——:

Did you expurgate my letters before allowing them to be read to school children? I am not always guarded in my language when I write to Dab.[28] No, Bill, we can't take pictures on the front. We would get shot if we did, shot by our own men, I mean. I do have one or two yarns to tell about but not much more. I could never last two weeks telling stories. That's not saying that I won't drop on you as soon as the occasion presents itself. This trench war offers few diversions. It's the recurring of the same two or three things. Most of the time we sit still in the ditch or in front of it. Periodically shells go hissing overhead, exploding behind. At night there are some of the damndest farces acted out that one could imagine. A sentry hears the rustling of a leaf or the starting of a hare or else imagines simply that he has heard steps and takes a few shots in the dark. Then everybody gets up and takes a look through the holes in the mud wall and seeing the flashes of the guns, everybody begins to send a few across. Then the machine gun men on both sides, though they see nothing at all, begin to turn the crank just for luck and both sides blaze away in earnest. It's a devilish racket for fifteen or twenty minutes, then the pandemonium stops as illogically as it began and everybody snoozes for a while. Then it starts again. No one gets out of the trench, usually no one is hurt. If it lasts longer than usual, one side or the other sends up a sky-rocket which illuminates everything for a minute as if it were day-light, then if everything looks normal, quiet reigns again. Rifle shooting at night is nearly always too high. I have been caught be-tween two fires on such an occasion, and I did not even hear a bullet whiz by. They all went skyward. Men, a mile back, way up on the mountain side, have been hit by bullets which were meant to strike a trench two hundred yards away. That's why the platoon cooks who do their work a half-mile to a mile back of the firing line, have to pick the spot for their fires pretty carefully.

I certainly should like to be at Bridgewater this coming June. No such luck, however, short of a miracle. There is no talk of peace here. The country is putting up a tremendous effort and neither men nor money will be spared to put our neighbors out of our territory and to clear up Belgium. We owe the Dutch a few and we are going to pay them in full. You can have no idea of the way they have treated our border towns and our border population. I have not seen the worst by any means, still I went through a town two-thirds of whose houses had been burned to the ground, and without any military necessity, neither had the civil population done anything to deserve such a treat-ment. Near here there are eight hundred women refugees from the North. Two hundred of them are about to give birth to children who are the result of rape, committed by German soldiers last Fall. These women are only a few of the victims. The government is going to establish great orphan asylums to take care of the little Dutch bas-tards. It's clear that in the majority of cases the mothers will refuse to take care of the poor kids or at least will never consent to bringing them up with their families. So you see that if there is real trouble ahead for Deutschland, it's not altogether a pity.

Tell Dab that, at our next meeting, I shall kick him where he wished to have me wounded.

Givors, as usual, April 19th, 1915.
To B——:

Your sister having secured a parrot with a dog's mind and fidelity, I dare say that the next letter I shall receive from you will be dated *en route* to Central America. Such a trip may become necessary to get away from the responsibility of the garden about which you are as reticent, in your last, as an official *communiqué* about the loss of a trench. I don't say those things in a mean spirit or with any idea of taunting you, but simply because such seems to be the situation to me.

Nothing new at Givors. My wound is so reduced in importance that the only dressing it requires is a piece of pink court-plaster as big as half a postage-stamp. It is too bad. I can no longer feel like a victim of the Great War. A few weeks ago I could still hold my arm stiffly and tell friends to slap me on the other shoulder. But now it is all up. Well, no one can expect to have a good time all the time. Resuscitated patients are sent away to Lyons, then on their week off, every other Monday. They may ship me Monday next, April 26th, and if they do not I am absolutely sure of going May 10th. I shall be perfectly willing to go, as hospital life, when one is well, is exceedingly tedious.

It is with increasing delight that I see the Germans and German-Americans getting in wrong with Uncle Sam. It is fortunate that Wilson and not the Colonel is at the head of affairs.[29] It would be too bad if the United States gave up their allegiance to Washington's advice to keep out of European imbroglios. In due time you may have trouble enough with Japan to satisfy any natural craving for excitement that you may have.

Are you coming to Europe this year? The French papers are starting up talk, in a mild way, tending to reassure frightened tourists and frequenters of watering-places. It looks as if the San Franciscan exposition might look more attractive to your compatriots than Aix-les-Bains.

After much rain and cold winds, we are having perfect weather. The valley of the Rhône is, south of here, one great orchard. And in my innocence, I used to think that the Santa Clara valley was *unique au monde* [unique in the world]. Every afternoon, we go out, a young *Auvergnat* and I.[30] He is a kid twenty years old, belongs to the *alpins*. He had two bayonets shot off in the course of five charges up the side of the Hartmannsweilerkopf [*sic*]. He came here with me, in the same train, having a toe badly frozen. We go in the hills back of the hospital, lie in the grass and discuss the war situation, which is always the same. Diversity is brought into these proceedings by my friend's destructive spirit. He starts on the run and with great yells at all animals. Last time but one, he brought discomfort and even pain to one black cat, one otter, one hen-pheasant and two water-adders. He is a young savage from the forests of the *Massif Central*.[31]

By this time you must know that my trousers are not red. I have felt humiliated to think that you thought me capable of a following low enough to wear red trousers. Don't fail to acknowledge having been correctly informed on the matter.

It seems that the *chasseurs à pied* are now receiving round, pancake shaped caps like the *alpins*. They can be pulled over one side of the face, hiding completely the cheek and the eye. Calabrian bandits never look more rakish than our *alpins*.

Givors, Rhône, April 22d, 1915.
To Miss H——:

First of all let me thank you again and allow me to say once for all that it is very comforting to find that one is well thought of by those who one respects most. Don't think that I am getting to be a conceited ass. I only wish [you] to know that you and your father have given me, at the right time, the right kind of strength. I shall write to your father as soon as I shall have seen again what is going on in the world. Hospital life is necessarily uneventful.

My famous wound has kept me out of trouble much longer than I possibly could have hoped. On coming down from Steinbach I kept wondering whether I would "draw" two or three weeks off. Now it is the end of April and the surgeon told me yesterday that I would not be shipped out of here before May 10th! That means no firing line before June 1st at the earliest, since we have a week's permission then take two weeks as a minimum to regain some training. It takes at least that time to get back into the habit of carrying the "ace of diamonds," that is, the knapsack, with any degree of ease. If they are not through with the ditch method of waging war it'll show that the war is definitely a deadlock and that it's time for peace. It is very hard to see how the German lines can ever be knocked out of condition. So far

Robert Pellissier wearing new *alpin*-style headgear
mentioned in the letters.

he who attacks is at a tremendous disadvantage. The English at
Neuve-Chapelle lost heavily and about thirty thousand of our men
were laid up in the capture of Les Eparges.[32] Every time the Germans
try to come back at us they get slaughtered. As a friend of mine, who
helped beating back a counter-attack two months ago, was telling me,
"It's real sport to see them coming along four deep." That kind of
"sport," however, working both ways, as it does, is bound to become
unpopular.

The one decent thing that may come out of this horrible mess may be the final discrediting of war in Europe, and perhaps elsewhere. It's an idea which keeps up French soldiers at present. One often hears them say, "Well, whatever happens to us, our children at least will be freed from the curse of militarism and all allied curses!" It is strange to see how the country at large seems to take the state of war for granted. Except for a few stores that are shut down and for the fact that only boys and middle-aged men work in the fields, together with some women, one would never guess that the country was at war— unless one lived near the railroad track. Troop trains keep coming up the valley, while Red Cross trains keep going South. All peace talk is looked upon with suspicion at present. The general feeling is that perhaps the Germans have enough of it and spread rumors of peace to unnerve the civil population. Everybody knows that there can be no peace as long as the Dutch are still in Belgium and in the North of France. Roosevelt who had not made a very good impression on France at the time of his last trip because he gave advice right and left and without being requested to do so, is now becoming quite popu- lar. I am wondering if in the Colonel's pronouncements there does not enter unconsciously or subconsciously somewhat the desire to get Wilson into trouble. The colonel has certainly a virile, masterful per- sonality, but he is also such a good politician!

Do you feel haughty toward poor Amherst and draw unfavorable comparisons between it and Easthampton? I don't know Amherst very well.[33] Only was in it a few times with B——, and the "touring" I did there was strictly restricted to the space between his office and X-rays electric appliances and the barn where he kept his two horses, Tuck and little Nell, I think they were called.

It seems to me that now that you have a farm you are getting lazy. At one time you spoke of nothing less than dairy farming on a scale to supply the milk trust. Now you only mention a few hundred hens. Perhaps it is the pleasure given you by driving the new horse which has temporarily made you forget greater enterprises.

If you need expert advice on farm matters, ask my second niece. Her *fiancé* having had to give up the selling of strings and thread has bought some land in Delaware, and M—— thinks she can paint a buggy and discipline hens.[34] Brooklyn is no kind of a place to train lady farmers.

Givors, Rhône, April 27th, 1915.

To B———:

Nothing new since four days ago when I wrote. Nothing ever happens here.

We seem to have been licked on three points of the front this week.[35] Still that's nothing more than usual. We advance a few yards one day, then lose the same distance a little later, to drive them out again. Perpetual see-saw all along the frontier which must be fairly red with blood.

I don't see, can't see, how that war can end by arms alone, the advantage always remaining with the one who does not attack.

Your President is making a name for himself in Europe. The press commented his message to Germany in very admirative terms.[36] I am wondering whether Theodore will get in wrong ultimately. Since the United States will not fight, and may not be able to fight just now anyway, what is the use of calling Wilson names? Theodore's language strikes me as altogether too violent and self-contradictory. He says in the same breath that Wilson ought to have shown fight and that the navy is not ready.[37]

Your saying that the plants of your garden were nearly drowned out shows that you did some planting. Now I wish that I could call back a certain letter mailed some time ago. How utterly foolish to try to peep into the future!

Givors, May 2d, 1915.

To B———:

Nothing at all to write about. Absolute penury of matter and of thought. Only the assurance that your garden is now rivalling Mrs. Jack's and that my prognostics were all off. Still as you could have thought for months that I wore red trousers, I may be forgiven for having misjudged your ability as a gardener. By the way, the French government has taken up your suggestion and red trousers are now abolished. All infantry wear a bluish uniform which blends with the landscape. It is not called Alice blue. It is known as horizon blue. The chasseurs are distinguished by something or other from other infantry but I don't know what exactly. We may be given the same kind of caps as the *alpins.* Theirs is the flat Basque headgear such as are worn by the heroes in your pet story, *Ramuntcho.*[38]

Nothing new in the war except that the Dutch are bombarding Dunkirk and killing civilians.[39] Imagine fourteen-inch shells falling all about the streets of Auburndale. One, all by itself, would blow up the seminary, your aunt's house, and the home of Reggie all at once.[40] When they fall in a field they make holes each big enough to hold four or five Reggies at their fattest.

Some say the war is going to last another winter. Others claim that by the end of July we shall begin to see the last of it. "I give my tongue to the cats," as the French say, and expect, at best, to get stranded in the middle of the year and simply have to live in Paris for six or eight months.[41] I shall rent a room 8 x 10 feet in darkest Quartier Latin and have one *petit pain* for breakfast with chocolate; shall work until 1 P.M. in the Bibliothèque Nationale, then go to lectures and straighten out notes after a frugal lunch of *cervelle au beurre* [brains and butter], shall walk on the *bullyvards* [boulevards] after a dinner the menu of which will vary.

By the middle of the week I shall know when to go to Valence. Whatever week I am going, on one day of that week, my brother and I are going to have a great banquet, just the two of us. All kinds of wines and smokes. Will return to 30 Bd. St. Jacques in the happiest mood. Warriors, in all stories, are high livers and I shall make use of the prerogatives of the calling.

This morning I had a hard task. One of the victims of the Great War has a girl—a normal school student, who studies English—and to impress her corporal, she casually drops or rather slips in an English phrase in her correspondence with him. To get vengeance he asked me to translate his latest letter into English. So I did, with a few additions and distortions. It is really a flamboyant love letter.

Well, I have no more to say; besides my cigar is all smoked up, and that is about the length of letter one should not exceed.

Givors as usual, May 10th, 1915.
To B———:

Will your country and my country No. 2 declare war on Germany? The *Lusitania* wholesale murder is not the worst but one of the worst.[42] For cold-blooded cruelty it compares well with the sacking of Louvain, Malines, etc. The Prussians must really be stark mad. I have just written home that I would go back to the front with considerable vim and determination since in a way I will be fighting for my two countries at once, even if your government manages to keep the lid on the part of the United States which is not pure Dutch.

A few days ago my aunt wrote me that my sister would doubtless come to see them and me this summer! I wrote to her that the sinking of liners was bound to take place sooner or later and that the ocean was no place for ladies, these days. She will think me a great prophet.

It looks as if I might leave here a week from to-day. Will write again in the middle of the week to give the latest bulletins and *communiqués*.

Life here continues to be flat and idiotic but quite painless. I go out every afternoon and beat it all over the neighboring hills. The thought of going away Monday next wakes me up a little. Last week I thought I would go into a complete nervous collapse I was so bored. Monotony in life is the hardest thing to stand after moral anguish.

My brother is peeved. He had hoped that the worst of the war would be over by the time I went back, and now he sees that the end has not yet begun. He accuses the government of procrastination and felony.

In a moment of enthusiasm and grandiloquence I bet with the surgeon here that the United States would declare war on Germany within seventy-two hours! Now that I have slept over it all, I have a feeling that I am in for three bottles of *vin fin* [fine wine] of some kind because I don't believe Wilson will fight—though, by Jove, he has had a good a reason to as any head of a government ever had. If Theodore were at the helm, you would already be flying—mixed but expressive metaphors.

Do you know that the Germans are kicking out of the departments of ours which they hold, all the old men, the old women and the youngest children, sending them starving and half-naked back to us by way of Switzerland? I have an idea that a great deal of the woolen things sent by your people for soldiers have been saved up for those poor wretches, who are a thousand times more than any soldier the victims of the war.

Well, having nothing more to say, I quit. The wisest man in the world could not do more wisely. Be good and remember that nothing too mean can be said about the government of the Germans. In my heart, I still believe that there may be a few good Germans, but it's no time to talk about the exceptions that prove the rule.

Regards to Reggie. Tell him that I don't believe in fat horses and that if I ever get on his back again I'll make him lose ten pounds an hour for three consecutive hours.

Translated from the French

Givors, the 13th of May, 1915.

To A——:

American heads must be pretty hot. Just now it must be rather un-comfortable to be even the grandson of a German. I fail to see how the American government can be satisfied with an exchange of diplomatic notes.[43] On the other hand, it is very likely that if the Americans were to leave their coasts defenseless they would within a fortnight receive a Japanese ultimatum concerning the Philippines. Wilson is an honest and courageous man. He will know how to get out of this scrape.

Aunt L—— asked me a short time ago if you were not coming to Europe this summer to make us a little visit. I answered that the season was not propitious for a sea voyage. This answer was made previous to the last *Boche* crime.

I start for Valence next Monday and I shall be at the military dépôt on the 25th. O joy! I am already preparing to say disagreeable things to the non-commissioned officers who are expecting me over there.

No doubt you know that we have made a slight advance in the region of Arras and that Italy is still ready to join us. Have you read d'Annunzio's speech, the one he made while standing on the steps of the *Monument des Mille?*[44] Do read it. It is to be found in *Le Temps*. It reminded me of Victor Hugo, only much worse. I have never read anything which so closely imitates the empty resounding of utter inanity.

CHAPTER 5

⌇

Resting

Valence, May 20th, 1915.

To Miss H———:

Thank you for the little book which plunged me very pleasantly in New England atmosphere, made me spend an hour or so in New England, a part of the world which I like very much indeed. The blossom of mayflowers added to strengthen the local color of Mary Wilkins' story.[1]

Madam, the French army is inoculated against typhoid. It's a mere accident that I have not undergone the process yet, but I expect to be put through it at the dépôt next week. Coming in irregularly as I did is the cause of my having been overlooked so far.

The indignation of the United States about the *Lusitania* must have been something formidable. Even now, I dare say, it would take very little additional German cussedness to bring the United States navy across the ocean. The message sent by Wilson to the Imperial Government has created an excellent impression among the Allies. French, English and Swiss newspapers comment admiringly its excellent form, its courtesy and its undoubted firmness of tone. I have an idea that Wilson is going to do big things for international peace. He combines very firmly patience and courage. He may be big enough a man to give international diplomacy a brand-new character which will be a reflection of his own integrity and courage.[2]

I left Givors three days ago to spend a week here. I go around inspecting buildings with my brother. We also watch the artillery recruits who are boys nineteen years old being trained. They are pretty sturdy looking youngsters and are having a great time trying to stay on horses recently imported from Argentine. Tuesday next I shall be at the dépôt and shall immediately try to direct the activities and mould the intentions of my petty officers, a set of men who greatly need to be educated, great as their native qualities may be.

I must run up street to rescue my brother from his office, so goodbye, and thank you again for your kindnesses—in the plural, you will please notice.

Amagny, Besançon, June 5th, 1915.
To Miss H——:

Since the arrival of your last letter we have been sent out into this hamlet, in the backwoods. There are twenty houses and four fountains. We camp on the inhabitants who do not object too much, so long as we buy enough stuff from them to pay for the straw which we steal. My platoon has a nice barn to sleep in. Not as nice as a New England barn, not being nearly so high. It belongs to two farmers. One half of it has a new coat of paint and the other a coating of what must have been paint once. That's because one farmer is rich and the other poor. We are right in the valley of the Doubs among beautiful hills, but as we have to overexercise among said hills, in spite of a pretty hot temperature for June, we enjoy the landscape only at intervals. To-day my platoon is on duty, keeping the peace and seeing that the laws are obeyed. I am writing in the guard-house, which is really the school house transformed. We have nice white pine boards to sleep on. Our supposed business is to run in such members of the French army who might do more than look upon the wine when it is red. We have one in the lockup now. As he was wounded recently and in addition saved, under fire, first his lieutenant, then his corporal, we pass him cigarettes and see to it that his stay on the humid straw of the jail is not too bitter.

We leave in two days for some other places where we won't stay long. They keep moving us all the time and no one knows why. We are all being vaccinated against typhoid. It takes four infections to gain some degree of immunity. I give up prophesying when I shall go back to the front—not for a month I guess—but that is a prophecy.

Our friends, the Russians, are beating it away from P-r-s-mysl, however it is spelt.[3] The undaunted Italians are climbing many hills—with the hot weather—a most creditable performance.[4] We have sent them a lot of artillery, so that they may not come back too fast. Will the United States get mad at Bill?[5] These days are trying all right. Some say the war will be over in July, but I can't see it. I think it's an all summer job and into the fall. The Lord wants the nations to decide that war is no kind of an occupation for any one. As soon as something worth while happens, I intend to thank your father for his kind letter—but now life is too flat and sordid.

Amagny, June 5th, 1915.
To B——:

I may not hear from you very regularly for a while since we keep moving. From Besançon we came here, then we were told that we could move Tuesday next and heaven knows where we will go after. We are getting some training. The actions we go through seem so silly and futile compared with the real article of last winter. Still it's quite necessary to get into training again. No answer has been given yet as to my application for an interpretership. I'm living in hopes. I should like a change of occupation.

The village where we are is beautiful and—miracle—pretty clean—though several miles from the nearest railroad station. It's in the valley of the Doubs—Doo, not Dubs—fine meadows surrounded by long hills. We live in barns, sleep on clean straw, eat *boeuf nature*—and rice then rice and *boeuf nature*. But we can buy wine, cheese, etc., besides. I am *"chef d'escouade"* [squad chief], and have powers of life and death over nine men and a cook—male cook, if you please.

Now, the Russians have received another licking and are strategically beating it.[6] The Italians should soon begin their strategic retreat on Nice and Marseilles. We nearly retook Lille but did not. Those who prophesied the end of the war for the end of July may see their prophecy go following after all the others made since August first, last year.

The papers say that the United States is full of fight. It is not surprising. I am fully looking forward to a diplomatic rupture between you and the Kaiser—unless the Kaiser lies down flat and crawls on his stomach before Wilson.

It is as hot as pepper out here in day time, but cold at night. I find that lots of places have California's climate without leave from California.

We are much more free here than we were in Besançon. Yesterday I took the Oxford Book of French Verse—which Marie (a niece) gave me years ago—and reread what there is in it of Verlaine especially and *Le ciel est par-dessus le toit—si haut—si bleu*—very much to the point these days, since we are prisoners of the nation. No dishonor connected with this imprisonment, however.[7]

Well I quit being exhausted. My best regards to your family.

Roche, Doubs, June 11th, 1915.
Dear B———:

Leading the most foolish life imaginable. All those who came out of hospitals up to May 20th have gone back to Besançon to leave for the front within a few days. The others remained here, so that now we are thirty-five men at the company, that is about two men by *escouade*. I have a barn all to myself and I do nothing at all; just wait for hours to roll by and they are slow rolling. This state of affairs can't go on very long. I dare say the company will be completed in a few days. At any rate we are happier here than in Besançon, being much more free to go about as we please. The country is beautiful. The Doubs is much smaller than the Connecticut, but its valley reminds me in spots of the Mt. Tom region. And it's as hot as it ever was in New England—boiling hot—as the humidity is very high and trying.

It's difficult to imagine the condition of the men who are fighting now. It looks as if fighting was a rotten occupation in summer as well as in winter. Italy has not yet begun its strategic retreat and we are much pleased. We get little or no news from the front these days. Something must be going on, which either must not be talked about or will not bear publishing. Oh! The monotony of this confounded war. One wonders at times whether life will ever be normal again. . . .

Now that Bryan has retired to civil life and is going to start wild propaganda for Peace and International Benevolence, you may end up in civil war, because Germany will feel safe and will sink more neutral vessels.[8] The war party and the peace party in the United States will have abysses between them and trouble will come out of them. Then I shall go back to your country and reëstablish peace. In years to come there will be a group of La Fayette and me in the Public Garden and in Golden Gate Park. . . . [9]

My people talk of going to the Pocono Hills for the summer. They leave New York this week. It makes me sad to think of it. To be sure I used to go camping nearly every summer, but somehow, this year, I am sick of camping.

This is a muddled and muddling letter—not due to softening of the brain, but to the heat and to the inactivity—and to the surroundings—a wretched cabaret room with clouds of flies which do lessen the pleasant effect of the fragrance of roses that comes through the open window over which hangs sackcloth in guise of curtain. A hen just came in. Rural is it not?

Roche, Doubs, June 15th, 1915.
To Mr. G——:

I asked the superintendent of the gas plant in Besançon to read your letter; he is an intimate friend of my brother and he receives me at his house as if I were one of the family. He jumped up when he came to the word indemnity, and although I am not excitable I agreed with him. You said that were the Germans to keep their colonies it would be immoral. It would be still more immoral if they were to keep what they have stolen from us and from the Belgians. If by indemnity you mean war expenses, I agree with you, for although we were blameless this time, our share of responsibility in this war dates back to our little military orgies of one hundred years ago.[10] On the other hand, an indemnity, which would cover the value of property stolen by the Boches, would be perfectly fair. They have made a clean sweep in the North of France and in Belgium. I do not see why they should not be held responsible for having so carefully packed and shipped to Bocheland the machinery of all our mills and the furniture of all our castles, before they set fire to the buildings themselves. They also flooded our mines in the North. It will take a considerable amount of money to put everything in working order. I can not tell whether the loss is to be figured in millions or billions, but it would be fair if all this wealth were returned to France and Belgium. Whether the payment of such a debt is to be called indemnity or described under another name, the face remains the same.

On all other subjects, I thoroughly agree with you. I am not at all yearning to cross the Rhine, the cost would be too great, and I desire still less to take a trip to Berlin, unless I were to go as a tourist under the protection of *Cook's Agency*, if it is still in existence after the war.

June 18th, 1915.
To B———:

Yours of June 2d at hand and contents noted. Nothing doing out here, but much brewing. We are only thirty-five at the company and we live in luxury, having a barn for two and doing nothing to speak of. The brewing comes in from the fact that rumors are all about us to the effect that we may be sent to a camp near Lyons to form a new battalion—*de marche*—so called, why no one knows, as all battalions do march more or less. Some say that unit would go to Italy, but no one knows—we are as ever—*comme l'oiseau sur la branche* [like a bird on a branch; ignorant]. A circular from the Secretary of War has been sent around. It calls for student officers called *aspirants*. Requirements—a *modicum* of education and horse sense. Chances of success greatly increased by wounds received in battle. So I modestly presented my name and have already been looked over by a dépôt commander and by a brigadier general. If they have not ruled me out already, I shall be made to try three written examinations (geography, mathematics—arithmetic to be plain—history). If I pull through these I shall go to some camp and get drilled until I can command a section, that is sixty men. Later I may become a second lieutenant, but that is in the dim future and it's to be hoped that war won't be long enough to bring me military success, fame or glory. At any rate, if I pull through the various *épreuves* [examinations], I shall have a change of occupation altogether, for the better. On the other hand, since I did not do regular military service, there are millions of chances of my getting tripped up—furthermore as I have hardly opened a book for a year I know neither history nor geography. I have not done an addition these last twenty years. So don't feel hurt or surprised if I go back to the ranks and end the war with a rifle and a *sac* [pack]. What I wish would happen is that having gone through O.K., I might be appointed *officier de liaison* with the British. No *liaison* in the worldly sense, you understand. Troops, not ladies, are in question.

Your cousin is a very generous person. I am not now in the position to see any family in want because of the war. All the women

whose husbands received daily wages and who are at the front receive
so much for themselves and an additional sum for each child, so that
there is no misery just now. That will come later when taxes will have
to be paid to cover war expenses. Here we see none of the families
ruined by German depredations or French precautions. D——, my
brother's friend, who has been so good to me in Besançon, gave me
some money when I left for the front, to help out anyone whom I saw
in need. It proved very useful as many of my comrades and friends
came from the North or from poor families, and, literally, did not have
a cent in their pocket. One of them, coming from Douai had not been
able to buy anything whatsoever since August last. D——'s money
came in handy, you may be sure. If, when I go back to the front I meet
cases which might interest your cousin I shall help them out in her
name and tell her about it later.

I am glad the Dutch have queered themselves in the U.S.A. and
I am equally glad that your country will remain at peace. There is
enough misery as it is.

My friend, C—— Chicago W. O. Gay & Co. (Boston) has sent
me four hundred and eighty expensive cigarettes and fifty aristocratic
cigars (Henry Clays). His brother shipped them to me three months
ago from London—just received them!

Roche, Besançon, June 23d.
To L——:

What do you know about the war? The Russians seem to be rapidly disappearing from the eastern horizon and the fighting in our
neighborhood is worse than ever. Yesterday we were told that the
Fifth Battalion had participated in the doings about Metzeral and had
lost six hundred and twenty men. As a result a big lot of men will
leave Besançon to-morrow for Alsace. If I had not applied for admis-
sion to the examination leading to the job of apprentice officer I
should have been sent with the lot and could count on being near
Munster three days from now. I feel kind of cheap at being here while
the others are going to take their chances. The examinations come
July 6, 7 and 8. If I pass them, I shall go to a school near Paris or else
to a camp not far from here. If I flunk, I shall go to the front P.D.Q.
To tell you the truth, I have no desire to come out as a section chief
and to lead men to Heaven knows what with the possibility of blunders and of remorse for a life time. My ideal is to get in as an *officier*

de liaison with the British. That I would enjoy immensely but no one can tell what calls in that line there will be. That kind of job does not mean responsibility for the life of others—just your own, and the carrying of orders. The great advantage is that you are not loaded down like a mule and are much more free. I am doing arithmetic, geometry and sub-elementary tactics in the hay-loft where I now have my residence so as to be prepared July 6th and following. Life is a funny thing all right. A few days ago a brigadier general looked us over, asked a few questions and made us manoeuver a section. He decided we might all (about eleven) try the examinations.

Some of the men going to Alsace to-morrow are returning to the front for the third time, having been wounded twice. It's pretty tough. The newspapers talk about men eager to get back to the firing line. Let me assure you that that's confounded nonsense. Most of them are stoically indifferent, others are determined and also disgusted.

A few weak sisters shout that they don't worry, but they get drunk and that's a bad sign. For all it is a heavy sacrifice; still taking all things into account, they show a good spirit. They are a brave lot and their courage makes war only the more damnable.

Will leave you now, having spoken my mind.

Roche, June 27th.
To B———:
Life at Roche, for me, is a pipe and a song. I do nothing but read in preparation for the examinations of July 6, 7, 8. I brush up history, geography, arithmetic and allied sciences; also I learn what to do when bringing a troop in a village, how to protect it on the way, how to protect it while camping, etc., etc., how to go next to the enemies' lines and rubber, etc.—all things about self-evident but wrapped around in words.[11]

If I had not had myself registered as *aspirant* or *élève* [student] officer, I would be in Alsace at this moment. At Metzeral, my battalion lost six hundred and thirty men, including all our officers. The commandant was wounded in the mixup. He fell and the Germans pounced on him and finished him up with the butts of their guns. Then our men became enraged, cleaned out the Germans and did not make a single prisoner. I leave to your imagination what this last statement means. Of course, a detachment had to be sent immediately from Besançon to fill in and it was my turn to go but as I had registered and passed the first two tests, I was not taken along.

I wish I could tell whether the friends I made in the trenches last winter are still alive or not.

With the swiftness of the Russian retreat and the small advances made by our great efforts it looks like another winter campaign or else peace negotiations on unsatisfactory terms, unsafe peace. Our hope is that the Germans having pushed the Russians off the map, will attack us again and try to cut our lines—attempts which would undoubtedly fail and cost the Germans enormous losses. But this is no war; it's a long continued butchery.

The Stanford people have renewed my leave of absence so my job is safe. Long live the U.S.A., where people do always the right thing by one!

I am going to Besançon to dine, sup and talk with Dulac. Train at 8.45. Letter written at 6.30 A.M. What do you think of that?

Roche, June 29th, 1915.
To Miss H———:

The Vermont picture was certainly very New Englandish. Mt. Sterling is an old stamping ground of my brother-in-law's. It's a part of the world he makes for during the short vacations of the school year and into which he makes raids sometimes in summer. There are days when I wish with great intensity that I could climb into a canoe, even though I have done quite a bit of camping, first and last, this unacademic year.

Nothing very new out here, but the same painful state of tension, increased now that the Russians are beyond the horizon line. There are going to be special examinations for St.-Cyr, the French West Point. I modestly applied for the privilege of trying them. They are coming off July 6th, 7th and 8th, so I am plugging upon them. Any one might have thought that the Ph.D. examinations would be my last.

If it had not been for those examinations I would be in Alsace now. My battalion attacked at Metzeral and lost six hundred and thirty men, so that reinforcements had to be rushed from Besançon last week. Our little success in the valley of the Fecht cost us dear. The four thousand beds in the hospital here are again occupied and more

Red Cross trains keep going south. It looks like complete mutual destruction and is disheartening, but every once in a while something happens that braces one up. Two days ago, one of the men here had his wife and three children come down from their home which is at St.-Dié in the Vosges. I had a talk with her. She was in St.-Dié during the seventeen days of German occupation. She saw with her own eyes a soldier go by her house with a baby stuck on his bayonet. She showed me the baby carriage which has a rifle ball streak on it. She and her children and six other women had taken refuge in the cellar, and the Dutch fired into the cellar. Her youngest was in the baby carriage at the time and escaped by a miracle. Other babies did not escape.

When the French retook the town, there was, of course, a final bayonet charge. That woman was made to stand against the wall of her house—all the women were lined up that way along the street so that the Germans could fire and the French could not, but fortunately the bayonet proved sufficient. Also women and old men were tied to chairs and placed across the streets to form human barricades. Those things took place last fall and the German soldiers may be sobered up by now and behave better, but their debt is heavy. So, if money lasts, war may go on through the winter again.

Besançon, July 7, 1915.
To B——:

Great business, all over. The three examinations passed without great difficulty. I'll know in a week or so, more likely two, whether I have passed or not. Speaking modestly I will tell you that in my professional mind there is no doubt about my having passed. On the other hand, there are some three thousand candidates all over France and many factors come into the business besides the passing [of] more or less childish examinations. I am going to wait in great dignity for the final outcome. If you were only here we would go off on a bat this very afternoon.

It seems to me that your press is boiling over once more about Mr. Morgan's misadventure.[12] That man, Holt, is clearly crazy. The Germans are not lucky with the United States. Reputations that need being plastered with a mask of innocence to keep before a decent public should not be bolstered up by impudent bluffers like Dernburg and by maniacs like Holt![13]

Here I am living at Dulac's who are as hospitable and charming as ever. These last two days, it has not felt much like war time, though the fighting seems to have started up again on the whole front with renewed intensity.

Roche, July 10th, 1915.
Dear B———:

Just two words—French *deux mots,* since I have swamped you with communications this week. Nothing new, except that this company is being reformed with all kinds of human odds and ends— infantry from various regiments, men once pronounced unfit for service, then called after second examination, and M.D. second thoughts of doubtful sincerity, territorials who are nearly forty and who ought to stay at home. It is somewhat depressing. Where in thunder are Kitchener's three million men?[14]

I hope that next time I write I shall know about the result of the examinations I tried to pass last week. . . .

To-morrow, Sunday, I am again going to Besançon. So far I have been very lucky to get away from this town. I should like very much now to take a trip to America.

Did you see my book? The Oxford press, American branch, sent me a copy of it. My sister did all the proofreading, so there are no mistakes in spelling. Thanks to her and to me the Great American Public has now a School edition of Racine's *Bérénice.*[15] I may make $5.00 on it, this coming academic year; nothing like prospect of great wealth to make life rosy.

July 10th, 1915.
Dear B———:

Nothing at all to relate. We had a nice lieutenant. He has been replaced by an ass of a captain, the type of the perfect fool. He does all he can to make life unpleasant and we can do nothing but smile on his doings.

No news yet from those examinations; hence no way of telling whether I shall ever be able to have my picture taken in another uniform. You probably have forgotten what I told you about my present garb and think of me again as wearing red trousers, which is doing me great injustice. Nothing but dark blue, please recall, with a few very fetching canary yellow trimmings—a charming combination.

We took an eighteen-mile walk between breakfast and dinner to-day; that's probably a great deal more than you did in the same time. We got drenched, which added to the pleasure of the ramble. We went by a place where a signpost, pointing to a trail in the woods, said "To the greatest tree in the Franche-Comté." I went out of my way to see it. It would have looked like a toothpick, or more politely, a diamond match, side of any self-respecting American tree. And I said, "America first. The Biggest in the World." That, I said to myself, naturally, so as not to hurt the feelings of the natives. The French are touchy.

No news from America. My Chicago friend tells me that the Allies, barring the slaughtering of civilians, are doing as much harm to American trade or rather much more, than the Germans with their submarines. I am ashamed of us but, no doubt, there cannot be a war of this size without general injustice all around. The only thing I can think of in way of excuse is that this war in a way is also your war, for if Germany were supreme in Europe, you would see yourselves in trouble with that power before many years, and you would very soon suffer in the administration of your country on account of your large German-American population. So, we are all doing it for your good and it hurts us more than it hurts you. So saith the hypocrite.

Roche, Doubs, July 15th, 1915.
To Mr. H———:

Thank you very much for your long letter and let me also thank you for the shorter one which came at a time when the feeling of being trusted and "believed in" by others was particularly precious. It is a letter which I will feel like reading again if I have to spend again any considerable number of days in a ditch with shells kicking up dirt all around. I shall read it as a moral tonic, not because I believe what you say in it, but in order to know what I must try to live up to in such moments. The "Billy" referred to was the Kaiser, but the information about Bryan was very welcome. He belongs doubtless to the great mass of utopists who know what they don't want, but don't know what they do want and are sincerely grieved because people at large, giving up all hopes of understanding what they are driving at, end by accusing them of hypocrisy or of insanity. They are the plague of the Peace Movement. Such men are useful in arousing the public conscience, but heaven help the land that tries to follow them in the execution of its business. It is in part thanks to them that the line of forts along the Belgian frontier, a set of defenses for which army men had been clamoring for years past, had never been built. And yet had we enough guns at the battle of the Marne, the Germans would now be thinking it over on the other side of the Rhine. That battle will always remain a puzzle. How did the Germans ever manage to get licked? They had everything in their favor, organization, numbers, enthusiasm? Yesterday was the 14th of July.[16] It was celebrated very mildly. The stunt of the day in normal times, is a military parade and review, everywhere where there is any body of troops. A year ago some 700,000 men took part in the performance—all strong, healthy boys between the ages of 21 and 24. How many of them are alive now? Perhaps 50,000, perhaps less—alive and well, I mean. In my battalion once in a great while a man from the years 13, 12 or 11 turns up (having reached 20 on these years) and he is looked upon with amazement and admiration. As a rule he was very severely wounded last fall or else he is going to the front for the fourth time, perhaps, after having had numberless escapes and a very respectable number of small wounds. When these men formed the nucleus of the army we had an immense reservoir of strength. It may be that the secret of the battle of the Marne lies in the tremendous energy of those boys who felt that it was their business, their own special avocation to protect their country. Our army is still good, but it is not made of the same stuff. Its intentions are just as good, but it is no longer in the twenties. Still it is wonderful to see the spirit of the boys of 18 to 19 who have just been called to the colors—it is wonderful but sadder than any one can imagine.[17]

Well, may this nightmare end soon.

July 15th, 1915.
To Miss H——:

I ought to have acknowledged your kind letter of June 24th sooner. Still if you knew how tiresome life is these days, you would not blame me very much. It is one long drawn-out bore. Last week I went to Besançon to pass three two-hour examinations which may or may not give me a chance to go to some camp of instruction and be trained for the work of "aspirant," which is the round below second lieutenant. Ever since I have been waiting for results to be published and results are always fabulously slow in coming. Any way the thing

was competitive and as there were more than 150 candidates by military sector and as there are twenty-one such sectors my chances of being ignored by the authorities are very great. I tried for these examinations not because of any particular faith in my military genius, but
because of the following piece of reasoning. The war is now a deadlock and it will either end in two or three months or else it will last all
winter and also next summer. If it ends in a comparatively short time,
leading to an unsatisfactory compromise, I don't care to get killed or
maimed in the last meaningless and purposeless skirmishes. If it is
going to develop into another winter campaign, I should very much
appreciate the relative freedom which is the lot of any officer. I don't
see myself spending again any number of months staring at a loophole in the mud wall of a trench. My reasons as you see are not heroic, but they are reasons, I think.

All the men whom I knew last winter have already gone back
to Alsace. After three weeks only, some are already killed or made
prisoners. The battalion took part in the capture of Metzeral and
lost five hundred and fifty men. Then it lost more men in repulsing
the German counter-attack that followed our advance. Now it is
somewhere back of the line "resting," which means that having lost
practically all its officers and being reduced to about one-third of
itself it has to be completely reformed. I dare say not one of my last
winter's friends are now at the front. The horror of this war comes
to one in full when news of this nature is received. Out here things
would not be bad if the men in command were not the leavings and
scrapings among officers. It stands to reason that the really good
ones are not kept in the back country. The chap now over us went
crazy last winter when a shell exploded too near him. I can assure
you that he has only partly recovered. His presence does not tend
to make Dépôt life either glorious or pleasant. Still it is more dull
than actually disagreeable.

The slushy German note seems to have stirred a pretty hornet's
nest in your country.[18] It's hard to see how it could be otherwise. In
everything the Germans seem to be outdoing themselves in rascality
and flat-footedness. The strange thing is that with their terrible military strength, they did not need at all to be grossly criminal and then
sneaky. If they had attacked us by way of Belgium, but without committing every kind of crime on the way, why, in spite of the violation
of Belgian neutrality, the world at large would have become accus-

tomed to the situation and their purely military successes would have finally won the admiration of all non-combatants. But it seems to be a rule without exception that all great rascals are also sooner or later great fools—so the Prussians sank the *Lusitania,* carried on a ridiculous campaign in the United States and even were represented by insane criminals who made attempts on the life of your most preëminent men. These actions, together with the asphyxiating gases, compensated the fact that they caught us unaware and half prepared and also destroyed the moral effect of their really splendid fight against Russia.[19] We, the French, are grateful for these little favors.

Well, some big gun is in the neighborhood inspecting our barns, so I must be on hand.

July 27th, 1915.
To B——:

Life is but one long examination. M.A., Ph.D., A.B., Normal School examinations, then *aspirant* examinations, then finally, yesterday, English interpreter's examination. It will be funny if I don't get anything out of all that; it will also be sad, very sad. Since the Russians have taken to the tall timbers around Warsaw, there are rumors to the effect that the English are going to get busy and take a sizeable portion of the front, giving the French troops or armies a chance to have more depth. Well, to resume, that may be the reason why they are suddenly calling for interpreters. I passed the examination as you may imagine, but have no way of telling whether I shall be chosen or not or when. Uncertainty is the motto of everything in the military.

The way I feel now, I should very much like to go with the English. At first, I wouldn't hear of anything except returning to Alsace, but since the capture of Metzeral no week goes by without my learning that some friend has been wounded or killed and at present there can't be anybody left of my last winter's friends, so that returning to the Fifth Battalion does not mean much to me any more. Being with the Tommies would be new and interesting for a while anyway. I should like it better than being an officer, as I have no way to tell whether I have any leadership in me or not. I can do what's to be done, but I don't like to drive others, especially when life and death are in question.

Roche, August 5th, 1915.
To Miss H——:

No, no, indeed! I don't intend to give up the joys of teaching for those of an officer's Kingdom of Boredom. To tell the truth strictly, joys should be replaced by freedom. As you suggest, it would be idiotic, at my time of life, with thin gray hair, to change profession. Besides, military life, in peace time, and on the lower rounds, must be fatal to brains and all.

What seems certain is that I am sure to get out of this blamed little town which is not very pleasant to inhabit, especially when one's home is forever a barnloft overlooking pig-pens and the like. The farmers out here don't raise only strawberries and honey-suckle, I assure you. To-day I learned that I was admitted at the military school of St.-Maixent where I must betake myself so as to start business August 25th. The course lasts four months, so that the Dutch will not see my face and its wrath until December. By that time the Russians may have started on another round trip of seeing East Prussia. I also passed the English interpreter's examination. What will happen if I am claimed in both places? Excuse this hurried note. The newspaper clippings you enclosed interested me very much. The colonel is the same old boy![20] As for the Germans and Bryan they seem to be "in bad."

Roche, August 6th, 1915.
To Mr. G——:

Your letter from Boston was received with joy and read with still greater joy—specially after your confession and expression of repentance in connection with W. J. Bryan. Your preceding letter had positively astounded me. I do not believe that W. J. Bryan is a rogue (*farceur*) after the French style; he is an Anglo-Saxon rogue. Whatever he may do, he will always be in his own eyes the righteous. Every time he is going to do a mean trick he begins by justifying his deed, wrapping it all up in fine, generous sentiments, beautiful virtuous commonplaces, an easy thing for him to do, as he is the kind of orator for whom only those words count which awaken some good strong sensation, preferably pity or indignation. The French rogue who meets with success is usually an intellectual knave (roué) who has hardly any illusions and even fewer about himself than about anybody else. His Anglo-Saxon counterpart begins by tricking himself into believing in his own probity, he has to an uncommon degree the typical fault of the Puritans, selfrighteousness. He is full of empty high-sounding sentiments, "whatever his enemies may say about him, his purpose is beautiful, beautiful."

The fall of Warsaw has been officially announced to-day.[21] It has not stirred in the least the inhabitants of Roche-les-Beauprés, as they are very much engrossed with harvesting. I believe that the general state of mind in France is more or less what it was last September, during the retreat of the Marne. People used to think: Evidently it is a very unpleasant experience but the end must be and will be a success.

These wretched Boches are pretty strong. Had it not been for the Belgians and other atrocities, from a moral point of view, they would have thoroughly beaten us by their prestige and their successes would have won for them the enthusiastic support of the neutrals, and we would have been materially defeated. If it had not been for the destruction of Louvain, the violation of Belgium would soon have been pardoned and it would have been all up with us.[22]

Paris, August 24th, 1915.
To Miss H———:

The newspaper clippings were very interesting. It looks now with the *Arabic* affair, as if the United States must break with Germany.[23] Whether you fight or not, does not matter now. The moral effect is what is needed. Germany may apologize but that is not likely. In the Paris *New York Herald* I see that camps for training are being formed in the United States. Looks like business. Hardly any lights in the Paris streets at night. Saw Notre-Dame by full moon yesterday, a sight not seen for many decades. The Louvre was dark as pitch. Shall be in St.-Maixent to-morrow morning.

CHAPTER 6

St.-Maixent

August 29th, 1915.

To Mr. C——:

The letter and the baby's photo came. He is a fine husky little chap who will soon be able to lick his father, thus avenging his god-father for many involuntary trips to the bed in Normal Hall and in 53 College House. I am safe from all harm until November 15th. I am now at St.-Maixent Military School. If I did first-class I would come out as a second lieutenant—quit laughing—but as I am with a lot of sharks it's more likely that I may come out as a humble sergeant. They are working us pretty hard physically and intellectually. I feel about the way we did twelve years ago when we landed in Cambridge; strange subject, no background, etc. Will write more fully later.

St.-Maixent, August 29th, 1915.

To B——:

Can't write a long letter because they have inoculated me again for typhoid and the result is a general befuddling of the brains and stiffening of the body.

No mail this week as my brother has not had time to forward my letters as yet, for we are now nearly at opposite ends of France.

We are to be here until November 15th. The work is hard physically. We are on the jump nearly all the time. I have no sure feeling about coming out as an officer. If they give me a sergeant's stripe I'll have done fairly well. The men who study here are all pretty able. Great many lawyers, some artists, some sports, but all men with a good deal of education and push to them. So don't scorn me too much if I come out humbly. I have only six weeks of regular military training to back me up in my aspirations.

Life here is one of great regularity. We have no time to ourselves except Thursday night after supper and Sunday. The rest of the time is all taken up with drills, practical exercises out in the woods, lectures and readings. To think that I should have come to what Dante calls "the midway point of life" to get into this.[1] One good thing among others is that we are nearly all the same age. Also we are splendidly fed—really very good—no longer the sad alternation of beans or potatoes with beef as at the Dépôt. There, you have my life down to the smallest details.

It looks now as if Germany would back down on the *Arabic* question; which would naturally lead to apologies about the *Lusitania* crime. To have Germany crawl would be the best thing, the best solution. I still doubt that she will crawl enough to give you people adequate satisfaction. Will get myself photographed one of these days, but not to-day, being too sad with punctures.

St.-Maixent, Sept. 5th, 1915.
To Miss H——:

I am tickled to death that the Germans saw fit to back out before Wilson and the United States in the *Arabic* case. It's a good lesson for them and fortunately one that will not leave an heritage of hate such as would inevitably have been the case had Wilson been forced to drastic action. The French press is suspicious of Germany's meekness. They see in it a desire to get peace talk well on the way while Russia is seriously in distress and while we are stuck on our lines. Everybody in France is resigned to the idea of a winter campaign No. 2 and no one wants to hear about peace now.

Nothing exciting at St.-Maixent. We work, more or less intelligently, about all the time. We work so hard physically that reading or thinking are extraordinary occupations. Nearly all the time we dig model trenches or take trips, so as to be able to use the map accurately (no joke in this country which is a complicated maze of sunken roads cutting through woods and fields surrounded with high hedges). This is an old Protestant center, depopulated more or less since the days of the Edict of Nantes. Still the "temple" looks in a very dignified way at the cathedral which is at the other end of the street.[2] We are not far from La Rochelle, the mother of New Rochelle, U.S.A.

We are being called to dinner, so excuse this hasty ending.

St.-Maixent, Sept. 12th, 1915.

To Miss H——:

No, don't believe what Miss Addams is telling or rather what she has been told. French soldiers don't get drunk each time they go into a bayonet charge.[3] I took part in one, and not only had we nothing in our cans except water, but we had had nothing to eat since breakfast (and it was two in the afternoon), and we had no supper at all and breakfast only at 10 the next A.M. I saw a charge start right from the very part of the trench where I sat and what struck me was the perfectly cold determination of the men who were to my left and to my right and in front of me. Those who cut lanes through our wires hit rhythmically and with perfect aim. There was no barroom atmosphere at all. The men in the school here come from all corners and quarters of the front. I have asked a dozen or so of those who have charged with the bayonet what they knew about systematical distribution of whiskey or what not and they told me that they knew nothing about it, had always gone to it in the full possession of their powers. One, a zouave, said that at "Vauquois" they had received a half-pint of brandy the night before the attack.[4] It may very well be also that certain units which come from tough parts of the population, such as the marines and other colonial troops, the "foreign legion," etc., do get royally drunk on all occasions, but they are the exception. The so-called "Gay-Ones" who are military convicts may also have little weaknesses of their own. But you may feel certain that when the majority of French soldiers charge, they go to it because they want to and not because they are crazed by drink. Where men do drink a good deal it's in the "Dépôts" when they are bored and discouraged, having nothing particular to do and being commanded by officers who cannot be trusted with a command at the front. The papers have reported often that the Germans did fill up, at times, on combinations of whisky and ether. A corporal from the supply service (I was with him at the hospital) told me that he had smelled ether in the cans of

German prisoners—but that's all pretty uncertain. It looks as if Mr. Dumba might go home and be followed soon by Mr. Bernstorff.[5] Good for Wilson.

This is a hastily written note, excuse its messiness. We are rushed all the time for one reason or another.

One great event since yesterday. There are chasseurs à cheval [cavalry] in this town and they are our enemies. Yesterday I was on guard at barracks where those gentlemen are not supposed to enter and one of their sergeants (*maréchal-des-logis* [sergeant of artillery or cavalry], if you please) went in, in spite of our objections and we are going to get him locked up for his trouble and impertinence. This, then is a great victory of infantry against cavalry.

You see that our life is not made up of important events.

St.-Maixent, Sept. 12th, 1915.
To B——:

No mail from America this week; not very surprising since the Germans are sinking our steamers off the roads of the Garonne and since Bordeaux has replaced le Havre. Two small ships were torpedoed off La Rochelle, a harbor fifty miles from here, and the people of this region who know of war only what they read in the papers were pea green with emotion. All the Saintonge and Aunis squashbugs thought that it was all up with them.

Nothing new here, but there is a general feeling that something important is going to take place at last on our front. English troops still keep coming and our own men are being shifted from west to east so that our "line" is getting deeper and deeper. Maybe I'll get out of there for the final licks, that is, at a time when things will be very interesting. Perhaps I will be sent with reinforcements from France to take Milwaukee. It looks like business in your country, and my one-half country. Mr. Dumba must be peeved and Mr. Archibald must "envisager" his landing in his native land with some degree of anxiety.[6] There is no doubt that Wilson did the right thing. It might have been better if he had acted sooner. Perhaps now, there will be sensational developments.

Well, having nothing more to say I quit. Life here is pleasantly monotonous. Have not learned anything new as yet. We have been having a kind of review of all ordinary military stunts. Later it will become more interesting. We work more physically than with our heads.

St.-Maixent, Sept. 19th, 1915.
To B——:

Again just a few words as life is slow as cold molasses—though it is really hot as Tophet these days.[7] This region is supposed to be very rainy and there hasn't been a cloud in the sky for weeks. Every time we go off on a march we sizzle away at an awful rate. We are always dressed for a Polar expedition and the result is startling. Well, we will have a winter campaign on our hands soon and I shall have something else to whine about.

No great news of any kind. We belong more than ever to the Nation—body and soul. When will that kind of voluntary servitude end? My friend C—— writes me from Chicago that the steel men whom he knows look forward cheerfully to two more years of campaigning! Ye gods! Well, the Stanford Trustees are still holding my job open for me; the Lord bless them.

My sisters are back in Northampton and Brooklyn respectively. M——, my second niece, gets married October 7th. Somehow or other my nieces always get married when I can't be on hand. Such is life.

Two months or so from now, I shall probably be going through Paris again.

Don't be surprised at the way the stamps are placed on this envelope. Being absent-minded for just a minute I pasted the complete series on a letter destined for my Paris cousin, then transferred them to yours with above result.

St.-Maixent, Sept. 28th, 1915.
To Miss H——:

Thank you for all the news, which praise be given are not war news, and for all the clippings. I should judge from the letter that a considerable portion of the United States' population would not object to having a little fight. Well, it may be just as well if you keep out of the mixup. It would be really too bad if, after Europe had received such a lesson concerning the craze of armament, you people had a spell of militarism! The only *raison d'être* of this hideous war is that it is the end of European militarism.

Yesterday we heard that a big blow had been struck in Champagne and that we had made about twenty thousand prisoners and captured some seventy guns.[8] But it seems that we advanced only two miles on an average and no one knows how much it all cost us.

If the prophecies of your brother's acquaintance about Constantinople could only come to be realized soon! If we held the Boshphorus, etc., things would be ended much more quickly. All these German victories over the Russians have a very bad effect on our little friends in the Balkans and all the Russians need is ammunition and more guns. To think that France worked hard to close up the Dardanelles under our dear Emperor the Small![9]

I am writing this at a time when I should be studying how many bricks it takes to stop a rifle ball! A scandal as you see. But I needed a rest, having passed off three examinations this week. O! you school days—How to be a kid after you have your Ph.D.!

St. Maixent, September 28th, 1915.
To B——:

I am late, two days late. No fault of mine. We have been having examinations and as we have hardly any time to study, Sunday was wasted in reading dry-as-dust rules and regulations tending to facilitate the murdering of Germans. Now those examinations are over; they will begin again in two weeks. Life here is intense. Most of the men who are in charge of courses are good; one is a blasted ignoramus.

We have just learned that our troops in Champagne made twenty thousand prisoners and captured seventy guns. We don't know how much it cost us, but the proof that our generals are not absolutely inactive is a relief. They probably started on an "offensive" to try to balance Bulgaria's butting into the game.

You are right in feeling that Americans can't as a rule appreciate the solemnity of European scrapes. It's impossible for them to understand because they have too little history back of them. People in New England may dislike England because they still feel a personal interest in the Revolutionary war just as they have set opinions about the South because of the Civil War. But you take the people of the Middle West and what do they care for Plymouth Rock or for Gettysburg?

So we are all the creatures of our environment and it's no wonder that Americans politically isolated and with the good fortune of having had so far only men of a pretty high moral character at the head of affairs, could not make out the duplicity of Germany which beats all existing records.

It's·hard to write just now. We are made to keep a company's books. We put in the names of the men of this company then make up fictitious meals—there goes the conversation. *"Moi je leur donne des sardines—et du sel. Moi je leur fiche des tomates—50 Kilos—Tu es fou! Faut bien une livre chacun! Des vermicelles, du fromage de gruyère. Si je leur donne des pommes et du bifteck il ne me restera pas d'argent pour demain"* ["I'm going to give them sardines—and salt." "I'm going to give them tomatoes—50 kilos." "You're crazy! Better give each of them a pound!" "Give them vermicelli and gruyère cheese." "If I give them potatoes and beefsteak I won't have enough money for tomorrow"]—etc., etc.

I'll have to entrust this to the sergeant as we get out of the school only Thursdays and Sundays.

This is a messy letter, but you will understand why.

St.-Maixent, October 2d, 1915.
To B——:

We licked the Dutch in Champagne and we feel that this is a proof that they will be licked again, then again, until they get out of our country. It may take months, but we will do it. There has been no excitement over the matter for the horizon is still too dark and our losses must have been heavy, though nothing like what the Germans lost.

Nothing new here. We go on shooting, marching, scattering, attacking hills where there are no enemies. It's perfectly healthful as an occupation, but it is neither remunerative nor elevating. Seven more weeks of it!

You had hard luck in your Adirondack's trip. My family went to Big Moose, a fine little lake near Saranac. They liked it very well except my brother-in-law who had no mountains to climb, only lakes to walk to, blooming little lakes as he scornfully called them.

I passed all my examinations last week, but we have another set coming off in eight or ten days. Ye gods, what a bore! And you can't even tell the examiners to "go to," without exposing yourself to being court-martialled.

When I get out of here, I may get six days off. I shall bat in Paris and across France to Valence. Then off to Alsace and the reconquest of Strasburg, Metz, Berlin and Leipzig.

The sergeant has just butted in on us for the "appel" [roll call], and in a few minutes the bugle will play the *extinction des feux* [lights out] so I must quit or run the risk of going to bed in "pinch" darkness as my kid niece used to say. She gets married Thursday next. Ye gods, but time flies!

Translated from the French

St.-Maixent, October 3d, 1915.
To Mr. G———:

At last the Boches have been beaten on our front. Nobody as yet thinks that a final victory is at hand, but the country has heaved a deep sigh of relief, on hearing that their trenches can really be turned topsy-turvey. Now, people face the future with less anguish. They say the Germans are beginning to worry. Their turn has come.

You talk as a philosopher, a house pulled down; that is nothing compared with the shelling of a town, but nevertheless it is not a cheerful sight at all, especially if the house was a model house, a tailor-made house, if I may borrow one of W———'s pet expressions. And by the way, you spoke of some of my friends rather slightingly. Do we select our friends because of their bright intellects or because of their hearts? My friends are perhaps not geniuses, but at all times I can count on their giving me advice, sympathy, help. It is not because you write books that I cling to you and keep writing letters to you. Your wife misunderstood me. All I meant was that you not infrequently took the counterpart of a given question merely because you liked to juggle with ideas and I, being a simpleton, used to take your paradoxical statements for Gospel truth until one fine day I discovered that your greatest pastime was trifling with ideas.

This part of Poitou is Protestant. Twice I went to the Protestant church. It gave me food for thought. The custom of writing Bible verses on the walls is a very good one. While reading the verses we think we hear old voices, ever so sweet, which bring back to our minds in crowds childhood's memories. But the devil take theology and dogma—the official creed so cheerless and narrow. After all, these little churches have a great deal of dignity, a cold dignity, to be sure, but touching nevertheless. Here the congregation is mostly made up of peasants and on Sundays you see nice old women wearing their beautiful white caps.

October 10th, 1915.

To B——:

This week has been very rainy so we have spent most of our time changing our clothes and cleaning our guns. Friday we went on a far-off expedition to attack a town with blank cartridges and shoo off some real cavalry (chasseurs à cheval). It rained, then fog came. The captain got twisted in his bearings and the section heads lost sight of the captain. Result, half the company attacked from the wrong side and the other half attacked and brilliantly captured—the wrong town. Hence great *parlez-vous* gesticulations, some swearing and a bad lunch because the *cuisine roulante* [mobile kitchen] which was to feed us got distressed and stopped between the two towns and we had to go to it instead of it going to us. Besides, the cavalry who manoeuvred against us said we were in too large bunches and claimed they could have killed us all to the last, which is only a lie as cavalry is no good at all in our days with all due respect to Reggie.

Last night we were out again. It was pitch dark. The lieutenant who is trying to train us attempted to cut through our lines, but I caught him as he was sneaking in and reaped great glory, in my own mind, from that gallant act.

Otherwise life is pretty stupid. It may be different on certain parts of the front.

There is great satisfaction felt here at the way the United States met ours and England's borrowing. The idea is that it is not a financial venture so much as a proof of sympathy and friendship on your part towards us.[10]

To-morrow we dig ideal and perfect trenches and later go off shooting. I am getting to be a reliable shot in spite of my biconcave lenses. Still I may come out of this school only moderately well as there are really too many things to get on to and also one has to make believe he has a spirit of authority verging on tyranny which I despise and which I can only put on as a cloak.

I close for to-night, life being empty of interesting personal details. Can you tell me what is going on in the Balkans? We can make neither head nor tail out of it.[11]

St.-Maixent, October 24th, 1915.
To B——:

No great things out here. The lectures *et cetera* go on for three weeks more. Then there may be ten days given over to examinations, then we will have a few days off, then we will, according to all probability, be again at the nation's beck and call.

Things look queer in the Balkans.[12] It's quite clear that the Greeks don't believe in our ultimate victory. It does not matter at all. We are going right on and we'll get them sooner or later. The financial and moral backing which you as a nation are giving us is a very encouraging feature in this dismal business.

If I come through this war, I shall fight for the United States in all their wars to come in my life time. California may have one with Japan before I am made a full professor at Stanford. You always were mixed up on the respective values of instructor, assistant, associate and Full Professorship, so you really don't know when that war is coming.

We are going to get forty-eight hours off at the end of this week. Too short to go to Paris. I shall go to La Rochelle if I have my way to have a look at the Atlantic and try to look over to Coney Island and Bass Point.

Can you recognize me on the postal? I am in the back kneeling—fourth from the left—hard to recognize because of my huge moustache.

The reason why I have not had my picture taken is because there is a professional photographer at my *escouade* who keeps promising that he is going to take us all—and who never does it.

I am fifty million letters behind, so will cut it short now; must tell my family what I am at.

Palace-Hôtel et
Du Commerce, Place d'Armes
La Rochelle, October 31st, 1915.
To B——:

A half-dozen of us are here batting around over All Saints' Day—which coming right after Sunday gave us a forty-eight hours' furlough. This is precisely the ninth day of vacation which your servant has enjoyed since September 6th a year ago. Where are the happy

Squad in training at St.-Maixent, a different photograph from the one
that is mentioned in the text. Robert Pellissier is in the back row
at the extreme right.

days when the Trustees handed over three months' vacations at frequent intervals?

This is a very interesting town—old as the hills. The harbor is
guarded by two towers dating back from the sixteenth century and the
city gate is over the thirteenth. The harbor is nothing now but a tiny
basin filled with fishing schooners, with red, drab and écru and blue
sails. The real harbor is four miles from here. Just came from it. To my
joy and amusement the first boat in sight was a tank steamer from Portland, Oregon, and Los Angeles. It had come on its innocent way
loaded with oil and cases that looked as if they might contain something that was not oil. It was being unloaded by German prisoners
under guard so that I could not speak with the skipper, much to my
sorrow. The Germans were not worked hard. They looked well fed so
that my conscience is at rest concerning the way we treat prisoners.

Your card showing the Washburn House reached me the day before I came here. I passed it all around to show to the French that free
America knows how to bring up children without keeping them under lock and key all the time and that a dormitory was a pleasant home

whereas a *dortoir* [dormitory] is very much like a prison ward. The French need to be taught lessons.

No one knows how I am going to come out of St.-Maixent. For whatever has to do with getting along in the woods and sneaking behind hedges I am all right—but for all parade stunts which I can't take seriously I am a joke. That's what my lieutenant told me and he was grieved. So was I, but who is going to give me a new kind of voice which will allow me to bellow like a bull? If I flunk out on the examinations and you make fun of me or despise me I shall never forgive you.

Please tell me what we should do in the Balkans. It strikes me that the situation is getting to be exceedingly muddled.

Just precisely a year ago to-night I was in the train on my way to the front! Perhaps, in a month I shall not be far from doing that again. Such is life—and it's no use trying to understand it. I can tell you with perfect sincerity that I do not look upon that trip with very much anxiety being dead tired of hanging around Dépôts and schools.

November, 1915.
To Miss H———:

Just back from a two days' bat, for we had forty-eight hours off, over Sunday and All Souls' day that followed. Did not bat as royally as you did in the White Mountains, but still enjoyed a little freedom which seemed extremely sweet as a reaction from the state of quasi penal servitude in which we live here at St.-Maixent. Four or five of us having no very good reason for going to Paris at this time of the year spent the day at La Rochelle, New Rochelle, N.Y.'s mother, and the once famous Huguenot stronghold. The old harbor is good only for fishing boats now as it is filling in with sand, but it is very picturesque with its two fourteenth century towers guarding its entrance. The real harbor is three miles from the center of the town. It is a brand-new one with all modern improvements. It was very busy as there were boats in from South America unloading horses and an innocent looking tank steamer from Portland, Oregon, and Los Angeles was being unloaded of its cargo by German war prisoners. Some of the cargo was oil to be sure, but there were also a good many boxes which any unbiased observer would have been tempted to call ammunition cases—rifles, cartridges. The boat had a huge American flag painted on both sides of the bow and two more astern. This to pacify possible submarines. In front of the city hall which is a very remarkable building of the fifteenth and sixteenth centuries, there is a statue of the mayor who was in office when Richelieu took the town. That statue was erected with money subscribed in New Rochelle, N.Y. That mayor was a great boy. When told that he would have to give up the keys of his town he emphasized his refusal by hitting the marble table in front of him with his dagger and making quite a dent in the stone. We saw the table and the dent, so we know it was so.

November 7th, 1915.
To B———:

Since the last time I wrote, the Prime Minister has decided to keep us here a month longer, so that we shan't get out of St.-Maixent before December 15th, so that I may spend Christmas with my brother. We may bat around Paris together in a modest way or else around Lyons. That is worth looking forward to, though life is such a bore here that there are times when I wish I could be anywhere except here. Still there were two great doings this week. We fooled with hand grenades and weeping-gases-shells. The latter are wonderful. They fired a few cartridges at us while we were in a sham trench. We did not expect it and all of a sudden we had, just had, to beat it, with our eyes shut and groping our way. The other great doing was the giving of two or three *croix de guerre* an occasion for which we were all gathered in our best finery and the cavalry in the region was massed side of us.[13] At about the moment when the colonel was to start his speech, the soil being soaked with rain and very slippery, the horse of one of the captains fell all over himself, while the mount of another of those gentlemen started to buck very stiffly like a wooden horse mounted on wires. Our joy though silent was immense. I'll tell you in secret that the army is made up largely of men who are hoping and piously praying that something ridiculous may happen to their betters.

Except for these little events, life is as dull as a rainy day in the Warren House, Cambridge, Mass.

That makes me think of what you said about Grandgent and his lecturing at the Sore Bone next winter.[14] I promptly wrote to him asking at what time he intended to be in Paris. It would be a great treat to see some one from America. You asked whether he was French. His father or his grandfather came from France, but he himself is American born and protected by the Stars and Stripes.

What is going to happen in the Balkans! We don't begin to have enough men out that way. That is probably why the Cabinet went out of commission.[15] We have made some terrible blunders. The worst was in believing for months that Greece and Roumania would never let Bulgaria loose on Servia. We may even have supplied ammunition to those nations! We are darn fools, but we are going to stick this fight out and come out on top.

Two cards from you when you were at Williamstown. Went through the place years ago—when I was still at Williston. Had gone up Greylock with my brother-in-law during Spring vacation and we got stuck in snow when on top of the mountain.[16] Western Mass. is a beautiful part of the world. It is at once pretty, as all well cultivated regions are, and there is also enough of the wilderness left to make it mysterious.

I must write to my brother before they bugle us to bed. Nine-thirty here, all lights out. Much more rigid than Smith College.

November 12th, 1915.

To Miss H———:

Thank you ever so much for the letters and for the clippings. Have not yet received the woollen things which you mentioned in your letter before the last. You may be sure that they will be welcome as we are pretty sure of having a rather rough time of it this coming winter. There is some talk of our being sent to Servia. It may be only talk, but on the other hand there is nothing at all impossible in the matter. Yes, there are such things as interpreting officers. But I am not an officer yet and as for interpreters there are plenty of them. Every business man who had dealings with London jumped at the chance at the beginning and there are very few calls now. As far as danger goes, it is always the same tobacco—to use a French idiom. A New York man who came about when I did and who was in exactly my case went to the front as interpreter with one of the American field hospitals in the Verdun region, where the front makes a V with St. Mihiel at the base—well he was killed in March in front of his field hospital. Interpreters who went to the Dardanelles must have seen something, too. And for that matter, any one who gets mixed up in such a business as this must not think too much about what may happen. It's as useless as it is cowardly. I could have been done away at least seven times last winter and yet I came out O.K. I mean that number of times there was no very good reason why I was not banged up—and many others with me. It is no use thinking up schemes for going to war safely. It's the ancient story of dancing and the pipers. It is very necessary to dance in the present case. The stronger Germany reveals itself, the more it becomes evident that life with a victorious Germany would be very hard for any one, anywhere on the planet and absolutely unbearable for any of us whether in Europe or out in sunny California. It is very fortunate, therefore, that there is no intention of giving up the game on our part or that of our pals. The Kaiser may go to Constantinople if he wants to, that won't help him out in the end though the trip may give him much personal satisfaction.

Did I tell you that here at St.-Maixent, I have lost the record for distance? One of us came back from Tiflis by way of Moscow, Stockholm and Arkangel! Another who was brought up in San Francisco started for France from Yokohama, where he was in business— a third, a banker—was looking up oil property in Wyoming at the time of the mobilization. The first and last of these three I met officially. Not so with the third. One day last month, we were off on a day's trip. It was as hot as pepper. We stopped at noon in a pasture to cook our dinner and it was hotter than ever. Behind me there was a man fighting with his kit, apparently trying to unstrap a refractory pan, when to my amazement I heard the man say in a low but exceedingly wrathy voice and exactly as I quote—the following words— "Will that ———! ———! ———! ———! ——— pan ever get off this ———! kit!" It seemed very good to hear straight from the shoulder American cussing. I sympathized with him in your language and we have been friends ever since. My apologies to your father.

Well, about four more weeks here. The chances are that the war will not be over by then. Will send you the latest from the front about Christmas time or New Year's. Wish I did know from what part of the front though, but that's asking too much.

St.-Maixent, November 13th, 1915.
To B———:

No very great news. Life is as flat as a pancake and not nearly as palatable. It's raining most of the time and the work is a perpetual repetition of things we half know, but which we shall never know much better. They would have done well to send us away when they had said they would. It does not pay to plan things one way and to carry them out in some other manner.

One named Georges just stepped from desk to desk to cover the ground faster in the room where I am writing and incidentally put his iron-shod foot on the left hand upper corner of this letter. He sends his apologies so I don't start again.

To-morrow we are going to have a banquet—those of us who are in the same *escouade*. We have retained a small room in a small hotel in town and after great deliberations and confabs decided upon an elaborate menu. One of us is a man from Lille. His house is burnt down and he has not seen his parents since a year ago last August. He is an extraordinary chap who had never been in the army before this year and who has not been at the front. He is fat and always late. No matter what we do he is the last one on hand. We have called him *Le Désespoir de l'Escouade* [the Despair of the Squad]—as we spend a good deal of time getting him out of scrapes into which he innocently wanders periodically, having brought all his civilian habits and ways of viewing life into this military servitude which is now our lot. What I started to say is that he has a very good mind for everything that has nothing to do with our present business and he has an endless Montmartre, Quartier Latin—*pas convenable répertoire* [improper or indecent repertoire]. He will be our toastmaster to-morrow and we expect huge things from him. To give you an idea of his abilities, at odd moments, and in a casual way, he will take two or three stools and balance them on the tip of his chin. While in the room, fooling, he roars like the bull of Bashan, but on the drill ground, when he has to command, his voice is feeble and gentle as a girl's—a mere quaver.[17] When he is off duty he can imitate to perfection the colonel's roar when that deep-chested gentleman gives forth commands to the whole battalion!

How long will the Dutch blow things up in the United States?[18] If they don't look out they will greatly facilitate Mr. Roosevelt's election to the Presidency. Wilson's chances are pretty feeble, I dare say.

Letters from Stanford tell me that they have a new president out there.[19] I don't know the gentleman and he does not know me. I wonder how he will take my prolonged absence from duty. He may be pro-German for all I know.

I am enclosing an unfinished proof of a group picture of my *escouade* taken by our Lille friend. Will send the finished product in ten days of so—as soon as I get it. Am sending only a few heads.

November 21st, 1915.
To B——:

This is going to be a short and foolish letter as life is made up mainly of nothingness. One more week of the same stuff, then the examinations, then *La Fuite* [the Flight; escape from training]—but that will be in three weeks only when all things are added up.

Too bad for the ladies of Eastern America. Still you will doubt-lessly get the vote in a year or two.[20] There is no reason why you should not have it and merrily misgovern in co-operation with us men. Some things will be better attended to with women voting, but some others may be worse off. When you once have the vote, the hardest thing will remain to be accomplished, to-wit: to keep women interested enough in their newly acquired right to think about it and use it. An extra-ordinary proportion of men don't care about what is voted and the same thing will be true of women unless they make a special effort and a long continued one. Votes for women may at worst be negative in the United States and it may be very good because there is more freedom and more higher education among American women than among their continental sisters. In France, such an extension of the franchise would undoubtedly bring about a deplorable Catholic, clerical reaction, one of the most stifling things that might happen to our poor republic.[21]

I don't believe that your country would lose very much by hav-ing something of an armed force. The rich must be strong, they must be willing to sacrifice something to remain rich. If France were a poor country, the hungry Germans who have grown too fast for their own good and for that of their neighbors, would not be bothering us from Dunkerque to Gallipoli. I don't believe that armies bring about war. If a man has a dollar he puts it in his pocket, if he has several hundred he puts them in a reënforced concrete, iron-clad, steel-rimmed, double-bottom bank and burglars immediately surround the bank and get busy with dynamite and all kinds of jimmies.

Yes, Marm, I was hit with that kind of a thing you describe, only it was not very big and came from a small shell or a bomb. One day,

I few days before I got laid up, a pretty big piece fell within ten feet of me and sizzled on the snow. We called them *les mouches* [the flies], because as they whirl through the air they make exactly the noise of a fly or beetle caught in a bottle—they buzz—whereas the shell itself, before exploding hisses.

We are not very brilliant in the Balkans from what leaks out. Started too late, and with too few men. If Italy comes in, something may be done for Servia—and as long as we hold the sea and as long as the Germans can do nothing more on our front nor on that of Russia—things are really not very bad. The Kaiser can go to Constantinople and be d——ed, that will not free his towns of Hamburg, Bremen, Lubeck, etc., etc., which are not doing very much business these days, praise be.[22] Are you really going to send us, at one and the same time, Mr. Roosevelt and Grape Juice Bryan?[23] The papers are announcing the coming of both—each in his specialty.

From some newspaper clippings received there seems to be in formation a German-American Party in the United States. That may complete the discrediting of the Dutch in your country and my second country. So let Prof. Walz do his worst.[24]

The German prisoners looked peaceful enough. They were clean and fat. That's the second lot I have seen. They surely are well treated and in no way overworked.

The details about our late attempt to do something in Champagne made me think of Miss Addam's saying concerning bayonet charges. We had some two hundred thousand men charging at the same time over ground kicked up by shells. Could that number of inebriated gentlemen go three miles right ahead of them and mind their officers?

To-day we were told that the courses would be prolonged to December 10th, so that with the examinations we shall stay here until Christmas. It's good for us, but also depressing, as the military school life is a frightful bore and a strain on one's nervous system which I give up trying to describe.

There are rumors that we will be sent to Servia when we come out—but that's almost the logical rumor to spring up at this time.

[The following two letters were not included in the original collection but clearly belong here. The first was written to Pellissier's niece Louise Alden, the editor's great-aunt, the second to Marie Alden Brown, the editor's grandmother.]

[*Undated, but written late November, 1915, at St.-Maixent*]
Dear Louise:

Thanksgiving Day, and we are having a half day off—a mere co-incidence as the great majority of the French know nothing about the tribulations of the Pilgrim Fathers.[25] We are really turned loose on the town to facilitate our participating in the latest National Loan—good soldiers with money will have a chance to invest in uncertain securi-ties; good soldiers without money will simply write letters to their families and drink tea.

Last night was the final grand blowout of the course. We have spent three months digging ideal trenches in a field near here and last night we made a night attack on them. It was a spectacular affair, planned elaborately by the gent in command here. We fired blank car-tridges, we fired 80 illuminating sky rockets, we sent no one knows how many genuine hand grenades which blow up with impressive din, we cut real wire with real wire cutters. As a matter of fact it all was so very realistic that two are now in the hospital with grenade frag-ments in their anatomy and several are nursing minor cuts and bruises. It reminded me very vividly of certain nights in Alsace when German rockets made the snowy landscape as brilliant as in day time and when our own rockets soared over the valley of the Rhine and came down slowly, slowly describing a spiral. Still it would seem as if the price paid last night for such emotion was a little high. Most of the company commanders had warned the gent above mentioned that he had assured them that there could be no danger in any exercise planned by him.

Monday the examinations begin and two weeks from to-day I should be starting for Besançon and my beloved Dépôt. We will have some days off undoubtedly as we have been held down here since August last. Where we will be sent after is not clear. Maybe to the same region but surely not to the same battalion. May not be sent to the front for a month after getting out of here.

I am sending you a picture of my "escouade"—a very pleasant one. Violin teacher side of me; then a Franche Comté bank clerk; then a Lille photographer whose house is burned down, then a typogra-pher, then a Parisian lawyer who speaks English very well, is some-thing of a journalist, has a peach of a mind and a will of steel; in front of me a business man—mirrors—very good mind, next a big kid whose father is a wholesale grocer in Montpellier, will be very good after a few whippings—then a sort of Mr. Smith (Chicago) but from Paris—good as [undecipherable] and very rich; then a school teacher who has not yet gone to the front—we say that he looks like a Central American general—then an engraver who is crazy over machine guns. Allow me to introduce my friends. With the exception of the general and the photographer, we have all called on the Dutch and been sent to the hospital after sojourns varying from three weeks to 8 months among and near the Dutch. Now it seems that I have forgotten our real Marseillais shown between the violin teacher and the bank clerk—he is our prize liar and exaggerator as befits one of his town.[26]

Give my love to all. Here's hoping that next year we will have Thanksgiving on the same continent.

Yours with much love,
Bundy

Please send one picture to Tante Adeline. Will send picture postals to Peg and to Marie.[27]

[*Undated, but written early December, 1915, at St.-Maixent*]
Dearest:

Your letters are a joy for ever. It is fine to really feel that you are well, substantially, finally settled and that you take hold of the new kind of life with such real pleasure. Talk about adaptation to new conditions—and for both of you—because after all it was not so very long ago that you were both citified persons, as useful on a farm as any two professors of theoretical phonetics could possibly have been.[28] That said without any offense you understand—merely a respectful remark of admiration. I brief (French idiom) with impatience to see you in your new surroundings. By the way, Louise sent me some very pretty pictures of the farm [rest of paragraph faded and unreadable].

Thanksgiving is always associated in my mind with a song that your mother taught you once before going to Marshfield when you were small; some of the words were, "Over the river and through the woods, to grandfather's farm. . . ." Not that you are any grandfathers, but you will understand what I am driving at.

Great relief here as all exams are over. They were somewhat in the nature of a farce, a trying farce at times. It's quite clear that we are going to be judged in the last resort by things which don't show in examinations. Some perfectly good men for instance may be too old, others may not have been at the front long enough, the shape of the nose of others may not be [undecipherable] enough.[29]

The men in charge of us have made up their mind about us rather subjectively. So don't be horrified if I come out as a sergeant instead of an aspirant. Still I have by no means given up hope and once at the front it won't matter at all what I am. Have already been at the front as long as the average here.

We may stay here as late at the 20th. Everything after that date is wrapped in the deepest mystery. One thing is sure, I shall be delighted [undecipherable] to get out of here.

Give my love to Mort and tell the Billings family that I have written.[30]

> With best wishes—ton affectionnè [your affectionate],
> Bundy

Postscript

St.-Maixent
December 5th, 1915.

Mighty glad that von Pap and Boy-Ed got their walking papers.[31] Those people have been really too free and easy and casual-like in their treatment of your government. Have nothing against anyone German but the methods of the ruling class must be treated as they deserve.

Translated from the diary

To speak only of the training received at Saint-Maixent, it is just to say that we were made to do certain things very well, but that we never had a chance to really learn how to command. The manoeuvres, by ourselves or one company against another, might be called attack of a wood, of a village, retreat, march under artillery fire, etc., they always were about the same thing. We went to some village five or six or eight miles away, walking on the road, then we broke up into sections and marched on our objective taking as we went along less and less vulnerable formations until we finally scattered as "sharp shooters" and after shooting many blank cartridges, we stormed the positions in question very brilliantly—à la baïonnette. The officers did practically all the commanding. We profited by these manoeuvres mainly because we saw how individual sections kept their direction

and kept in touch with their neighbors even when very much subdi-
vided. What we did by ourselves was going off on patrols of all kinds.
We fairly stripped the skin off our hands in the course of those exercises for the country about Saint-Maixent is one inextricable maze of
live hedges in which thorns and brambles of all varieties intertwine
into nets of great resistance.

The first of these manoeuvres lasted through the morning and the
afternoon of one day. The weather was perfect; for six weeks we
scarcely had a drop of rain and the clearness and warmth compared
with the best of California climate. Under such conditions, even when
the work was very rough—which was the rule—the mid-day rest was
very pleasant. We either cooked our meals in the open or else the field
kitchen supplied us with bouillon, boiled beef, steamed potatoes and
hot coffee. We preferred to do our own cooking, several of the men
in our squad being first-class cooks and very willing to work for the
rest of us who simply helped by cutting wood, carrying water and
peeling potatoes. Later in the season the trips were made to extend
over two days or part of two days. We would leave in the afternoon
or else be awakened at two or three A.M. and thus do half of the walking before sunrise. In one or two cases we were quartered in villages.
At Chevreux our presence was imposed upon a Protestant family who
gave us the free use of their kitchen, before allowing us to retire to
their hayloft and we spent a fine evening listening to the songs and the
stories of our official entertainer B—— at St.-Maixent, called the
squad's despair, because of his utter heedlessness in all things military.

We were less fortunate at Salles. Our hosts had a wretched home,
damp and poorly furnished. There were only women in the house, the
men being at the front. The mother at first would not let us settle for
the night in her kitchen. As it was very cold the lieutenant made her
take us in and, much to her distress, we carried in enough straw and
clover to make something of a bed on the stone floor. The poor
woman was full of bitterness. She thought that we were taking advantage of her loneliness and made nothing out of the lieutenant's speech
in our defense in which he spoke of "tactical necessities" and other
matters that were Greek to her. Her great fear was that we would be
in her way in the morning and that she would not be able to get breakfast ready for the farm hands. We knew that we would be off before
her time to awake had come, so we did not worry very much about
her distress. As it turned out, by 4 A.M. we had replaced the straw on

the stacks and swept the kitchen, made our coffee and buckled our pack; she came out of the living room just as we were starting on our way to attack a detachment of cavalry stationed across the river.

That kitchen was strangely dingy and sombre. Jary remarked that it must have remained thus for centuries and that we had before us the hearth of a Mediaeval Jacques.[32] Two small windows flush with the muddy yard let scanty light into the cellar-like room. At the end there was a huge fireplace over which swung a crane. There were a few pots scattered under the flue. In the ashes two crickets chirped and chirped and chirped. The floor was roughly paved. Such must have been the home of Joan of Arc. This thought forced itself on my mind as I looked at the oldest daughter. She was a girl of sixteen who was born handless; the sorrow of her life had given a strangely intelligent and wistful expression to her delicate features.

December 4th, 1915.
To Miss H——:

Some note of mine must have gone astray, for I am sure that I have written during October or else letters will come bunched, for, as you noticed, boats leave in bunches; probably to facilitate their protection across the ocean. One or two torpedo boats can take care of several liners which are only a few hours apart.[33] Please thank your brother very much indeed for the woollen socks. They are fine. I have already tried them one very cold night in the course of which we did fool stunts in neighboring trenches dug especially for our education. They keep one's feet as warm as toast. The socks, not the trenches. All the examinations are over. The practical test came last Monday. The written and the oral examinations were to-day. No telling how I came through. Too many things come in to make guessing possible— age, a little pull now and then, nerve, number of months spent at the front, number of times wounded, etc. At any rate in two weeks we will be out of here. We were to leave December 10th, but a new move on the part of the War Secretary's office put off our liberation from this kindergarten life until December 20th. May yet spend Christmas with my brother.

My friend Allen B—— shipped me a fine Colt automatic and a letter full of gentle reproaches.[34] He thought that I had gone in the army for good, giving up teaching. Can you think of a more crazy idea?

Thank you very much for the clippings. They are always very in-teresting. Yes, indeed, there is *some* difference between the Massachu-setts press and the Middle Western shrieking sheets. The Middle West always made on me the same impression as a very big, overgrown, uncouth and disagreeable boy. It will take a good licking, or several such, before it is toned down. That doesn't mean war, of course. This, of course, is being written during study time, since we know it all and don't have to study now.

December 5th, 1915.
To B——:

The papers announce to-day that your government has de-manded of Wilhelmstrasse the immediate recall of von Pappen and Boy-Ed.[35] That's good, very good. It was high time that the United States showed its teeth. The Germans have taken advantage of your good faith and of your patience in a scandalous way. It was pretty bad to have all the German professors in the United States turn out to be political agents—the Waltz, the Munsterbergs & Co.[36] Imagine Grandgent or Guérard or any other gentle French professor touring the country to defend the cause of the Allies.[37] To be sure our cause does not need to be defended so desperately.

Servia seems done for and we were fools not to send out enough men in time to help that poor little country.[38] On the other hand, if we had sent men before the German-Bulgarian attack, people out here, politicians rather, would have shrieked that we were leaving the fron-tier undefended to launch into hazardous adventures. Those same gentlemen are the ones who now raise to the heavens scandalized and horrified hands at the criminal hesitancy of our present masters.

But on the whole, things go pretty well. No one wants to give up the fight and that is the main thing for the present. We must last longer than they. Whether we cut through their front or not or whether they go gallivanting to Constantinople or remain at Monastir makes no great difference.[39] They may get, temporarily, a lot of fun out of those exercises, but it's wearing fun.

CHAPTER 7

Alsace

December 30th, 1915.

To Miss H——:

Having travelled madly these last few weeks I have neither sent nor received mail. Hope soon to have an address to which letters, which must be accumulating at Valence, may be forwarded.

I came out of St.-Maixent a sergeant, but may be boosted to an aspirantship soon, as I am now on my way to the front. Same region where I was last year in spite of all they had told us about going to other parts—going to the same battalion, also unexpected.

Will tell you about the front when I get there. It's more honest than doing like war reporters. Just now I am almost dropping from sleep, having ridden all night in a wheezy accommodation train to get to the Vosges, whence I proceed Rhineward by autobus.

As to-day is the 30th of December, I still have time to wish you a Happy New Year, even though the letter will be a trifle late in getting there.

January 1st, 1916.

To Dr. J———:

Back in Alsace after nearly a year's absence. To think that when last leaving this valley, I sincerely thought that I would be back in three or four weeks at the most.

Life out here is about the same. The same mud, the same never ending lines of autos, pack mules and troops going up and down the valley.

Last week, just before I came back, my battalion had a hard time of it in the attacks against the German positions in the Northeast. As a result we are now resting; may not go up into the mountains for several days,—a state of things to which I do not at all object. While going from St.-Maixent to Paris I saw Professor Grandgent, who is giving lectures at the Sorbonne on Dante, and also on phonetics. He gave me most useful information concerning the state of public opinion in America.

Spring will soon be here and the war is not yet ended, nor even is the end in sight. If my long continued absence works injustice to anyone, please do not hesitate to consider my contract with Stanford ended. I wish for nothing more earnestly than to return to Stanford and take up my work there once more, but I realize that a leave of absence prolonged over three years may not be the best thing for the department, and I want you to feel that if you wish to give me a permanent successor, I shall understand the justice of the step perfectly well.

January 6th, 1915.

To B———:

No very huge news. We are waiting for more men and not doing much in the meanwhile. My main occupation is to get used again to mud and straw. As for food, the valley is much better than last year. We can buy all manners of cheeses as well as fish, oysters, and glory of all French culinary art, snails! Had snails to-night with parsley; also mushrooms and *rognons sautés* [fried kidneys]. Will be broke soon.

Even being a sergeant is much better than being a private. Much more freedom if a little responsibility. My captain is a boy twenty-three years old. Very capable, a born leader. The kind I should like Americans to know about. Which does not mean that there are not many of the other kind. May the censors overlook this line.

No mail at all as yet. Can't expect to get any for several days yet. It's very long to get connected again with the real world. My first mail ought to be a monster as my brother must have hoarded many epistles since I left Valence.

On clear days, the Dutch send us a few shells night and day. They aim at us, but they hit anything. The schoolhouse a few days ago, with some children badly scared and a teacher killed.

We probably won't go any nearer to them than we now are for a week or more. We may be kept thus resting.

Well, will try to write real news later. For the present good luck and many best wishes.

[*Undated*]
To Mr. G——:

If I pull out of this long drawn out scrape, I shall have gained one inestimable thing, absolute faith in the soundness of our race. How utterly ridiculous the decadence yarn seems, in the face of facts, of deeds. When the Germans attack us they are often drunk as drunk can be; they howl and shriek; they come in hordes. Our men go at it in full control of their faculties and without the imperious need of feeling the comforting touch of the elbows of neighbors. By the way, I may add that we have only one kind of bullet and that we don't turn them in the cap so that the big end may hit first and tear worse. It is a common thing to find German *chargeurs* [magazines] with every bullet turned.

Thank you I have plenty to read. We are quartered in a schoolhouse. I have been delighted to learn that every progress which in the last twenty years or more has blessed the human race has been due directly to the genius of the present Emperor of Germany.[1] Also a very dear old aunt of mine keeps sending me small editions of the Gospels slipped in between tablets of chocolate and boxes of crackers.

I wish your nerves stayed where they belong. You are in the right place where you are now. If you had left your family you would have been a damnable coward. Your usefulness back of a pine tree or in the mud of a trench would have been even more "infinitesimal" than it is now in a country which is in danger of being run off its common sense by a wave of militarism at any time, and where men capable of setting an issue with absolute clearness are not too numerous. I see why you feel badly, but I am decidedly glad that you are tied down. This is a crude way of putting things. Don't keep it against me. The thought is sound, I believe, even if the form is poor.

January 11, 1916.
To B——:

No great news. We are up in the hills watching the Dutch who fire shells at us and we fire some at them. We wear fine steel helmets which give us a mediaeval air. Will have myself photographed with my new headgear at the first opportunity. I must look very picturesque—it comes down to my ears and may give me a Bowery air. We also go about with little bags around our necks. They contain each a mask against gases. War grows more and more complicated and ugly.

I live in idleness, having two corporals who boss the men as I tell them to. I am free to come and go through the woods—a big change from last year when I was always glued to the same spot.

We are having snow, rain, fog and wind all at the same time—but we can build fires.

Hope to get a letter from you soon. Our mail is again disorganized—only a card from Kansas.

The Back Woods, January 18th, 1916.
To Mr. G——:

Once more in the mountains of our long lost province, in the very region where we were a year ago. After a year's absence there are but a few changes to be noticed—some pleasant, some otherwise. In the valley, the stores are now full of all good things from steak to oysters and snails. One no longer has to stand in line once a week to snatch a half pound of chocolate at the arrival of the necessary ox-cart bringing supplies to the one store. On the other hand the valley towns are shelled at night; they were not last year. This shelling is hideous, thrown perfectly at random. In the last village where we were quartered a shell fell in the schoolhouse—children injured, teacher killed. Once in a great while a chasseur is hurt; nearly each time civilians are the victims. A little girl had her leg severed. She insisted on having it buried in the military graveyard so that she might carry flowers to the grave later. For the last ten days we have been in the mountains occupying various positions in second line as the battalion is not complete, having participated in the last fight on the too famous kopf.[2] I came the day after the fight ended, so I saw nothing of it, for which I am not very sorry. It seems to have been botched in style.

Life is easier than last year. The weather is very mild and the authorities have hit on a type of plank house which is very satisfactory. They can hold a section, have two stoves and are water-tight. All can lie down at night and the straw is dry—also the straw is changed fairly often. As for the lines they are about where they were, only it's no longer possible to go off on patrol duty; everywhere they are a few scores of feet apart. As a sergeant I am leading a parasitic existence, watching my half section work, doing nothing myself. I get into trouble periodically with my immediate chiefs who really are boys, and I have not given up all hope of being retrograded one of these days. In the meanwhile I practice as honestly as possible the kind of imposture implied by any command in this d——— business.

The spirit of the men seems to me better than it was last year at this time. They play cards at night and sing. The spirit of the regular army does not rule as it did last year and that may account for the diminution of gloom—also, to be sure, war as a life condition is taken more or less as the normal thing by men who are in it for from eight to ten or twelve months on an average and who have been wounded two or three times apiece.

If there is any call for volunteers for Suez, I shall speak up.[3]

January 19th, 1916.

The British captain who wrote in the November *Atlantic Monthly* strangely exaggerated the value of life in war time to the average man.[4] He sees in it a dipping into real life, life next to nature of a mass of men who lived a few months ago either cramped or selfish lives. He does not realize that the private's life when there is no fighting is dull and purposeless. The physical labor, the tasks imposed are often as bootless as the construction of a fleet of ships by the Roman Army spoken of by Montesquieu; ninety per cent. of the work done is useless or so badly done as to become useless.[5]

20th of January, 1916.

The captain told me that to his surprise I was doing well with my men and that contrary to his expectation I had the making of an officer in me. Flattering. He is twenty-three years old.

The men know it and they work to humor us. It is really ex-

tremely funny to watch carpenters, farmers, mechanics, being bossed
by officers who are innocent of any mechanical training.

January 25th, 1916.
To Miss H——:

Thank you for the letters and the many clippings which are always very interesting. It is fine to keep in touch with the American
opinion. Nothing much doing out here. A few days after I joined the
battalion we were sent up in the mountain and for the last three weeks
we have been leading the life of the lumber man. We are in the back
woods living in houses that remind me of the New Hampshire and
Maine log houses. We spend our time digging artillery shelters, but
are ready to leave at a minute's notice if there is trouble in the neighborhood. So far no trouble at all. A few shells fired at random by the
Dutch blow up on the road below; a few aeros buzz overhead on clear
days and try to see what we are at. It is not very exciting—thank
goodness.

I have a very friendly and quiet gang of men to boss. Bossing is
the biggest imposture; even I spend whole days doing absolutely nothing except chat with this or that man who stops digging or sawing
wood for a minute.

In a few days we may go up to the trenches or go back to the
valley. All is very indefinite. We are much more comfortable here than
in the town where we were before, as said town was being bombarded
every day. One day a shell fell in a school house, wounding several
children and killing the teacher. If that's war! . . . The sick and
wounded were carried away up to last week by Harvard and Yale
men, running little Ford autos.[6] A fairly risky business, since several
places on the road are bombarded. One of those American boys was
killed this month; another wounded.[7] I had quite a chat with several
of them. The socks sent by your brother are very useful out here as
you may imagine. It was pretty cold for a while; now nearly all of the
snow is melted! The winter will set in again in February and March
probably.

February 10th, 1916.
To B——:

Nothing very new. Am writing to you at 3 P.M. by candle-light,
being in a hole that is about ten feet below the level of the ground. I

sleep in another hole about twenty-five feet below the level. We don't do much. We watch and dig and get bombarded—they pour or rain shells on our hill for half an hour two or three times a day—the rest of the time is serene. In our holes we fear nothing—only it is time we went back to some village. It's over a month now since we have been in a town and we are in great need of getting next to civilization. We have seen this treeless hill enough.

February 19th, 1916.
To M———:

The blanket, which is my door, was pushed aside a few minutes ago and your letter was handed to me. You bet I was glad to know about Louise or Robert as the case may be and about the young Virginian.[8] Great-uncle and godfather all at once. Well, there is something cheerful to reflect about indefinitely.

You would be interested to see the place from which I am writing this. It's a shack roofed over with tree trunks and rocks. It's about seven feet and three feet to the ceiling. It opens right on the trench, which is as far from that of the Dutch as the Brooklyn house is from that across the two back-yards. Three sleep while three watch. My business is to see that they don't sleep while out of the shack, that they look over enough to see, but not enough to be seen. It's bright moonlight and there is snow on the ground, so the matter must be looked out for. This is the third or fourth time I take up this letter. I may add that we are on top of the long-named hill which ends with the Dutch for head, and which has appeared so often in the papers. A year ago it was a finely forested little mountain (2,700 feet) overlooking the valley. Now there is not one whole tree on it; a few stumps only and those full of holes and shaky. The rocks kicked up by last year's shelling show everywhere. We have been here for three weeks, but there is nothing much doing—just watching and watching. It is now nearly a month and a half since we have been in town or anywhere near one and a trip down begins to look attractive. We expect to be relieved in a week or ten days.

Yes, it would be idiotic for the United States to start arming madly. You had enough of a navy to fight this time had you wanted to. I don't see how any sane man can talk invasion after the examples of Gallipoli, Cattaro, the march to Calais, etc. If you ever have to fight it will be with Canada or Mexico; fight on land, I mean. Stories of Japs in California landing hundreds of thousands of men in San Francisco, etc., are idiotic. With a good fleet, the United States ought to be able to steer clear of militarism as easily as England has done so far. But you must be strong on the water, because you are so very rich. Your main problem now should be to make Americans out of all the damned foreigners on your shores and back country. You may send this to Wilson if you see fit.

Writing is often a difficult enterprise nowadays, so don't be hurt or *inquiète* [anxious] if you do not hear from me very regularly.

From the diary

February 22nd, 1916.

Skyrockets were fired, but the Germans did not notice the disturbance and we received no shells.

The troops in front of us must have been changed, for they fired few shots and no grenades—they popped their heads innocently over their loopholes and gave other signs of trust and joviality unknown to date.

From the diary

February 23d.

Two nights I spent over an hour with men on the parapet placing chevaux de frise and never was fired on once, though we must have been heard working in each case.[9] Still all was not rosy. The Germans talked so much and so loud that a fool corporal requisitioned the interpreter—a fine, brave Alsatian boy, twenty years old, who came up to listen. He heard, of course, nothing but futilities—schnell! schnell! [hurry! hurry!] by two who were placing wire—then the illuminating statement, "We were better off where we were last week than we are now." The boy, eager to hear more and to see more clearly, finally climbed on the ladder until his head and shoulders were in full view over the parapet—he then received a bullet in the cheek which killed him instantly. What a price to pay for such a result! That boy was from the region; he had run away at the time he ended his first year in the German army, and enlisted in the French army.

Marie Pellissier Alden Brown (1890–1972), Robert Pellissier's niece
(the editor's grandmother). "M" in the letters.

From the diary

February 26th.

    Peaceful day and night close to our new and unobtrusive friends across the way.

Translated from the French

February 27th, 1916.
To A———:

    You must think that I am sadly neglecting my correspondence—and it is true—but dear me, under the circumstances. We have been for nearly seven weeks in the mountain and the longer it lasts, the less enjoyable it is, for in the Vosges, February and March are accompanied by sudden storms of snow, rain and wind. Moreover, as we are on the firing line we are always eight where there is only room for six. A move is as complicated as in the game of chess.

    If I am able to write to you now, it is because our section is on duty; half the men are at the loopholes and the rest are asleep. Even then I am partly sitting on one of the corporals. As it is almost always like this, do not wonder if you do not hear from me as often as when we used to have a rest more frequently. We were to be relieved from duty this week and we were looking forward to going down into the valley, but how could we go now? With what is going on at Verdun there is no possibility of a let up for us.[10] We have to bear it patiently.

    Good news from our brother, who keeps sending me weekly packages which are very welcome, of course, for our mountain sector is very quiet, a most remarkable thing in these days. Explain to our Brooklyn family my apparent lack of feeling.

Translated from the French

March 6th, 1916.
To Mr. G———:

    For the last half hour I have been searching for your letter in all the pockets of my cloak (for since very recently cloaks have pockets), but I cannot find it, and I shall not be able to answer your questions in the regular order.

Do not for a moment think that I have had any misgivings concerning either the interest your family takes in me or the friendship you have for me. Often it is very difficult to write either because life, on account of an over-accumulation of horrors, pales on one, or because the conditions of daily life make it possible to write just one postal card and no more—but the idea of sending a postal card way out to Texas seems a trifle ridiculous.

No, I do not hate wholesale fashion. I even believe that I do not hate at all in the literal sense of the word. If on a fine night when crossing the campus on my way back from Palo Alto, I should encounter a hold-up man, thrusting his revolver at me, I should do my best to smash his face, but once the deed was accomplished, I should be perfectly willing to have him taken at my expense to the Peninsular Hospital. It is the kind of feeling I have when fighting the Boches. Against the Boches taken singly, I have no grudge, but I am perfectly determined not to allow my linguistic and idealistic family group to be swallowed up by theirs, which at the present time is certainly far from showing moral superiority. Have you read *Above the Strife*, by Romain Rolland?[11] I have not, but the title appeals to me and the author has been attacked so unanimously by the most sensational newspapers that I dare say he must have voiced some kind of truth in a vigorous manner. The Boches, however, are disconcerting to a degree when it comes to knavery and fanaticism. Well, what I ask of you is not to consider me as a blind monster, for it is not with joy that I put my finger on the trigger but I go through with that motion, whether I like it or not, and I shall continue to do so. It is a disgusting job, but it has to be done—so help me God!—if in so doing I incur everlasting condemnation.

I have had the luck to join a company under command of a young captain who is really a fine man and life is very different from what it was last year. For the last thirty-seven days we have been on the top of the worst one of the Alsatian Kopfs, and we cannot hope to be relieved as long as the fight is so fierce around Verdun. After all, our worst troubles here come from the cold, the snow and vermin; we are literally eaten up—but the shelling is infrequent and of short duration, while from the Swiss frontier the roaring of cannon never stops.

This furious German attack on Verdun was launched very early in the season. Let us hope that the meaning of it is that our enemies are yearning to come to a conclusion. If such is the case, and if they cannot take Verdun, they may soon reach the end of their tether. Their rulers will not have a leg to stand on and possibly we may see the end of the war before next winter.

If you have interesting articles, do send them to me. Quite often I have time to read at night and I am yearning for intellectual food.

From the diary

March 7th, 1916.

Had dinner with the captain who was very kind—ate eggs, ye gods! Talked of America—and of the men. He is a very altruistic man—thinks a great deal of what he can do to help his men keep up their courage, makes a definite effort to know each one individually— and the troubles of each.

From the diary

March 10th, 1916.

Galvin, alias "Turned up Nose" (*Nez en l'air*) was killed; he was not on duty. Was very nervous, ran around the trench, wanted to use firecrackers and hand grenades—then suddenly he dashed to the sentry's post, and ran up the ladder. The corporal rushed to get him down and got there in time to receive his body—the boy had received a bullet full in the head.

March 13, 1916.
To Miss H———:

Your Mass. Central letter came to-night—eighteen degrees makes one thoughtful—or grateful that no such temperatures occur in this part of the world, for under the circumstances we would be up against it; still we have been having pretty mean weather,—snow for days and days, regular blizzards, but without the very low temperature which accompanies these "feasts" in dear "old" New England. We are still on the top of our long-winded named Kopf and are wondering whether we shall ever come down. To-morrow will be the forty-third day spent here in close proximity to our friends the Dutch, very close proximity, since we can and do throw hand grenades at one another, and it will be the fifty-eighth day since we left the valley or have been in any town. We do not complain, however, because this apparently undue prolongation of service is the result of the fighting which is now raging around the best fortified part of our front—and that fighting may be the beginning of the end, for it's clear that the Dutch are suffering losses out of all proportion with their ground gains. Their attacking with so much determination at this time of the year was a big surprise to everybody. It looks now as if all their Oriental moves had been but a bluff and a foil, and as if the finish would be on our front after all. Personally, I am having a pretty good time as one of the lieutenants is away just now and I have taken his place, being in charge of a section, that is one-quarter of a company. It is pretty good sport and gives one a little additional freedom—if there is such a thing as freedom in this infernal business. Except for hand grenades and a little bombardment on clear days, life has been rather eventless. We did have one scandal. A man was taken sick. He was sent to the hospital—from which he ran away. He had just wanted a few days to get married and had taken them. Of course, he now faces court-martial for desertion, and the joke of it is that he won the war cross for bravery last summer. This afternoon, there was quite a serious bombardment for a half-hour or so. I went out to see if everybody was on hand and I found the chap in question comfortably settled at his post writing a letter, using the bottom of his loophole for a table! Another case of court-martial, if I "peached" on him, for sentinels are not placed in the ditch for the purpose of cheering lately acquired wives by mail. The chap is twenty-one and a case! One can't get away from America. I am writing to you from an underground room— about ten feet below the level—we have a nice stove and berths arranged like those of a ship. Behind the stove I have just spotted a tin can—Napa, Cal. California Fruit Co. St.-Helena brand of peaches!— The Best! We used to go on bats to Napa and St.-Helena from Stanford. My sister sent me once the *Review of Reviews* and a few days ago our *Current Opinion*. Ye gods, but the Germans hold your press well in hand. About every article contains an insinuation against us—and those which are in any way material for condemnation of German methods are hidden away in the advertising matter! Pretty clever. Are you going to fight Mexico?[12] It looks a little bit like it. This is a rambling letter, but as it is being written between 3 and 4 A.M., please excuse me.

March 14th, 1916.
To B———:

A word to assure you that all is well in the best of worlds and that the Dutch don't seem to have taken Verdun and that we are still on our mountain but that we may be relieved soon by another battalion.[13] It will be high time. Men ought not to be made to live like cave-dwellers much more than two months—winter months at that. The weather is quite pleasant in the middle of the day now, quite warm, but our sun baths are spoiled by the actions of the Dutch who bombard us every clear day. Such is life in war time—not much of a life, believe me.

One of the lieutenants is still away so I am bossing his section, being grand commander in chief of one quarter of the company. Not very hard work either, at least at present.

It was not at Monterey that I used to gaze upon Bohemian life, but at Carmel-by-the-Sea near Monterey—a very pretty place full of scandals.

This is merely a note telling you that all is well and not a letter—hope to be able to write one soon, if we get back to the valley. Have completely lost the habit of writing, or eating at a table as well as that of sleeping in a bed.

My sister—Brooklyn—sent me the *Review of Reviews* once, and lately *Current Opinion*. Very interesting, in reading the articles, to see where German money comes in giving facts and conclusions a pro-Dutch twist—*sans avoir l'air d'y toucher* [acting innocently; literally, without appearing to be touched by it].

I blushed, violently, reading your compliments on my un-militarized handwriting—thank you, as I should never forgive myself were I to become really and truly militarized.

Have been able to order canned jam and condensed milk, so am living like a prince—hot milk chocolate at 2 A.M. when on duty!

March 22, 1916.
To Miss H———:

I am writing to you in a sort of hut, six feet by six—in which we are four. We are about forty feet from the Dutch whom we can hear cough and putter around. We are hoping they all get bronchitis. We have been bombarded very violently two or three times, but otherwise life is uneventful. We look at the Dutch with a periscope—they do the same to us. It's now five weeks since we have been in a town and we "need washing." Hope to go down next week, but can never be sure of anything.

March 24, 1916.
To B——:

When did I write to you last? Impossible to tell as days in the trenches are all alike equally blank. The one great topic of discussion which never fails to arouse interest is concerning what day of the week one is on. You, being only a civilian, can have no idea of the sameness of things existing in war time.

Now we are in a village, the first time in nearly three months, and out of that time we spent fifty-three days in the trenches, which really is too much.

Our leaving the H——kopf was fortunately quite uneventful. The Dutch must have suspected something, for they bombarded fiercely the day and the night before and at noon on the day itself, but as we started down at 6 in the evening, we slipped between the showers, as it were, and came out on the other side of the range without any losses. We had to go it all night long to get here, but we did not object as this town is sheltered from artillery fire and we live here peaceful as shepherds. To be sure it's pouring great guns, but we have real houses to live in instead of leaky shacks and we are so glad to have several complete nights' sleep ahead of us that we don't mind the weather.

We may be here two or three weeks. The only cloud in the sky, speaking very metaphorically, is that we are being inoculated once more against typhoid and we are consequently under the weather.

My lieutenant has not yet returned, so I am still in charge of my section. The main work is to get new shoes, trousers and neckties for all those who are really too shabby. I feel as if I were dealing in ready-made clothing.

March 25th, 1916.
To Miss H——:

At last in the valley and living nearly like a white man after two months spent in the hills and in close proximity to the Dutch. It is a fine sensation to be able to walk straight on a road after weeks of worming one's self in and out of crooked, narrow trenches covered over with logs placed so low that you can't stand upright. We are in a very pretty hill town, quite clean and containing a good many friendly inhabitants. For a wonder I was able to get hold of a room containing a real bed. We also have a dining room in a house and the use of a kitchen. In other words we live like kings. This cheerful state of affairs will last until the middle of April, at which date we may be expected to go back to call on the Dutch.

The trouble around Verdun seems to be over with or nearly so. It is a great relief to us to have proved that they can't walk over us at will, as they did over Russia for a time and over the Oriental parts of the front. It looks now as if the time had come for them to stop sacrificing their men ruthlessly. They can't afford to attack again as they just have—and without results.

Thank you for the many clippings which I read with much pleasure.

Blizzard time must be over even in New England. Over here the fields are already beautifully green.

The cook has come to set the table, so I must quit. This is just a note to tell you that all is well.

From the diary

April 3d, 1916.

One of our men took me to the farm where he and the liaison were quartered last summer—most cordial greeting by six little children—the youngest, five years old, disappeared in the dark bedroom and sang (??) La Marseillaise. Very friendly people reminding me of the three women of Neuhäuser near Goldbach.

From the diary

April 10th, 1916.

Drill in the morning, then a sudden announcement: there would be a review by the president of the Republic and we were expected to decorate the village in style—hence hecatomb of firs and pines of Christmas tree size—great harvesting of moss and yellow flowers, hunting up of flags and banners to be put up at the Mayor's house—result superb.

While at attention before the cock of the walk, the visiting officers saying "splendid battalion, elite battalion," Poincaré said nothing at all, according to his manner in the Bussang hospital. Franchet d'Espéret was there—a fine, tall, white-haired man.[14]

From the diary

April, 1916.

The woman who has a little store next to the *Lion d'Or* is a refugee from Thann. A bullet went through the upper story of her house, then one through the lower floor, then one in the cellar. She found the head of one of the children in the garden.[15] She told me about it in a monotonous tone of voice, but at the end, "Sir, it is too much, you know, sir; it is too much, it is too much." And these simple words told me more than if she had been a trained speaker and reciter.

From the diary

April 11th, 1916.

In the morning, sham attack and in the afternoon grand review and parade before a Servian Prince and a Servian general, two enormous big fellows with coal black whiskers, our Major who is not a dwarf looked like a mite before them—but a pretty spunky and wiry mite.

From the diary

April 12th, 1916.

In the evening I went upstairs at the *Golden Lion* and had a talk with an English ambulance driver—very friendly—we complimented each other on our respective nations, then he drew an illustrated postcard—made to order—representing a lady in Eve's blameless costume—on the back of the card was the following message which my British friend, with his limited knowledge of French, had been unable to translate. "Mon shery chtai envoyé un koli de un kilo yapa gran shoz dedans parsque pour un kilo pa si tu veut quelque shose depplus dilmoi ta chérie." [Deary, I have sent you a two-pound package; there is not much in it, because in a two-pound package, you cannot put much. If you want something more, tell me so. Your Dear One.]

Translated from the French

April 24th, 1916.
To A——:

Nothing new here. Out of the three weeks I have to spend at
Military Headquarters, one is over. We are left very much to ourselves, I assure you, and life here has nothing much in common with
the wild and dishevelled existence we were made to lead at St.-
Maixent, a place which has left in my mind the most unpleasant
memories. I am studying new things and I hear other things which I
have heard a great many times, but on the whole the work is interesting and well supervised by people who know their business. Moreover, I enjoy my three meals and my beautiful room in a way which
might lead the casual observer to believe that your brother has sunk
into a deep-rooted and remorseless materialism. The truth is that I am
making up for lost opportunities and I distrust the future more than
I can tell. Now, this excellent Wilson seems to be speaking plainly and
firmly. Perhaps it is high time he should do it, but, of course, he has
had and he still has on his hands a very complicated situation. It is
what I am doing my best to explain to our country-people who, in
spite of Red Cross ambulances, hospitals and even volunteers from
far beyond the sea are tempted to believe that in the United States
there is an overwhelming feeling in favor of the Teutons. "C'est tout
boche" [It's all German], a judgment which is rather summary. Do
you remember one of my Williston boys named Henderson? He enlisted in a Canadian unit and the poor boy was killed at Loos.[16]

May 2d, 1916.
To A——:

The less one has to do the less one does, that is why I did not
write to you last Sunday—since I live as a citizen and as a Christian
in this happy valley I have entirely neglected my correspondence.

The day before yesterday I dined in great style, having been
invited by the Protestant chaplain to whom our cousin had rec-
ommended me. From a theological point of view, we might have di-
vergences of opinion, but nevertheless we spent an hour together talking very pleasantly—at least from my own point of view. He is an
excellent man, very courteous and gentle—qualities which do not

keep him from appearing in first line trenches whenever he is not in the hospitals.

We are working here very peacefully; our courses will last one week longer; after that time there is a possibility that we may be sent to third line trenches for a while.

From the diary

Call by the Protestant army chaplain—for the division—all churchmen seem to expect a great change in the hearts of men after the war—they see an excuse for the war in the future reform and conversion of the individual. For my part, I don't believe very much in it. The intellectual élite will see things more clearly and modify the leadership of nations. The masses, once the suffering and hardship [is] forgotten, will live much as before.

The captain, speaking of the wreath bought for Galliéni, said that he would prefer fifty francs' worth of mass![17]

May 7, 1916.
To B——:

No mail from America this week. Letters from across the ocean come in bunches of six or eight to the amazement of the mail man and to the scandal of my companions; then days follow quite newsless. That shows that there are not so many boats gadding about as in peace time. As my captain frequently remarks we too often forget that the war is still on—but then he should not worry too much as there are frequent and powerful reminders of the real nature of life these days.

Nothing much going on here. The lectures are over—this sounds like Harvard or Bridgewater days—and we expect to go back to the hills Tuesday next or Wednesday, hills not of the vacation variety, but full of trenches, without trees, leaves, or flowers. The three weeks just spent in the valley have been an oasis of comfort and quiet, but I don't object to going back with the battalion. I am interested to see what life in the trenches is like in good weather. I have always seen them when the days were short and cold and forever threatening snow or rain—and there was always a lot of mud, a very important factor of demoralization. Cold feet in the physical sense create the moral cold feet of American slang.

May 15th, 1916.

To Miss H———:

Your April 20th came almost together with its predecessor, from which can be judged that the mail steamers had an uncertain and incoherent existence. Thank you very much for the news and for the clippings—and most of all for the letters which are always very, very pleasant messages.

The Diary of Evolution is awfully funny—where is it taken from?[18]

I have now been back to the front for a week. It is not the real front either, but about third lines where our business deals mainly with the pick and the shovel. If we did not get a few shells once in a while we might think ourselves at a camp of instruction miles from the front. I get so bored watching men work that I have taken to the shovel and fill gabions for a pastime.[19] We work from 3 A.M. until noon, resting for the balance of the day. 3 A.M.! Think of the sacrifice to one's country. I who never could make any of the breakfasts on time either at Bridgewater, Williston, Harvard or Stanford. War does bring out the heroic in one.

May 26, 1916.

To B———:

Late again in my correspondence—this due to the fact that we left our mountain fastness two days ago and that such operations always take time before and after—before to get ready, after to get over the effect of the effort.

My lieutenant has again gone off and I am taking his place, which is all right in its way, but as it happens, my turn for a ten days' trip—furlough—comes to-morrow and I can't go. Had a pow-wow with the captain and I shall go in the middle of next week if nothing happens. Think of getting a look into the interior of the country! In a way I am glad it was put off as this has given me a chance to tell my brother of my coming. Now I am sure to find him in Valence.

We are in a pretty good village. Since I do the work of a lieutenant, I got busy and found a room—rather the room was all found when I got here. The cook of my section is my friend. Those gentlemen, of course, come into a place before their body of troops so that the first meal may be ready when it comes down hungry and tired.

Well, my cook got busy and hunted me a room without my having asked him anything at all. Pretty good of him.

We are now just getting over our stay in the hills—that is getting new clothes, etc. A great business getting everybody satisfied. After the war, I'll make a first-class dry goods clerk.

This is not much of a letter, but I will write again from Valence if I get there next week as I hope.

P.S.—do my letters get to you stamped? I don't stamp them any more as the *vaguemestre* [military postmaster] has told me over and over again that I did not have to, and he seemed very hurt every time I did.

June 4th, 1916.
To Miss H———:

Just a few words to thank you for the *Life*'s which were really very good and refreshing and more for the letters. Have had difficulty in writing of late because we have moved so much and I had again a lieutenant's job. Much to my surprise I was granted the fourteen days off which the nation had been owing me for sometime back. I left the front May 31st and have been travelling ever since and looking up relatives. This is the end of the trip—the most extreme point I mean. I am here with my brother getting a dip into city atmosphere before going back to the pine hills of the Vosges where I am due June 9th. Don't know just where I shall find my battalion as it has been travelling of late.

Marseilles is full of life. In addition to the usual rush of trade there are many colored troops—Australians, Senegalese, English, Servians. Have not seen any Russians yet. The coast is beautiful—as beautiful as any Carmel-by-the-Sea or any other Californian locality—and it's the same kind of beauty.

Grand Hôtel de la Poste
Marseilles
June 4th, 1916.
To B———:

You may be wondering what has become of me as a person and as a correspondent. Got my furlough signed and my bag packed May 31st in the morning and left the Valley of the Thun just as the battalion was also leaving—probably for the Munster Colmar region, where I shall be by the time this letter reaches you—if I am not somewhere else. Things are moving rather fast in the military world these days. For the present I am enjoying life. Have looked up and investigated all the relatives in the Rhône valley. Just now I am in Marseilles on a bat pure and simple. Am going back to Besançon and the mountains and the Dutch by the end of the week.

You will excuse me if I don't write more at length, as I am having a great time getting a plunge into urban and civilized life. It seems awfully queer to see with your own eyes how normally the other half lives.

Good bye for the present—Had never written to you from this country so far—a new record.

CHAPTER 8

∼

Munster/Colmar

From the diary

June 9th, 1916.

Roussel was killed yesterday with ten others in a cagna [dugout]. One shell did it. Day spent in getting straightened out—the sector is a maze with German lines above and below. Mean sandy ground, saps not very safe can be shelled from all directions.

We have pioneers with us who direct the work—a great improvement over past conditions when school teachers, business men, watchmakers tried their hands at the mining job and were the laughing-stock of the farmers and laborers. This place is all sand on rotten granite. The trenches are braced with planks all along the front. In the rear there are constant slides, bags filled with dirt tumbling down at the least provocation. A fine view down the valley, except for the three villages riddled with shots. Patrols are possible in places. They came to our wires a few days ago and placed a poster telling about the great German naval victory.[1] We placed another in their wires telling them what is what and more in French and German.

June 12th, 1916.

To B———:

It is an age since I have written you or anybody else a real letter having indulged in *cartes-lettres* [postcards] in a shameless fashion. *Que voulez-vous, c'est la guerre* [What do you want, that's war] and I have been moving around a good deal. First they moved us from the trenches to the valley, then from the valley the battalion moved to another valley, while I quietly beat it to France on a six days' furlough as already stated, and those six days allowed me to beat it all over the Saône, Doubs and Rhône valleys. My brother and I looked up all possible relatives and ended by a bachelor bat in Marseilles—very *convenable* [proper; appropriate].

Coming back was a little sad as the more one sees of civilian life, the more it looks preferable to the military mode of living, especially in war time.

After going over mountains which are all unknown countries to you I caught my battalion settled in this sector, a queer set of trenches all mixed up, where you would think that the lines were two threads from two spools with which a kitten had been playing. The Dutch are in front and above and on both sides in places and we go all around them in other spots. We see all their ditches and they see ours, but as there is nothing which they can do us which we can't do them and *vice versa* we remain in a state of watchful waiting which, as you know, is a perfectly safe occupation. You have asked once or twice about the fighting in the Vosges reported in the papers. There have been one or two scraps through the winter but not where I was, or at least we never had anything beyond bombardments and it's probably all we shall ever get up this way. There is nothing to be gained by us or by them in these mountains. If there is anything done it will be in the flat country, where artillery can do its damnedest—not swearing, but a truthful statement. There are vague rumors that we may be sent to other parts, but it's pretty vague.

You also asked me about my Spanish friend, de A———.[2] Not a word from him. Our parting, you may remember, was stormy. He got into trouble with a recently acquired brother-in- law whom he spotted as a Jew and insulted grossly. That got him in wrong with his wife who defended her sister's husband. de A——— got regally drunk on white wine to forget it all—took me out for a ride in his buggy while in that state and once home, after the ride, made motions with an axe which were not reassuring for my head nor for that of his gardener. The next day he apologized, sold his furniture, bought a ranch in Mendino county or such and disappeared from my flabbergasted gaze. O! you Latins! He is a very bright man, but balanced on a razor's edge.

Yet after all I am glad the United States did not fight. Wilson followed Washington's advice and posterity may say that he did well.[3] It's too bad that he did not use all the diplomatic weapons which he had in his possession. He could have kicked out all the German officials and broken relations without firing a shot, simply using economic pressure as a club. In ordinary life, when you don't like people you simply close your door to them—that does not mean that you are honor bound to hit them on the head with a broomstick in addition to telling the family not to open the door.

I think that American influence will be diminished in Europe for some time to come because of the *Lusitania* and because Bernstorff and his gang did as they pleased without check and that will be unfair because the weaknesses of sincere pacifism are not any uglier or baser than the crimes of militarism and Europe will never be able to thank America enough for what Americans have done and are doing for Belgium, the Northern Departments and the wounded and orphans on both sides.

As for your little La Fayette debt, it is cancelled, I believe, by the actions of your ambulance drivers, of your aeroplane *esquadrille,* and by the sacrifices of Americans who have enlisted either in the *Légion Etrangere* [Foreign Legion] or with the Canadian troops.[4] So next time we walk along strange itineraries in Paris moving eclectically through the *Quartier Latin* [Latin Quarter] and *La Cité,* we shall hold up our heads very proudly and slap in the face people who may not look at us just the way we want them to. I shall be an American for the occasion and shall have my moustache shaved.

My lieutenant is again off to the races or some other place, so I am the boss, having a table, a candlestick and a berth in my cellar. Things would be pretty pleasant if it did not drizzle so in these blamed Vosges. It was snowing when I came across the range! Just like New England weather—you can't tell what the thermometer has in reserve for you.

The last good-sized town through which I came on my way here is a mountain summer resort, full of villas strung up along a lake—

flashy hotels—a Coney Island—Big Moose—atmosphere; no sign of war except for a few machine guns and the Red Cross on the hotel roof—but a few miles from there more hotels, perched on the mountain top and those all shot to pieces by shells. It made quite a contrast.

Well, this is a huge letter and I have exhausted all the news of the sector.

From the diary

June 18th.

Took a trip into the sap which extends Dutchwards—about fifty yards—no sign of any steps in the sand, but it is a dangerous highway. I had Boyden's Colt with me, but no rifle.

Translated from the French

June 19th, 1916.
To A——:

Not many letters from America of late. I dare say you are having Commencement in that happy land where life is spent normally. I am very glad to receive *Life;* it gives me an idea of what people say across the water. The propaganda in favor of "l'Orphelinat des Armées" [the army orphanage] is very interesting. It would not be a bad idea for you to adopt a little French boy. O, the poverty when everything will be ended, and what a shame if people do not do everything in favor of the victims, young and old. We are in a rather interesting and quiet sector. At one time there had been talk of sending us somewhere else, but now we no longer hear anything about it.

June 22, 1916.
To Miss H——:

Pardon me for not writing a letter, but we ran out of paper and the stores are just a few miles back. No great news out here. We are on a sandy hill and trenches built in the sand are much like the Biblical House, especially when shells fall plumb into them, which has happened twice to my tiny sector since I have been up here.[5] We expect to be going down or back to civilization soon. It rained for three weeks and now it is as hot as pepper—a weakening set of conditions; many are shaky. Thank you very much for the clippings. With them and *Life*, I keep in touch with the United States' way of thinking. Is it war with Mexico? Perhaps we don't feel like hugging the Russians! What next? Verdun is still a horrible gash.

July 2d, 1916.
To B——:

We have been travelling so of late that my duties as a correspondent are getting hazy. We left Alsace, for good probably, last Tuesday. We left the trenches Monday about midnight, sneaked our way in the dark to a safe place where the machine guns couldn't get us, then climbed over the Vosges, reaching the highest point about 9 A.M., then kept on and got into a camp by 11: pretty tired and wet (poured great guns) and hungry—but pretty glad to be in France once more and away from the *yaw yaw* and *nicks nicks* of the Alsatian *patois.*[6] The next day we came down the French side of the Vosges and paraded in grand style through one of the summer resorts of the region—summer resort minus the squash bugs, aeroplanes being fond of the place. The next day we rested. The two following days we went on and now we are here in a tiny village getting refreshed.

This is a rolling New Englandish kind of country and we are all glad to be out in the open, having nothing to fear and plenty of time to bask in the sun. We may stay here two or three weeks, then we shall go North to attack; according to all probabilities, there are going to be great doings out that way and we want our share of them. For the present we think of nothing but sleeping (I have a bed, glory be), eating and getting washed up in plenty of water, instead of in a tin cup.

We have a fine cook and a pleasant dining-room so life is rosy. They have come to set the table so I must quit—but let me warn you against your piano teacher. She is a theosophist or my name is mud. Look out, she'll want to convert you to the craziest form of mysticism on the market. The lady who had had green and purple husbands to whom I taught French for my sins in Easthampton—you may remember—handed me precisely the same line of talk. *Beware* lest you end your days at Point Loma.[7]

July 5th, 1916.
To Miss H———:

I am writing you from a tiny French village in the rolling country which forms the foot-hills of the Vosges on the French side. We are about eighty miles from the trenches and the battalion has never been so far back into the country and from the Dutch since war broke out two years ago. We are out here to get into walking training once more and to forget the trenches in case the attack in the North with the English should be successful. It is a very nice change, for the present at least. The summer so far has been very rainy and the trenches where we were in places were so sandy that we were kept building the walls all the time while in other spots the water did not drain off and the dugouts were very unhealthy places. There was so much sickness that at one time we were not more than one hundred men for eight hundred and fifty yards! I had never seen the men so played out though, when we were relieved in the night from Monday to Tuesday, everybody picked up and we managed to reach the crest of the Vosges before noon and to cross over into France without anyone's giving out, though some dragged along pretty sadly, making S's like drunken men, as they went along. Now everybody is fattening up and all the troubles are forgotten. We don't expect to go up North before the middle of the month and we fully enjoy our dip into civilized life without worrying about what may come later—the motto in this business more than in any other being "Sufficient for the day is the evil thereof."[8]

Yesterday was July 4th. That date must have had a special significance to the U.S.A. folk, this year, after these months of tribulations as a neutral nation, a narrowly escaped Mexican war and a presidential campaign ahead.

CHAPTER 9

Somme

[*Extract from a letter not dated but arriving at Auburndale August 3, 1916.*]

To B——:

I refuse to write a letter—it's too hot and besides there is nothing to say as life is as flat as a pancake or a Kansas town or a faculty meeting. We trot around and over the country in pursuit of imaginary Boches, then we sleep and eat and so days go by as alike as Siamese twins. A squash bug life of the purest Beverly type is more full of *imprévu* [the unexpected] than our existence.[1]

Did I ever tell you my opinion of cats? Well, for your sake I never killed any, but I may have betrayed my country in being so forbearing. At the last trenches where we were, German cats came across the line to us and we used to feed them and show them every courtesy, but with very few exceptions they would go back to the German lines and probably tell on us. I have thought since, that we should have put them in irons right away.

From the diary

July 20th, 1916.

T——, who had promised to be so good, stole a rabbit from the old people—then it came out that he had stolen a hen at Uriménil—

judgment—then platoon fire on the Marseilles road—pretty depressing performance. He is good for court-martial. He is a crook, but there is no proportion between the punishment and the crime, except in so far as war time compels the most rigid discipline. I never heard of any petty thievery being committed in Alsace. T—— is a Protestant. He told me very unexpectedly that he did not want to see the priest, from which I judge that he tried some sly trick with the Holy Roman Church. The liaison got a hen, too, but it has not been found out and that August body will not be disturbed. They are likely to be more cautious from now on from T——'s catastrophe. Our cook heard a hen cackle to-night as we were eating—dove into the hen house and came out with the "fruit" still warm—explaining that the lady of the house counted on four eggs a day from her hens and that he conveyed any egg over the regulation four. It was funny as the dickens, but it makes T——'s rabbit and even his hen less and less important.[2]

Translated from the French

July 23d, 1916.
To A——:

We have passed close by Paris and now we are settled in the flat country, quite a change after leaving Alsace. We are waiting for events. I hope we will coöperate with the British in the near future. We are living in a queer hamlet. The houses are poorly built—as no stones are to be had, the walls are made of the strangest compounds of bricks, mud, straw, nodules of silex, etc. The men from the Vosges, who are in the habit of seeing houses built so as to stand the severest winters cannot get over their surprise, and they show utter contempt for those wretched hovels. Moreover there is no water except in the wells, the billy-goats are called "matores," brandy is called "bistrouille." These men from the Vosges are positively scandalized because for them any kind of brandy is "gnole." All these things tend to confirm them in the belief that here we are not in France.

July 23d, 1916.
To Mr. G——:

That almost unanimous rallying of Spanish sentiment around the German cause is rather baffling.[3] To be sure we have played that country some pretty mean tricks in the course of centuries and the clericals have made the most out of history.

We went by Paris a few days ago and now we are not very far from the English. We may attack with them before very long. It may be dangerous and if anything serious should happen to me, would you write to my sister at Northampton? That does not mean that I am taking life tragically and that I am sending you my obituary. The morale remains good, as the papers take so much delight in printing. After two years of war the fact remains that if the Germans win out in a war which has so well illustrated their philosophy, the planet will be uninhabitable until there is an uprising which might be worse than the present catastrophe.

We are glad to be out of Alsace—for the present at least it seems to be enjoyable to be going along level roads instead of climbing up mule trails. Under bombardment we may miss the ridges and accompanying *angles morts* [dead angles; out of the reach of fire]. I don't believe in a spectacular *trouée* [breakthrough] any more than you do. There is no very good reason why we should perform what they have failed to accomplish, since it will always take men to attack and merely machine guns to defend.

July 24th, 1916.
To Miss H——:

It can't be raining in New England any harder than it is here. If it's that way all over the world we may yet hear of floods in July and August in California. Here it is getting quite serious, as the farmers—the few who are left at home—can't get the hay in, while in some places the wheat stands in swamps—rain every day and every night about continuous performances of showers with interludes of sunshine—we seem to be taking up our travels again bound, we don't know where to, but as there are great doings underway at about every point of our five hundred miles of front, life promises to be interesting wherever we are landed. We are no longer trench troops—we may have lots of trouble but little monotony, if any. At any rate, don't be surprised if I don't write very regularly from now on for a few weeks, as the mail autos may be hard put to it finding us to take our letters back to where things run normally.

The trouble with Mexico seems to have quieted down. It's just as well. It isn't a bad plan to leave some parts of the world quiet for the present. Thank you very much for the clippings—they are always most welcome. S.P. 190. We travel along with our sector.[4]

August 6th, 1916.
To B——:

Contrary to what might be expected, no great personal news. We are still in our hamlet awaiting developments. Some great things are under way undoubtedly for we have kept hearing the roar of artillery day and night for three days—a continuous roar, like that of a cataract. Those who are on the grounds must go half-crazy from the sheer continuity of the crash. We have no idea how long we are going to be left in peace and comfort. We had no idea when we left our late stamping-grounds that we would be shelved for such a long time. We may lose nothing by waiting.

What was my amazement a few days ago, while stepping in to the little one-horse local grocery store, to be confronted with an advertisement embellished with a photo of the Monterey Hotel, Monterey, Cal.! It was the same kind of surprise as when I caught sight of *Le Journal de Pontarlier* in a bar-room at La Honda, Cal.—my father having written for years in said paper. All going to prove that the world is tiny and that it is foolish to make such a rumpus on its surface as the Germans and the Imperial idea have started.

Your war with Mexico has ended agreeably. It is a good thing. You can gain no glory fighting Greasers and you have lands enough and you are in no danger from the south and you may do a lot of good to this misguided world by being patient and starting new precedents in diplomacy making it walk in the open and serve the interest of the nation in the broadest sense—instead of creeping in the dark to help out a few lucky shysters. In spite of the *Lusitania,* Wilson may loom big yet in the history of the world. I absolutely refuse to put a small dingy political motive back of his foreign policy. It seems to me that he acted logically as representing a Nation made up largely of convinced pacifists. It is not time to talk peace now in France, but after the war it will be a shame if all the fine and generous movements for general peace which were at the bottom of most political discussions are not taken up again and with more vigor. After two years of this fighting business I can't agree with those who say that there will always be war, and any man who has the generosity to fight for peace *envers et contre tous* [in spite of all opposition] seems to me most respectable. It's very easy for a Roosevelt to be popular. All one needs to do is to appeal to the cowardice of those who are afraid and to the passions of those who are, above all, proud or vain or greedy. Wilson could have been immensely popular with California, New Mexico, Arizona, Colorado and a good part of the Mississippi Valley simply by getting hold of a few Mexican border states, giving poor downtrodden promoters a chance to get fatter.

Romain Rolland is getting damned up and down because he keeps airing his belief that in spite of all things done, there may yet be a few good Germans in the world. He is very much more creditable to his nation than that ass of Saint-Saëns, who since the Belgian and Northern atrocities, has discovered that Wagner had no musical sense at all.[5] It would be too bad for France if there were a dozen Romain Rollands writing and talking, but it would be a sign of mortal disease in the nation if all thinkers and all professional men were of the Saint-Saëns stripe. A confirmed, unabashed, untractable idealist here and there is a beacon light, no matter how destructive his theories would be if applied without discrimination. It seems to me that Wilson is a Puritanical idealist whose mistakes will be more than made up for by the new orientation which foreign affairs in the United States may get from his principles of patience and forbearance. What made me write out this "tartine" [tirade] is the fact that I have often to explain the United States to the men here, who, being ill informed and not analytical, think that the United States were afraid to fight Germany! As foolish an opinion of you as so many of your *bourgeois* had of us *ante bellum*.

Well, this is an atrocious letter to send a lady. Fortunately it's getting dark and *Stio père et stio mère* [This father and this mother] want to eat supper and I must let them have their table. A few more weeks here and I [will] be on to their *patois*.

August 7th, 1916.
To A———:

Your letter came yesterday. All Western Massachusetts is indeed a beautiful region. The war over, you and I will take a fine trip through all the Hamptons. And next time you come to Europe I will show you all my haunts: Steinbach, Uffholz, Hartmannweilerkopf [*sic*], Metzeral, etc. It is possible that ere long I will have to add a few names to this list, though at present we are still leading a peaceful life in our hamlet. But of late I assure you it was lively at the front. For three days our artillery kept up night and day, and without ceasing for a moment the most frightful dance.

I did not find your name in *Life*. The work of the $73 is a fine one and I am glad you are participating in it.[6] Where has the father of the little girl been killed?[7]

Our brother is sending me now regularly one pound packages called: Victory packages. Because, if we were to start on a long march the small packages are the best.

August 21st, 1916.
S.P. 190
To Miss H——:

We are not very far from your English cousins. They and we are bombarding with a continuity which quite beggars description. There is a canopy of steel over our heads just about day and night. We are so used to the constant reports and hisses that we don't pay any attention to anything that falls not in our immediate neighborhood. You have had plenty of thunderstorms this year. Well a *barrage* is like the most furious thunderstorm you ever heard, only it goes on and on by the hour and when it turns to ordinary bombardment it's like an ordinary storm. (Living in New England is a fine preparation for war.) Will write you at length when we get back to some sane region.

Translated from the French

August, 1916.
To A——:

We are still at some distance from the front waiting for our turn to come and there are still a great many men ahead of us. Therefore, we have nothing to do save the usual manoeuvres. Since I am with the battalion I have never been so comfortable. The lieutenant offers me his bedroom and I eat with the quartermaster and the sergeant-major. I cannot give you any details about important things because we do not know what is going on and the papers are stuffed with mere trifles.

In connection with a remark you made in one of our letters, I wish to tell you that if some of my colleagues have returned to the United States it was because they were ill or because they had a pull. If one is in good health, at the present time, one cannot possibly leave the army by fair means. Possibly those belonging to auxiliary services may have special favors, secretaries, nurses, etc., but not so with fighters. But any how, when one has undertaken a task one should see it through.

August 10th, 1916.
To Mr. G———:
    I feel pangs of remorse for having sent you a letter foreboding fateful events in a very near future. The fact is we are still between Paris and the firing line mainly occupied in taking good care of ourselves. We fully expected to be sent right away to take part in some battle of epic character, "filer vers les épopées" [make verses for an epic], as my captain said, but now I am rather inclined to think that they keep in store for us some autumnal devil of a stroke. Nothing seems to indicate that we are soon to start for the region where there is a constant rumbling of cannon. And yet in our *Theory* we read, Any disengaged body of troops should right away march to the firing line (doit marcher au canon). How many inane statements are to be found in that blessed *Théorie?* It will be real fun to read it after the war.

Translated from the French

August 27th, 1916.
To Monsieur D———:
    It seems that we are going to attack and I do not wish to take part in this affair without writing a few words to you. It is perfectly possible that I may come out unscathed, like many others, but it is also possible that I may not. I am writing to my brother, John, a letter of general interest. If I should not come back, you would tell him that to the last my thoughts were with him and with our family in America and also that I do not regret the choice I made in returning to France. This will seem very foolish if to-morrow or the day after I should return as usual, but you will certainly understand that at this time I cannot refrain from looking at all the possibilities and be silent.
    Be also assured that I entertain towards your family and towards you a feeling of the deepest gratitude.

Your friend,
Robert Pellissier.

LETTERS FROM THE ARMY CHAPLAIN

Passage from a letter to Mme. S——

Cléry, September 6th, 1916.

I had seen him a short time ago and he had been present at a church service I had organized. I knew he held a trusted post (he being the connecting link between two battalions); he was very much exposed and his battalion has suffered heavily. In the course of many a conversation I had with him, I had learned how to appreciate in its delicacy and sensitiveness this outwardly reserved soul. He felt keenly the sadness of war. He saw the ravages made in the souls of men as well as the material destruction. He said to me: "Don't let people speak to me about the fine influence of war—about its regenerating power." But from a moral standpoint himself he had grown. One could not help being impressed by his faithfulness to duty, by the dignity of his moral character, by the keenness of his insight. As he was a thoroughly kind man, all those who knew him loved him.

To Mme. S——:

I dare say that by now you have received the letter I addressed to you at Vence. Grievous letter in which I told you of my fear with regard to my friend, Robert Pellissier. At that time I still had some hope, but with my last visit to his battalion this hope vanished. Your dear cousin has fallen a victim to his high conception of duty, for it was because he had this high sense of duty that he had been entrusted with a delicate mission. His lieutenant selected him to stay the last man, after his battalion was relieved from duty, so that he might give the countersign to the company which was to occupy their sector. Generally this duty devolves on an officer. He was to be appointed 2d lieutenant (nobody understands why he had not yet been promoted to that grade). He was the trusted man of his commandant. What happened while he was alone? I cannot tell. One thing is certain, he was shot through the chest by the ball of a mitrailleuse. Having been carried away by stretcher bearers, which I was not able to identify, he breathed his last a short time after reaching the ambulance. Wounded at 6 o'clock in the morning, he died on the same day and he was buried in the cemetery which is close by the evacuation ambulance of his sector's division.

I had the bitter regret of missing him. When I inquired about him from the men of his battalion, on the morning of the 29th, they did not yet know that he had been wounded. They said: "He is assuring the connection; he will be here presently." As he was not coming I went on. He must have been carried away to our stretcher bearers' post, while I had gone to another battalion. That is why I did not see him again. However, shortly before that time, I had a long conversation with him, and with great calm he had spoken to me of his eventual death. He assured me that he had no presentiment; he added: "I have no illusions, I know perfectly well that I may not return." He asked me to write to you, and I wrote as soon as I could find out something about him; and to his brother, I shall write to-night.

He has shown the most remarkable sang-froid. He was understood and loved. The testimony of his men and of his chiefs is unanimous. I was moved when I witnessed the emotion they showed on hearing of his death. They thought he was only wounded. The commandant of his company told me that he had been glad to think he was going so soon to have him as an officer. They already considered him as such. A lieutenant told me that he considered him as a brother. One of the chasseurs said: "I had never before met a man like him. The nobility of his character, the generosity of his heart, his faithfulness to duty had won for him the sympathy of all." They admired his intellect and his uprightness. He was a complete man. His chiefs had asked that he be awarded the military medal, for during the recent encounters he had shown that he had the qualities of a leader, and an absolute contempt for danger. He has upheld the morale of his men who placed in him absolute confidence. I did not even know he had been wounded, and as I had seen his battalion at the time when it was relieved from duty, I rejoiced at the thought that he had escaped; but when in my turn I was relieved from duty, when I went to look over the list of names in the ambulance, I found his name accompanied by the cruel word (dead). I went to the cemetery and when, by the last glimmer of twilight, I read on a cross the name of Robert Pellissier, all of the anguish of this horrible war filled my heart. On his tomb I prayed for his companions at arms. As for him, I feel that he is far above, in God's own radiance. How I wish that I could have been of more comfort to him! But he was a strong man. He had given his life. May such sacrifices hasten the time of deliverance for our dear crucified country.

H. Monnier,
Aumônier Protestant Militaire.
Groupe des Brancardiers Divisionnaires,
secteur 190.

Mr. J. Pellissier,
Valence, Drome.
Dear sir:

In order to comply with the wish expressed some time ago by your brother, when he gave me your address, I wish to inform you by a personal letter of the grievous news, which last week came to my knowledge and of which I have recently had full confirmation.

Having seen a great deal of your brother I soon came to esteem and love him. A courageous and generous man, he has rendered the greatest services and won the affection of all. I was cherishing the hope that he might be spared. But in the last encounter at the Somme, by Clery, his battalion suffered heavily. Remaining the last one in order to secure the connection with the battalion which was to replace his own, he was mortally wounded by the shot of a mitrailleuse. He died on the same day at the ambulance.

He was going to be appointed second lieutenant. His name is on the list of candidates for the military medal of which his unfailing devotion to duty had made him worthy.

He is not only regretted; his loss is mourned by all the men in the battalion who knew him.

His tomb, marked by a cross bearing his name, is in the cemetery at Etinehem (Somme). The place cannot be reached at present, but should we keep gaining ground, I think it will be reached easily. To your cousin I have given all the additional information I was able to secure, but what I cannot express is the deep feeling with which these testimonies were given.

I mourn in him not only a member of my church but a real friend. You are entitled to know that he has been loved and that he has rendered to his country the greatest of services. That is not enough to comfort. God alone can do it efficaciously and I pray to Him that he may allay the grief of my friend's family.

H. Monnier,
Army Chaplain.

FROM THE *Journal Officiel*, OCTOBER 14, 1916

Médaille Militaire, Croix de Guerre avec palme

Robert Edouard Pellissier, Mle 04682, sergent à la 1re compagnie du 5e bataillon de chasseurs à pied; Sous-officier d'une bravoure et d'un sang-froid remarquables. La section ayant été soumise pendant plusieurs jours à un violent bombardement, n'a cessé d'exalter le moral de ses hommes et de porter secours aux blessés. A été atteint d'une trés grave blessure lors d'une relève particulièrement difficile.

Translation

Military Medal, Croix de Guerre with Palm

Robert Edouard Pellissier, medal 04682, Sergeant of the 1st Company of the 5th Battalion of the *chasseurs à pied;* noncommissioned officer of remarkable bravery and fearlessness. While the section was subjected to several days of violent bombardment, he never ceased to lift the morale of his men and bring help to the wounded. Received a grave wound during a particularly difficult relief.

APPENDIX A

A Tribute by His Sister

Originally printed in the *Williston Bulletin*, October, 1916

Dulce et decorum est pro patria mori [1]
—ROBERT PELLISSIER

The Spirit of France as Portrayed in the
Life of a Former Williston Teacher
Killed in the Somme Offensive
By Adeline Pellissier
Professor of French in Smith College

On September 18th news reached us that Robert Pellissier, of the French chasseurs à pied, had been killed in battle. To his family his life has been and always will be the greatest inspiration. When I think of my brother's life, the picture which rises before me is that of a young horseman coming at full speed over hill and dale. He is neither dismayed nor halted by any obstacles; he clears them all lightly and with a joyous shout. At the end of his course, he meets death on a battlefield, bravely fighting for France.

One of Robert's chief characteristics was his profound attachment to his native land. He was born in 1882 at La Ferrière-sous-

Jougne, Doubs, in the Jura Mountains, and the severe and almost tragic beauty of the fir tree forests, extending for miles over the mountainsides, was so strongly stamped on his memory that he always longed for fir clad mountains and loved those landscapes best which came nearest to this type of natural beauty.

Robert was the youngest of a family of seven children, and as his father died when he was but six years old, in the course of his life, when he came in closer contact now with one and now with another of his brothers and sisters, he eagerly asked them for his share of the moral guidance left them by their father as their most precious heritage.

Robert's father, after having lived the greater part of his life near Grenoble and in Lyons, had finally become superintendent of a large wire and nail factory at La Ferrière. The owners of the mill, the employees, the eight hundred workmen constituted the whole settlement. As in this Roman Catholic community our family was the only one which was of Huguenot ancestry, and as the only Protestant church was several miles distant, our father, in his own way, gave us religious training. In summer, on Sunday, when the weather was fair, he often took us to a part of the forest where old fir trees, standing wide apart, left an open space as dark and mysterious as a cathedral, and there he would read to us either a psalm of David or a passage from the Gospels, and the reading over, he would tell us how, in olden times, our Huguenot ancestors had fought for their faith and how for centuries before the great French Revolution, they had prayed and worshipped in the wilderness, in some clearing or by the side of a stream. Sometimes my father would tell us about the Huguenots of the Cévennes, and sometimes he would describe the wanderings of the Waldenses, following them from France into Italy and from Italy back into France.[2] But the whole trend of this religious instruction was that external ceremonies are of but little importance and that the spiritual side of worship is the main thing.

An interesting story shows how this lesson was understood by my sister Marie at the early age of six. Having been invited with seven other little girls to hold the white ribbons of a pall at a child's funeral, in the Catholic church, Marie remained standing through the whole ceremony, although her little friends kept tugging at her dress, to make her kneel down. When they asked her the reason for such indecorous behavior, Marie answered: "I worship in truth and in spirit."[3]

Five years older than Robert, she handed down this conception of moral courage to him. It must be added that our father felt that whatever form of religion a man accepted he must live up to it, and he always urged his men to keep in touch with their church and with their priest, so broad was his spirit of religious toleration.

My sister Marie, who is no longer living, was Robert's earliest instructress. Long before Marie could read, she knew some poetry by snatches. She had picked up this knowledge at the breakfast table, for my father, who went to the mill at six o'clock in the morning, returned home at eight, to have breakfast with his family. From his office to the house, he used to read and, after he had sat down at the table, he would repeat to us, with fiery enthusiasm, the passages he most admired. Sometimes it was a passage from the work of a philosopher or an historian, Pascal or Michelet, but still more frequently he would recite a few stanzas from our great poets: de Musset, de Vigny or Victor Hugo.[4] Marie did not know the titles of the books, but she knew part of their contents. She had no difficulty in singling out, on the shelves, the book with the red binding which to her meant:

> Poète, prends ton luth, et me donne un baiser;
>> La fleur de l'eglantier sent ses bourgeons éclore,
> Le printemps naît ce soir; les vents vont s'embraser;
>> Et la bergeronnette en attendant l'aurore,
> Aux premiers buissons verts commence à se poser.[5]

She could tell also that in another volume was to be found:

> J'aime le son du cor, le soir, au fond des bois.
> Soit qu'il chante les pleurs de la biche aux abois,
> Ou l'adieu du chasseur que l'écho faible accueille,
> Et que le vent du nord porte de feuille en feuille.[6]

By Marie this poetical knowledge was imparted to Robert.

If I give these apparently insignificant details it is because, in my opinion, they account for an early sense of discrimination between good and bad literature, a certain natural sense of rhythm which in my brother seemed to be inborn. Every now and then there was a sad and gloomy day in our home; our father would come in and say with a look of profound despair on his face: "Le ministère est tombé"—the ministry has fallen—and, on such a day, even the younger children were made to understand that the French Republic was like a ship without a pilot; they firmly grasped the idea that beyond the family there was France, and that France was in danger.

After the death of his father, Robert went with his mother to Geneva, Switzerland, where they lived for a few years. Robert often told me that during the years spent in Geneva, he felt like an exile and as the suburb where his mother lived was very near the French frontier, he never spent a day without at least putting his foot on French soil. The thing which depressed Robert most was the turn of mind of the Genevese children; he saw their good qualities, but he found them morose. Robert, as his father before him, had a keen sense of humor, and he missed this spicy quality in the minds of his young classmates.

When his brother Paul came home after one year of military service, Robert took with him long walking trips. The older brother used to say: "You cannot begin too young to get trained for military service," and the little brother was trained with a vengeance. These walks were very interesting, for as Paul was studying to become an architect, he would point out to his brother, as they went, the characteristic lines in the style of an old chateau, or of a Gothic church, and besides, in his knapsack there generally was a book of historical memoirs or some poems. In the Geneva days, Robert once or twice spent a vacation in the mountains with an aunt, or rather a cousin of his mother, a lady of strong personality, who interested him in the work she was doing.

As this aunt was suffering from a nervous breakdown, she had gone to live in Aigle, a small town in the Swiss Alps. While living there, she noticed that a number of boys, who were under bad influence at home, were gradually becoming hopeless cases. All this happened before the days of Junior Republics. Mademoiselle T——— invited twelve or fifteen of these boys to meet at her house in the evening; and while they were seated around a bright fire on the hearth, she unfolded to them her plan. They would meet at her house regularly, in order to sing and roast chestnuts, and besides she would teach them to make fishing nets, to weave baskets and to cane chairs. By the spring the boys had become so proficient that they were able to have a sale, and their goods sold so well that they had money enough to take a little trip. Robert was invited to go on one of these expeditions. On the first day, it was discovered that some one had eaten somebody else's luncheon and filled the basket with dirt. On seeing this, the face of Mlle. T—— fell, and she showed such bitter disappointment that every boy stood perfectly still. As nobody admitted having done the deed, Mlle. T—— spoke with much force, reminding the boys that they formed an association, that they had to live up to the name of "fidéliens" or "faithful," that the F they were wearing on their sleeves stood for "franc, fidèle et fort" [French, faithful and strong], and that henceforth, if any of them did anything wrong, he would have to admit his guilt, be judged by his comrades, and if found guilty, the penalty would be the removal of the letter F from his sleeve until he had redeemed himself by exemplary behavior.

Robert was greatly impressed by this scene, and to the end of his life he kept up a correspondence with this aunt, and he often inquired about her boys. With the exception of one, all the boys turned out well. The "fidéliens" used to write an account of their trips and Robert used to like to read it. This aunt was to Robert a great inspiration.

During the same year, Robert had another thrilling experience, of a more worldly order. My sister Marie had become acquainted with her next-door neighbor, a very attractive Italian girl of twenty, who was even then a great singer. She gave the children tickets for a presentation of "Carmen." Robert, who was fond of music, was at first delighted, but when he saw the Italian singer, in the part of the heroine, misusing her influence, he became indignant and wanted to leave the hall. For a whole week after that performance he refused to speak to the singer, saying she was a bad character. The singer, much amused, said it was the greatest compliment she had ever received. Gradually Robert began to understand the difference between real life and its artistic presentation, and he saw how hard an artist has to work to come near perfection. Life's work, in this instance, was presenting itself to him under an entirely new aspect.

Several years later, in 1896, as Robert's mother felt very much depressed by the death of one of her sons, it was suggested by Robert's sister, that they both come to live with her in Brooklyn, because she thought the company of her growing daughters would be good for Robert. In course of time, the three nieces of less than ten years younger than Robert became very dear to him, and his brother-in-law felt toward him as would a father. Robert himself made all the arrangements for the sea voyage and it was certainly not by mere accident that the travellers crossed the ocean on a steamer belonging to the French Line. While on board, Robert had his fourteenth birthday, on the twelfth of May. On that day Robert made a vow: he would master French history and become thoroughly acquainted with the works of all the great French historians, past and present. This vow was kept.

Robert's first summer in America was spent in the White Mountains; he wished to enter school in the fall and he did not know a word of English. In the kindness of her heart, his sister suggested a private school, the Froebel Academy, which was connected with a kindergarten. Kindergarten!—this word filled Robert's heart with anguish. He a boy of fourteen, who had recently taken such a solemn vow, enter a school affiliated with a kindergarten! He resolved to enter the public school in the fall. He would study grammar by himself, pick up every day English from the conversations he heard, and study one book thoroughly. With the help of one of his sisters who was a teacher, he read and translated Dickens's *A Tale of Two Cities*.[7] After making both a literal and idiomatic translation, often covering several pages, he would commit to memory the whole passage. In the fall he entered the grammar school; it is true that in English he ranked seventy-third, but by June he ranked third. He was then able to skip one year of the grammar school and enter the high school. After the third year he decided to make up the work of the fourth year during the summer and enter the Bridgewater Normal School in the fall. With occasional help from our neighbor in the White Mountains, who was a professor of botany at Wellesley College, with a good text-book and a microscope he made up one year's work in botany.[8] He found relief from this rather strenuous work by going on long walking trips with his brother-in-law. It was his brother-in-law who taught him how to play tennis, and to swim, and as Mr. A——— was a professor of history, Robert would often go to him for advice.[9]

Robert took a four-year course in the Bridgewater Normal School; he remained there from 1899 to 1903. Mr. A——— thought that Robert in attending this school would have a good opportunity to get acquainted with both boys and girls. In the Bridgewater Normal School Robert met with no difficulties except when he wished to be excused from taking a course in beginner's French. The teacher of French, who happened to be a German, would not believe that Robert was a French boy and made him take the course. To offset the penance of taking beginner's French with a German, Robert decided to devote one hour to talking to himself on different subjects, in his native tongue, in order not to lose his command of French. Robert specialized in sciences, and, at the end of his course won a Harvard scholarship. In 1903 he entered the Senior Class of the Lawrence Scientific School.

Robert felt on coming of age that a man should earn his own living, and he set about to do it. But as he was following an almost entirely scientific course, he found that, beginning with the correction of French books at six o'clock in the morning, he was kept almost constantly occupied until eleven o'clock at night. Fortunately, during that year Robert had as a neighbor a Bridgewater friend, a very witty young Irishman, and there was, between them, many a bout enlivened by flashes of French and Irish wit. They often enjoyed retaliating on some young gentlemen, who, having entered Harvard for the life and sports, occasionally taunted them for having entered the University "by the back door." But on Commencement Day, the French and Irish friends after experiencing a few seconds of anxiety, on not finding their names on the first page of the programme, were greatly relieved and thrilled with joy when, on turning the page, they read them on the Honor List. After graduating from Harvard, Robert taught at Williston for several years (1904–1908), intending to earn the funds he needed for the study of medicine. Of these years I shall say nothing, because another has kindly undertaken to do it. Let it be said that Robert's health having given out after his first year's teaching he was obliged to give up his cherished plan of studying medicine and devote all his energy, first to getting well and then to preparing for advanced work in an entirely different line. On his way to the United States Robert had stopped in Paris and met his cousins; brief as it was, this visit made on him a strong impression, and he often said to me that the aim he had set before himself was to do, in a scientific line, as brilliant work as his cousin, G. P., had done in literary criticism.[10] When Robert returned to Harvard in 1908 he had brushed up his German, studied by himself French literature, and besides had acquired, with the help of one of his sisters, a knowledge of Italian and Spanish sufficient to enable him to do graduate work in Romance Languages. He took the Degree of M.A. at Harvard in 1909, and he was given for the following year an acting instructorship at Leland Stanford University. As he was in charge of only two courses he was able to keep on with his graduate work, and at the end of the college year, in May, he went to Mexico City, where he spent the summer studying, being the guest of his brother John, a civil engineer. Robert had a horse placed at his disposal by the company with which his brother was working, and every week he spent a few days with his brother in camp. While in Mexico, Robert acquired a practical knowledge of Spanish, and he worked in the public library. For exercise, he took long horseback rides and climbed high mountains. It was also a great joy for him to become well acquainted with a brother he knew so slightly and who was to become very dear to him. In 1910 Robert returned to Harvard to complete his preparation for the degree of Ph.D. For two summers he taught in the Harvard Summer School and worked on his thesis. His subject was "The Influence of French Literature on Spanish Literature of the Eighteenth Century." From 1911 to 1914 Robert taught in Leland Stanford University.

To complete his studies he had in between taken two trips to Europe; in 1905 he went to France by way of Italy and in 1913 he went, by way of France, to Spain, a trip which he thoroughly enjoyed. In the summer of 1914 his brother-in-law arranged to meet him in the West and they went on extensive walking trips in the California Sierras. Robert was looking forward with great pleasure to the work he was going to do in the following year; he had been appointed Assistant Professor of Romance Languages and he was to offer a course in comparative literature and one in the history of civilization. Writing to me, in the spring of that year, he said he could not conceive of any offer which could induce him to leave the work which he expected to enjoy so thoroughly. But the war broke out and, without any hesitation, although he was not called to the colors, he immediately sailed for Europe on the first steamer which conveyed home French reservists. Robert had been excused from military service because he had come to the United States before he was fourteen and had not visited France more than twice between the ages of twenty and thirty. His brother-in-law had even suggested that he might become an American citizen, but Robert felt that he could not renounce the country of his birth, at a time when France would certainly need the help of all her children. He was convinced that there would be a war, sooner or later, and he had resolved to offer his life to France.

He had so constantly trained himself in all kinds of physical exercises that, after two months of military drill, he was not only placed with the men of his class, but with the élite. He became a chasseur à pied. The chasseurs are the men who, on account of the stubborn defense they made in the Vosges Mountains and in Alsace, have been called by the Germans "blue devils." One of the men belonging to the same company said when writing to a friend "M. Pellissier est un homme très courageux; je me suis trouvé avec lui dans plusieurs combats, il est toujours le premier" [Monsieur Pellissier is a very courageous man; I have found myself with him in several battles, and he is always the best].

Robert was happy that his fate took him to Alsace, for as a boy he had read with delight the novels of Erckmann-Chatrian, two Alsatians, who, in their novels, have described the great wars of the first Napoleon. Robert was delighted to tread the ground where Madame Thérèse had once passed.[11] He was deeply moved when an old Alsatian woman told him, "Enfin vous voila il y a longtemps qu'on vous attendait" [At last we see you; we have been waiting for you a long time]. He was touched when, in Alsatian homes, he was treated like a son, and his hostess refused to accept any pay for his room or for the services rendered. Robert was naturally of a very gentle disposition and he often felt like the captain of whom he said "He wept when he saw the slaughter of Germans, for young men are young men, even when they are Germans."

Robert was wounded in the shoulder near Steinbach, at the end of January, 1915. After spending four months in the hospital he found that although his wound was healed he could not carry a knapsack. He therefore resolved to take the examination for admittance to St.-Cyr, the French West Point. He passed the examinations and spent four months in Saint-Maixent, a military school for officers. He went back to the front with the grade of sergeant and, on several occasions, he took the place of a lieutenant for several weeks at a time. It was during this period that Robert heard, with profound grief, that one of his former Williston pupils had fallen on the battlefield of Loos. When mentioning the sad news, in one of his letters to me, he could not help saying, "Pauvre petit" [Poor little one].

Robert felt very grateful to the Americans for what they have done for France, not only as volunteers and ambulance drivers but also for children orphaned by war. With profound admiration he spoke of the work done in this line by "Life." He was also grateful for the friends in America who refuted the unfortunate statement of Miss Jane Addams's that soldiers when they attack are drunk. To a friend

Robert Pellissier, prewar photograph.

who asked him what to make of such a statement he answered, "No, don't believe what Miss Jane Addams is telling or rather what she has been told. French soldiers don't get drunk each time they go into a bayonet charge. I took part in one, and not only had we nothing in our cans except water, but we had had nothing to eat since breakfast (and it was two o'clock in the afternoon), we had no supper at all, and breakfast at ten o'clock the next morning. I saw a charge start, right from the very part of the trench where I sat, and what struck me was the perfectly cold determination of the men who were to my left and to my right and in front of me. Those who cut lanes through our wires hit rhythmically and with perfect aim." In another letter Robert explained whence, in his opinion, springs the strength and determination of French soldiers: "The one decent thing which may come out of this horrible mess may be the final discrediting of war in Europe and perhaps elsewhere. It is an idea which keeps up French soldiers at present. One often hears them say: 'Well, whatever happens to us, our children at least will be freed from militarism and all allied curses.'"

I have tried to show in these pages what were the influences which helped give to Robert his stamp of character: his deep religious feeling, his moral point of view, his sincerity, his perseverance, his gift of adaptation, and the fairness of mind which enabled him to give everyone his due, his gratefulness towards the people who had helped him, his sympathy for Americans, and overshadowing everything else, his devotion to France. Of him may truly be said: "Qui patitur vincit" [He who suffers, triumphs (Latin proverb)].

APPENDIX B

~

A Colleague's Tribute

Originally printed in the *Williston Bulletin*, October, 1916

A Colleague's Tribute

By Sidney Nelson Morse

Professor Pellissier, who was recently killed in the Battle of the Somme, taught four years at Williston. He came here in 1904 direct from Harvard with the enthusiasm of a brilliant student. In Harvard the study of science appealed to him as well as the study of language. For a little time during his course there he was undecided which field to enter. Language, especially the French to which he was bred and born, he had a predilection for; it claimed his first attention, but science fascinated and challenged him to reveal her secrets. So interested did he become in biology during his college course that he was glad of the opportunity to teach it at Williston, his first year, in addition to his major courses in the French department, of which he later became the head and sole teacher.

Perhaps the number of his classes this first year, and the devitalizing work of correcting test papers overtaxed his strength. The following year, 1905, he found it necessary, owing to pulmonary trouble, to give up teaching for a time and seek bodily and mental refreshment. Westhampton air, a rigorous diet, horseback riding, and an indomitable will completely restored his health, much to the surprise and joy of his many solicitous friends. The fight he made against insidious tuberculosis was heroic. It was an earnest of the valor which for two resolute years just closed he manifested on the Western front in France.

In 1906 he was made head of the French department, continuing his work two years. During this time he enlarged and extended the courses in French. He added third year French.

In 1908 he resigned to take a post-graduate course for his doctor's degree in Romance languages at Harvard, which opened the way to an instructorship in Leland Stanford University.

In a general way what may be said of all good teachers may be said emphatically of him. He was faithful, conscientious, painstaking, helpful, and resourceful. But he was more than that. His ambition was to excel. His standards for himself and for his pupils were high. He was a zealous worker for the first-best and exacted high grade work from his pupils. His perfect command of English of the rational phrase, yet rich in allusion, enabled him to impart his discriminating knowledge of French.

In temperament he was intense. To his recreation, to his social intercourse, to his study, he brought an ardor that was contagious; and to his teaching he brought a keen appreciation of the accuracy, flexibility, beauty, and strength of the French tongue.

As a man, simple in life and warm of heart, he was genuine, plain and unostentatious. All shams he detested. Veneer and gloss without the substance had no attraction for him.

He was a knightly spirit. He loved honor; he was jealous of his honor and of the honor of his friends. In vivacity, wit, and repartee he had no easy second. At heart deeply generous and sympathetic in impulse, with a seeming abruptness of manner which was merely the necessity of husbanding time, so active was he, he was quick to discern a need and meet it. He unerringly recognized true worth where it was to be found, and though at times he did not reveal his real self to those who did not know him, yet to his friends and intimates he was always the trusted comrade, the cherished companion, the loyal friend.

His character, his career, his life—but even more, his death for his country—are a beneficent inspiration.

APPENDIX C

The Pellissier Memorial

Originally printed in the *Stanford Alumnus* 18.2 (October, 1916)

The Pellissier Memorial

The University has just suffered a severe loss in the death of Robert E. Pellissier, Assistant Professor of Romanic Languages. Dr. Pellissier was appointed Instructor in French in 1911 and three years later was promoted to the rank of Assistant Professor. On the outbreak of the European war he took out a leave of absence and enlisted as a private in the French army. His courage and ability soon won him recognition and in December last he was raised to the rank of sergeant. He was killed in the great Somme offensive on August 29th.

To do honor to the memory of Professor Pellissier, it is proposed to raise a fund among the members and friends of the University to be known as the Pellissier Memorial Fund. This fund is to be devoted to the furthering of the work of the American Field Ambulance Service in France by the purchase, or part purchase, of an ambulance to be maintained for one year. The total cost would be $1,600.

It is confidently expected that the faculty, students, alumni and friends of the University will embrace the opportunity to make possible the maintenance of a Stanford ambulance in honor of a Stanford man who sacrificed his life at the call of duty.

Contributions may be sent to the treasurer of the fund, or to any member of the Committee. Checks should be marked "Pellissier Memorial Fund."

Committee: O. M. Johnston,
                H. R. Fairclough,
                A. M. Cathcart,
                P. A. Martin (Treasurer),
                Paul Staniford.

From the plaque on the Ambulance:

AMBULANCE OFFERTE PAR LES MEMBRES & LES AMIS DE L'UNIVERSITÉ DE STANFORD EN CALIFORNIE EN MEMOIRE DU PROFESSEUR ROBERT EDOUARD PELLISSIER, SERGENT AU 5ME BATTALION DE CHASSEURS A PIED.

[Ambulance given by the members and friends of Stanford University in California in memory of Professor Robert Edouard Pellissier, Sergeant in the 5th Battalion of Chasseurs à Pied.]

A second ambulance was given to the American Field Service by graduates and undergraduates of the Bridgewater Normal School, Bridgewater, Massachusetts, in an effort organized by Mr. Sumner Cushing, Salem, Massachusetts.

APPENDIX D

Time Line of Events in the Letters

DATE	EVENT
8/25/1914	First letter from New York City
8/30/1914	In transit on liner *La France*
9/2/1914	Arrived at Le Havre; traveled to Paris
9/3/1914	Traveled to Lyons
9/4/1914	Traveled to Dijon
9/5/1914	Arrived at Besançon; stayed overnight in hotel
9/6/1914	Arrived at enlistment barracks in Besançon
9/6–10/30/1914	Drilled at Besançon
9/14/1914	News of the victory of the Battle of the Marne
10/12/1914	Injury in training
10/30/1914	Departed from training for the Vosges
11/6–17/1914	In the trenches in the Vosges
11/17–21/1914	Behind the lines
11/27–12/1/1914	In the trenches, probably at Hartmannweilerskopf

12/2–10/1914	Guard duty behind the lines, three miles from St.-Dié
12/14–16/1914	Attacked and captured Steinbach; captain killed; Steinbach recaptured by Germans; battalion lost 525 out of 1,400 men
12/16–19/1914	Rested in Thann
12/20/1914–1/14/1915	Guarded Sudel Pass in Guebwiller/Goldbach area; Christmas Eve at Goldbach
1/14–18/1915	Rested at St.-Amarin
1/18–24/1915	In trenches in Steinbach/Uffholz area
1/24/1915	Wounded; evacuated first to Weiler, later to Bussang
2/14–5/17/1915 (?)	In hospital at Givors
5/18–25/1915	On furlough at Valence
5/25–6/7/1915	At Amagny (near Besançon)
6/8–8/23/1915	At Roche, studying for aspirant examination
8/25/1915	Left for officer training
8/29–12/20/1915	In officer training at St.-Maixent
12/20–30/1915	In transit back to the front; visited Paris
1/1/1916	Back in Alsace, slightly back from the front
1/6–3/23/1916	On front line on Hartmannweilerskopf for fifty-three days
3/24/1916	Returned for rest to headquarters—possibly Bussang
4/10/1916 (?)	Review by President Poincaré
5/7–24/1916	Back at the front
5/24–30/1916	Rested behind the lines
5/31–6/9/1916	On furlough, mainly traveling with brother John in Rhône valley; went as far as Marseilles
6/9–7/2/1916	Back at the front near Munster/Colmar

7/2–19/1916	Rested behind the lines
7/23/1916	Battalion transferred to Northern front
7/24/1916	Arrived in Sector 190
8/28/1916	Killed in battle near Cléry

NOTES

FOREWORD

1. Jean Norton Cru, *Témoins: Essai d'analyse et de critique des souvenirs de combattants édités en français de 1915 à 1928* (Paris: Les Étincelles, 1929; reprint, Nancy: Presses Universitaires de Nancy, 1993).

2. Ibid., p. 491. All translations are my own.

3. I explore the case of Norton Cru further in "Jean Norton Cru, lecteur des livres de guerre," *Annales du Midi* 112, no. 232 (2000): 517–28. This piece was also published in English as "Jean Norton Cru and Combatants' Literature of the First World War," *Modern and Contemporary France* 9, no. 2 (2001): 161–69.

4. Raoul Allier, preface to *Impressions de guerre d'un soldat chrétien* (Paris: Fischbacher, 1920), p. 5.

5. Henry Bordeaux, preface to *Lettres d'un officier de chasseurs alpins, 2 août–28 décembre 1915* (Paris: Plon, 1918), p. lii. So far as I know, this is the only collection of letters from a French soldier of the Great War to have been translated into English. See *A Crusader of France* (New York: Dutton, 1919).

6. *Au Veil-Armand: Lettres de Henri Volatier, Chasseur au 5e Battaillon Alpin, à sa fiancé*, published by G. Mouterde, S.J. (Paris: Gabriel Beauchesne, 1919). It should be noted that numbered *chasseur* units could be referred to as *chasseur à pied* (light infantry) and *chasseur alpin* (mountain light infantry) at different times, for reasons that remain a bit obscure. See the history of this unit, *Campagne, 1914–1918: Historique du 5e Bataillon de Chasseurs Alpins* (Paris: Chapelot, [1919?]).

7. *Au Veil-Armand*, p. 10.

8. Class almost certainly played a role in determining the form in which the letters

of Volatier came to be published. Volatier was the child of peasants, and himself a shepherd. He then worked for a butcher, whose daughter became his fiancée. The letters of a man of such modest origins would not have been published without a patron, who would have felt obliged to provide additional guidance for reasons of class as well as religion.

9. The great medieval historian and World War II resistance hero Marc Bloch also served in the Vosges during the Great War. See Marc Bloch, *Memoirs of War, 1914–15,* trans. Carole Fink (Ithaca: Cornell University Press, 1980).

10. The long-discredited notion of German "atrocities" has now been given serious scholarly attention in John Horne and Allan Krammer, *German Atrocities, 1914: A History of Denial* (London: Yale University Press, 2001).

11. See *La dernière lettre écrite par des soldats français tombés au champ d'honneur, 1914–1918* (Paris: Flammarion, 1921).

12. Norton Cru, *Témoins,* p. 491.

CHAPTER 1. EN ROUTE

1. Lizzard: Lizard Point on the south coast of Cornwall in England, a landmark for ships.

2. Gargantua: See François Rabelais (ca. 1490–1553), *Gargantua et Pantagruel.*

3. William: Kaiser Wilhelm II.

4. turcos: Turks; i.e., Muslim soldiers from the French colonies.

5. The government was evacuated to Bordeaux on September 2, 1914.

6. Paul Pau (1848–1932), French general, later organized the Army of Alsace. Joseph Simon Galliéni (1849–1916), French general, organized the famous attack on the German Army using Paris taxis for transport; he was later minister of war from October 29, 1915, to March 16, 1916.

7. taube: German Taube airplane.

8. Blues: new recruits, so-called from their blue uniforms.

9. The French 75 mm. field gun was in use throughout the war. Designed in 1897, it was mobile and highly accurate and fired up to thirty shots a minute. The recoil mechanism, which has been adapted by nearly all artillery ever since, kept the gun aimed at the same point even after many shots had been fired.

10. Cyrano: *Cyrano de Bergerac,* a play by Edmond Rostand (1868–1918). Its first production was in 1897, only seventeen years before this letter was written.

11. 1902 soldier: one who turned twenty in the year 1902.

12. The French captured Mulhausen briefly on August 8, 1914. General Bonneau was dismissed on August 10.

13. The battle of the Marne was fought September 5–10, 1914.

14. Joseph Jacques Cesaire Joffre (1852–1931) commanded the French armies during the Battle of the Marne and for the early part of the war; he had also served in the Franco-Prussian War in 1870–71. He was replaced as commander in 1916.

15. Original footnote: Finding passage on a steamer homebound.

16. Original footnote: Enlisting. A—— sailed from Marseilles on the day he landed in Havre.

CHAPTER 2. BESANÇON

1. The Cathedral of Rheims, where thirty-two of the kings of France were crowned, was shelled for the first time on September 19, 1914, and suffered additional damage throughout the war. This act, which shocked Europe and America, became a symbol for French recruiting posters and a rallying cry for the war effort.

2. Romain Rolland (1866–1944) received the Nobel Prize for literature in 1915.

3. Dutch: one of Robert Pellissier's favorite terms for the Germans; anglicization of "Deutsch."

4. Adeline Pellissier, his sister, was a professor of French at Smith College in Northampton, Massachusetts.

5. Allemand: proper name in French for "a German," versus the slang term "Boche," which may come from "caboche" or "wooden head."

6. Alexandre Chatrian (1826–90) and Emile Alexandre-Chatrian (1822–99), authors of *Blocus: Episode de la fin de l'empire* and *Histoire d'un conscrit de 1813*.

7. Emélie, Marguerite, Marie and Louise: Emélie was Robert Pellissier's sister, married to Edmund K. Alden; Marguerite, Marie, and Louise were their children.

8. The Kingman family were cousins who lived nearby; Alice Sinnot was Edmund K. Alden's sister, married to Allston Sinnot.

CHAPTER 3. VOSGES

1. Domodossola: town in northern Italy.

2. Rutland: probably Rutland, Vermont.

3. to Brooklyn: to his sister Emélie and her family.

4. Caesar, Book I: a reference to Caesar's *Commentaries*. Caesar's troops occupied Besançon in 58 B.C.

5. Biblical characters looking for grasshoppers to feed: joking reference to John the Baptist in Matthew 3:4: "And the same John had his raiment of camel's hair, and a leathern girdle about his loins; and his meat was locusts and wild honey."

6. before 1870: before Germany occupied Alsace in the Franco-Prussian War.

7. this town Saintamarin: St.-Amarin.

8. Hearst papers: the newspaper chain controlled by William Randolph Hearst (1863–1951).

9. Eugène Brieux (1858–1932), French playwright.

10. Huguenot: The Huguenots were French Calvinist. Protestants, especially in the period 1550–1685. The Huguenots exercised considerable political power until the revocation of the Edict of Nantes in 1685.

11. Gustave Aymard (1818–73), French novelist.

12. That is, the movement of the alarmed birds betrayed the presence of German troops.

13. Mt. Tom . . . Titan's Pier: Mount Tom is a part of the Holyoke Range in western Massachusetts, not far from Northampton. Titan's Pier is a basaltic outcrop of Mount Holyoke. Both Mount Tom and Titan's Pier were favorite day hikes of Robert Pellissier and his brother-in-law.

14. marmites: French for "cooking pots"; joking reference to the large shells.

15. Thomas Corneille (1625–1709), French dramatist.

16. As the war went on, the French built the "Route des Crêtes" and the "Route Joffre" to supply the front.

17. Dante Aligheri, *Inferno*, Canto XV:

> Ora cen porta l'un de' duri margini,
> e 'l fummo del ruscel di sopra aduggia,
> sì che dal foco salva l'acqua e li argini.

> [Now one of the hard margins bears us on,
> And the smoke of the rivulet makes shade above
> So that from the fire it shelters the water and the banks.]
> See *Dante's Divine Comedy: The Inferno: A Literal Prose Translation*, trans.
> John A. Carlyle, M.D. (London: Chapman and Hill, 1839).

18. Alfred, Lord Tennyson (1809–92), *The Charge of the Light Brigade:*

> "Forward, the Light Brigade!"
> Was there a man dismayed?
> Not though the soldier knew
> Someone had blundered.
> Theirs not to make reply,
> Theirs not to reason why,
> Theirs but to do and die.
> Into the Valley of Death
>   Rode the Six Hundred.

CHAPTER 4. WOUNDED

1. in France again: i.e., not in Alsace.

2. Raymond Poincaré (1860–1934), prime minister from 1912 to 1913, president of the Republic from 1913 to 1920, and prime minister again from 1922 to 1924 and from 1926 to 1929.

3. Alexandre Millerand (1859–1943), minister of war, who resigned in October, 1915.

4. Kabyle: The Kabyls are a Berber people, mainly from Algeria.

5. Marshfield: Marshfield, Massachusetts, was the home of many of his brother-in-law's relatives and the site of many family gatherings.

6. "M——" in this case is his niece Marguerite Alden Walker, who lived with her husband John Scott Walker in Woodberry Forest, Virginia.

7. "There once were two cats of Kilkenny,
    Each thought there was one cat too many;
    So they fought and they spit,
    And they scratched and they bit,

Till, excepting their nails,
And the tips of their tails,
Instead of two cats there weren't any."

8. Emile Gaboriau (1832–73), novelist and writer of detective stories, created the characters of Père Tabaret and Monsieur Lecoq.

9. Kuno Francke (1855–1930), professor at Harvard while Robert Pellissier was a student. The article is probably "True Germany," *Atlantic Monthly* 116, Oct., 1915, pp. 550–60.

10. This is almost certainly Jean Norton Cru (1879–1949). His book *Témoins: Essai d'analyse et critique des souvenirs de combattants édités en français de 1915 à 1928* (Paris: Les Étincelles, 1929; reprint, Nancy: Presses Universitaires de Nancy, 1993) is still the standard text on French soldiers' wartime writings.

11. *La Vida de Lazarillo de Tórmes y Sus Fortunas y Adversidades* (1554), author unknown, attributed to Don Diego Hurtado de Menoza; *Histoire de Gil Blas de Santillane* (1715, 1724, 1735), by Alain René LeSage (1668–1747).

12. Something is going to happen to the valorous Turk: There were two naval bombardments of the Dardanelles before this letter was written; the first took place on February 19, the second on February 25. The landings at Gallipoli took place on April 25.

13. Ferdinand: his cousin, Ferdinand Pellissier, also known as F. P. in the letters.

14. *biffin:* footslogger; *pitou:* raw recruit; *pousse-caillou:* infantryman; *chasseur:* hunter; *chasse-bi:* hunter of gray (Germans); *vitrier:* literally, glazier—possibly a slang term for a glass-breaker or hell-raiser; *diable bleu:* blue devil (refers to the blue uniform worn by the *chasseurs à pied* and to their fierce fighting reputation).

15. Wolff Agency: popular name for the Continental Telegraphe Compagnie of Berlin, one of the largest news bureaus and financial data reporters of the day.

16. These wheeled litters were called *brouettes.*

17. spread terror among Parisians: The first German bombing of Paris using Zeppelins took place on March 22, 1915.

18. Original footnote: *Five Matters of French Romance,* by Albert Léon Guérard (London: T. Fisher Unwin).

19. Anatole France: pseudonym for Anatole François Thibaut (1844–1924), awarded the Nobel Prize for literature in 1921.

20. Marcellin Berthelot (1827–1907), Claude Bernard (1813–78), Louis Pasteur (1822–95).

21. Paul Bourget (1852–1935), Maurice Barrès (1862–1923).

22. Francois-René, vicomte de Chateaubriand (1768–1848), *Le Genie du Christianisme; ou, Beautés de la religion chrêtienne* (1802).

23. The English lost over twelve thousand soldiers killed or wounded in the battle of Neuve-Chapelle, March 10–13, 1915. Instead of the usual lengthy bombardment over several days or weeks, which would have warned the Germans and given them time to bring up reserves, the English used an intense bombardment of only thirty-five minutes, on a front approximately four thousand yards wide.

24. B. & A. expresses: Boston and Albany express trains

25. Joan of Arc was popularly considered to be a saint, although she was not formally canonized until 1920.

26. Spahis: native cavalry.

27. *réseda:* herb, also known as mignonette.

28. W. V. is probably William Vinal, former teacher or classmate at Bridgewater Normal School in Bridgewater, Massachusetts. "Dab" may be a German teacher.

29. the Colonel: Theodore Roosevelt, who served as a colonel in the Spanish-American War of 1898.

30. *Auvergnat:* person from Auvergne, in south central France, near Clermont-Ferrand.

31. *Massif Central:* high central area of France.

32. The French captured Les Eparges on February 19, 1915, after exploding four huge mines under the German positions.

33. Amherst: Amherst College, alma mater of his brother-in-law.

34. my second niece . . . her fiancé: His niece, Marie Alden Brown, was the editor's grandmother. She and her husband, Percy Mortimer Brown, had a farm in Harrington, Delaware, where the editor's father was born in 1920.

35. He refers here to the landings at Gallipoli on April 25, the second Battle of Ypres on April 22, and a third defeat not identified.

36. This is probably referring to Wilson's "America first" neutrality speech to the Associated Press in New York City on April 20.

37. Theodore: Theodore Roosevelt.

38. *Ramuntcho,* by Pierre Loti, pseudonym for Julien Viaud (1850–1923).

39. The Dutch are bombarding Dunkirk: German artillery shelled Dunkirk on April 28, 1915.

40. the seminary: Lasell Female Seminary in Auburndale, Massachusetts (now Lasell College).

41. Original footnote: "To give up guessing."

42. A German U-boat torpedoed the liner *Lusitania* on May 7, 1915, in the Irish Sea, with the loss of 1,198 lives, out of the 2,000 people on board. It caused widespread revulsion and anger against the Germans in the United States.

43. This probably refers to a speech President Wilson gave to Congress on May 10, 1915.

44. Gabriele d'Annunzio (1863–1938), Italian poet and nationalist, gave a series of speeches in May, 1915, that helped push Italy into the war.

CHAPTER 5. RESTING

1. This possibly refers to *A New England Nun,* by Mary Eleanor Wilkins Freeman (1852–1930).

2. This is a prophetic comment in view of Wilson's role at the peace negotiations after the war.

3. P-r-s-mysl: The gigantic Austrian fortress of Przemysl in the Carpathian mountains was besieged twice by the Russians. It was surrendered on May 22, 1915. The fortress was retaken June 9, 1915, by the Austrians with German assistance.

4. The Italian Army fought a whole series of battles at Isonzo in the Alps against the Austrians under terrible conditions. The attacks mentioned here took place on June 9–12.

5. mad at Bill: Kaiser Wilhelm II, popularly known as "Kaiser Bill."

6. The Russians retreated from Galicia after the retaking of Przemysl.

7. *The Oxford Book of French Verse: Thirteenth Century–Nineteenth Century,* ed. St.. John Lucas (Oxford: Clarendon Press, 1908), p. 458. The poem by Paul Verlaine (1844–96), is from *Sagesse* (1881):

> Le ciel est, par-dessus le toit,
>   Si bleu, si calme!
> Un arbre, par dessus-le toit,
>   Berce sa palme.
>
> La cloche dans le ciel qu'on voit
>   Doucement tinte.
> Un oiseau sur l'arbre qu'on voit
>   Chante sa plainte.
>
> Mon Dieu, mon Dieu, la vie est là,
>   Simple et tranquille.
> Cette paisable rumeur-là,
>   Vient de la ville.
>
> —Qu'as-tu fait, ô toi que voilà
>   Pleurant sans cesse,
> Dis, qu'as-tu fait, toit que voilà
>   De ta jeunesse?
>
> [The sky above the roof's
>   So blue, so calm.
> A branch above the roof's
>   Fanning the air.
>
> The bell up there in the sky
>   Makes little sounds.
> A bird up there in the tree
>   Sings its lament.
>
> Dear God, dear God, life's there
>   Simple and quiet,
> These soft and distant sounds
>   Come from the town.

What have you done, you standing there
In floods of tears?
Tell me what have you done
With your young life?]

Translation and editorial matter © Martin Sorrell 1999. Reprinted from
Paul Verlaine: Selected Poems, translated and with an introduction by Martin
Sorrell (Oxford: Oxford World's Classics, 1999), p. 111. Used by permission
of Oxford University Press.

8. William Jennings Bryan (1860–1925) served as U.S. secretary of state under
Wilson from March 4, 1913, to June 9, 1915; he resigned rather than sign the U.S.
diplomatic note to Germany protesting the sinking of the *Lusitania.*

9. a group: a statue or frieze.

10. our little military orgies of one hundred years ago: the Napoleonic wars.

11. how to go next to the enemies' lines and rubber: listen in to what is going on.

12. On July 2, 1915, J. Pierpont Morgan, America's biggest investment banker, was
injured when a bomb went off in a waiting room in the U.S. Senate. The bomb was set
by a man calling himself Frank Holt, later identified as a German tutor named Erich
Muenter, who committed suicide a few days later in his cell.

13. Bernhard Dernburg (1865–1937), German diplomat, wrote many articles
defending Germany's actions in the war; these are best seen in the collection *Search-
Lights on the War* (New York: Fatherland Corporation, 1915).

14. Kitchener's three million men: Horatio Herbert Kitchener (1850–1916) served
as British secretary of state for war for the first part of the war. He transformed the
British Army from a small, all-professional body into a volunteer mass army.

15. Jean Racine, *Bérénice,* ed. Robert Edouard Pellissier (New York: Oxford
University Press, 1915).

16. the 14th of July: Bastille Day, French national holiday.

17. Robert Pellissier was thirty-three years old at the time he wrote this, so he must
have felt ancient compared with soldiers in their late teens, though superior to the older
reserves and territorials who were in their forties.

18. slushy German note: Germany's second reply, on July 8, 1915, to the U.S.
diplomatic protest of the sinking of the *Lusitania.*

19. asphyxiating gases: The Germans first used poison gas on the Eastern front in
Poland against the Russians on January 31, 1915, and on the Western front against the
British at the Battle of Ypres on April 22, 1915.

20. the colonel: Theodore Roosevelt.

21. Warsaw was captured by the Germans on August 4, 1915.

22. Louvain, in Belgium, was taken by the Germans on August 28, 1914; many
buildings were burned and banks were taken over, and there were widespread reports of
hostage taking, rapes, and other atrocities.

23. the *Arabic* affair: The German submarine U-24 sank the liner *Arabic* off the south
coast of Ireland on August 19, 1915. Germany's apology, and an order on August 27 by
the Kaiser forbidding the sinking of passenger ships, prevented U.S. entry into the war.

CHAPTER 6. ST-MAIXENT

1. the midway point of life: This is a reference to Dante's *Inferno*, Canto I:

Nel mezzo del cammin di nostra vita
Mi ritrovai per una selva oscura
Chè la diritta via era smarrita.

[In the middle of the journey of our life,
I found myself in a dark wood,
For the straight way was lost.]

See Dante's *Divine Comedy: The Inferno: A Literal Prose Translation*, trans. John A. Carlyle, M.D. (London: Chapman and Hill, 1839).

2. Through the Edict of Nantes in 1598, Henry IV granted freedom of religious conscience. The Edict was rescinded in 1685 by Louis XIV and led to a massive emigration of French Protestants. The "temple" is the Protestant cathedral.

3. Jane Addams (1860–1935) had recently returned from a tour of Europe. On July 9, 1915, she gave an address at Carnegie Hall, sponsored by the Church Peace Union, at which she said that troops in Europe were given drinks before going to fight. She received widespread criticism for her remarks.

4. zouave: an Algerian soldier. Zouaves wore a very colorful, baggy uniform. Vauquois was a strategically important village overlooking Verdun, the scene of many attacks and counterattacks by both French and German forces, including the digging of mines filled with explosives that blew up the entire hilltop.

5. Constantin Theodor Dumba (1856–1915), Austrian ambassador to the United States from 1913 to 1915; Johann Heinrich, Graf von Bernstorff (1862–1939), German ambassador to the United States from 1908 to 1917. After returning to Germany when the United States declared war, Bernstorff was sent as German ambassador to Turkey.

6. Ambassador Dumba had written a letter to his government advocating that German Americans and Austrian Americans working in U.S. war plants be organized to strike and cripple munitions production. He sent this letter secretly via an American journalist, James F. J. Archibald. British authorities arrested Archibald on arrival in England, searched his stateroom, and published the letter, which made headlines in the United States. The comment about Milwaukee is perhaps referring to its large German American population.

7. hot as Tophet: an old New England saying, derived from Isaiah 30:33: "For Tophet is ordained of old; yea, for the king it is prepared; he hath made it deep and large: the pile thereof is fire and much wood; the breath of the LORD, like a stream of brimstone, doth kindle it."

8. This probably refers to the combined offensive of Artois/Loos, which began September 25, 1915.

9. To think that France worked hard to close up the Dardanelles under our dear Emperor the Small!: This probably refers to Emperor Napoleon III and France's

participation in the Crimean War. One of the goals of the war was to close the Dardanelles to the movement of Russian warships.

10. This probably refers to the "Loan of Deliverance" of $500,000,000 from the United States to France and Britain, which was finalized on October 4, 1915.

11. During the summer and fall of 1915, the Allies and the Central Powers made many diplomatic offers and military threats to the various Balkan countries to try and swing them over to their respective sides.

12. things look queer in the Balkans: Allied landings took place at Salonika on October 5, 1915; the Greek premier Venizelos resigned immediately. German troops invaded Serbia the following day, and Bulgaria invaded Serbia on October 11.

13. *croix de guerre:* French medal, created in 1915.

14. Charles Hill Grandgent (1862–1939), professor at Harvard; Sore Bone: Sorbonne University.

15. The French cabinet went through a major shake-up in late October; Millerand resigned as minister of war on October 30, 1915, to be replaced by Galliéni.

16. Greylock: Mount Greylock, 3,491 feet, in Adams, Massachusetts, is the highest point in the state.

17. bull of Bashan: Psalm 22:12: "Many bulls have compassed me: strong bulls of Bashan have beset me round."

18. How long will the Dutch blow things up: A fire on November 10, 1915, at Bethlehem Steel's munition works in South Bethlehem, Pennsylvania, was widely suspected to be due to German sabotage. Over eight hundred artillery pieces were destroyed in the fire, which caused $4,000,000 in damage. Another fire destroyed the Roebling plant in Trenton, New Jersey, which manufactured barbed wire for the Allies.

19. Ray Lyman Wilbur, dean of Stanford from 1911 to 1916, was appointed Stanford's third president in October, 1915, and served until 1943; he also served as head of the Conservation Division of the Food Division in 1917 and as secretary of the interior during the Hoover administration.

20. Too bad for the ladies of Eastern America: This probably refers to the defeat of a referendum on women's suffrage in New York in 1915.

21. French women finally won the right to vote on October 6, 1944.

22. Germany's ports were blockaded for most of the war.

23. Grape Juice Bryan: William Jennings Bryan was also a fervent campaigner for temperance.

24. This probably refers to John Albrecht Walz (1871–1954), professor of German at Harvard, who was active with the German National Alliance party in America during World War I.

25. the Pilgrim Fathers: This is a family joke, since Louise Alden, the recipient of this letter, was a direct descendant of John Alden and Priscilla Mullins, who came to Massachusetts in 1620 on the *Mayflower.*

26. he is our prize liar and exaggerator: Among the French, people from Marseilles have a reputation for stretching the truth.

27. Bundy: Robert Pellissier's family nickname. "Tante Adeleline" is his sister, "A——" in the letters, professor at Smith College and the original collector of the letters; "Peg" and "Marie" are sisters of Louise.

28. Marie Alden, the editor's grandmother, a Vassar graduate, had recently married Percy Mortimer Brown and moved with him to a farm in Harrington, Delaware. Neither one of them knew the first thing about farming!

29. shape of the nose: possibly a reference to anti-Semitism in the French Army.

30. Mort: Percy Mortimer Brown, husband of Marie Alden; the Billings family: her new in-laws.

31. Franz von Papen and Karl Boy-Ed, the German naval and military attachés in Washington, were expelled on December 5, 1915.

32. Mediaeval Jacques: an average French person in the Middle Ages; "Jacques Bonhomme," similar to the American John Doe or the British John Bull.

33. boats leave in bunches: This comment is puzzling, since the formal convoy system was not put in place until the late spring of 1917.

34. Allen Boyden, son of the principal at Bridgewater Normal School, where Robert Pellissier had been a student.

35. Wilhelmstrasse: the seat of the German government in Berlin. The German Foreign Ministry was located there.

36. Hugo Munsterberg (1863–1916), professor of psychology at Harvard, wrote many articles and gave speeches promoting German American relations and endorsing Germany's position in the war; he also founded and directed the Amerika Institut, a German government-sponsored organization to influence public opinion.

37. Albert Leon Guérard (1880–1959), colleague and contemporary of Pellissier's at Stanford.

38. The remains of the Serbian army began to retreat into Albania on November 21, 1915.

39. Monastir: city in southern Serbia, captured by the Allies in November, 1916.

CHAPTER 7. ALSACE

1. Evidently the schoolhouse was in formerly German territory, and he was reading German schoolbooks that praised the Kaiser.

2. too famous kopf: Hartmannweilerskopf.

3. The Turks had attempted to capture the Suez Canal nearly a year earlier, on February 3, 1915. Defense of the canal was a key part of British policy in the Middle East. This comment is an example of Robert Pellissier's dry sense of humor. The Suez Canal would certainly have been warmer than the Vosges in January!

4. "The Winter's War," by a British Captain, *Atlantic Monthly* 116, Nov., 1916, pp. 701–706.

5. This probably refers to chapter 4 in *Considerations on the Causes of the Greatness of the Romans and Their Decline*, by Charles le Secondat, baron de Montesquieu (1689–1755).

6. The ambulances were run by Section III of the American Field Service. For a very interesting survey of letters and other materials, see *Friends of France, 1914–1917: A History of the American Field Service in France* (Boston and New York: Houghton Mifflin Co., 1920).

7. The man killed was possibly Richard Hill of Ann Arbor, Michigan (Dartmouth 1915), who was driving ambulance 3153 and was killed by a shell on December 24, 1915.

8. "M——" in this case is his niece, Marie Alden Brown, the editor's grandmother, who was expecting the birth of her first child, Louise Brown, born in 1917. The "young Virginian" refers to his great-niece Marie Alden Walker, born in July, 1916, in Orange, Virginia, to his other niece, Marguerite Alden Walker.

9. chevaux de frise: literally "hair curlers"; iron stakes or sawhorses used to support coils of barbed wire.

10. The German attack on Verdun started February 21, 1916. Fort Douaumont fell on February 25.

11. This was originally published as *Au-dessus de la Mêlée* in the *Journal de Géneve* (Sept. 15, 1915).

12. The Mexican Pancho Villa crossed the U.S.–Mexico border on March 9, 1916, and attacked army barracks in Columbus, New Mexico.

13. the best of worlds: a reference to Voltaire (1694–1778), from *Candide* (1759), chapter 1: "All is for the best in the best of possible worlds."

14. Louis Felix François Franchet d'Esperey (1856–1942), French general, commanded France's Fifth Army in 1914 and later commanded Army Group East (1916), Army Group North (1917), and the French attack on Bulgaria (1918). He was made marshal of France in 1922.

15. The "bullet" may have been an artillery shell or heavy machine-gun bullet rather than one from a rifle.

16. Loos: This is most likely an error in the original editing, since this letter is dated April 24, 1915, and the battle of Loos took place later that year (September 15–October 8). A more likely battle would be the second Battle of Ypres, which lasted from April 22 to May 23. It included the first use of poison gas by the Germans on the Western Front. The Williston archives report that William Fast Henderson (1908) of the Twenty-Eighth Canadian Highlanders was killed at Ypres on April 24.

17. Galliéni died on May 27, 1916.

18. This probably refers to J. Mander, "The Diary of Evolution," *New Republic* 6, Mar. 25, 1916, pp. 211–12.

19. gabions: large baskets or containers without a bottom, filled with earth to make fortifications.

CHAPTER 8. MUNSTER/COLMAR

1. This probably refers to the Battle of Jutland on May 31, 1916. Fourteen ships were sunk on either side. Both the English and the Germans claimed a major victory.

2. Original footnote: A Spaniard in California.

3. Pellissier probably had in mind Washington's "Farewell Address" to Congress, September 19, 1796, which was a standard history lesson in U.S. schools for many years. The relevant passage is: "Europe has a set of primary interests, which have to us none, or a very remote relation. Hence she must be engaged in frequent controversies, the causes of which are essentially foreign to our concerns. Hence therefore it must be unwise in us to implicate ourselves, by artificial ties, in the ordinary vicissitudes of her politics, or the ordinary combinations and collusions of her friendships, or enmities."

4. your aeroplane *esquadrille:* The Esquadrille Américaine, squadron 124 of American pilots (later the famous Lafayette Esquadrille), was formed in April, 1916.

5. Biblical house: Matthew 7:26–27: "Every one that heareth these sayings of mine, and doeth them not, shall be likened unto a foolish man, which built his house upon the sand: And the rain descended, and the floods came, and the winds blew, and beat upon that house; and it fell: and great was the fall of it."

6. *yaw yaw* and *nicks nicks: ja* and *nichts;* German for "yes" and "no."

7. Point Loma, California, was for many years the headquarters of the Theosophical Society.

8. Matthew 6:34: "Take therefore no thought for the morrow: for the morrow shall take thought for the things of itself. Sufficient unto the day is the evil thereof."

CHAPTER 9. SOMME

1. squash bug life of the purest Beverly type: probably a reference to summer tourists at the seaside in Beverly, Massachusetts, north of Boston.

2. This diary entry is a little confusing. Apparently one of Robert Pellissier's squad mates was caught stealing, judged guilty by an officer or by a field court-martial, and executed by the roadside. The liaison, who had stolen a chicken undetected, got off scot-free, as did the cook.

3. Spain was officially neutral throughout the war but lost many ships to German submarines. Germany promised to replace them after the war.

4. S.P. 190: the military sector where Pellissier was reassigned.

5. Camille Saint-Saëns (1835–1921), along with other French composers, artists, and intellectuals, gave his opinion about Wagner in an article in *La Renaissance,* which was later reported in the *New York Times,* Feb. 14, 1916, p. 9.

6. Original footnote: Orphelinat des Armées.

7. Original footnote: Renée Halfer. Her father died of typhus in the prison camp in Cassel.

APPENDIX A

1. *Dulce et decorum est pro patria mori:* It is sweet and honorable to die for one's country (Horace, *Odes,* Book 3, II:13).

2. Waldenses: followers of Peter Waldo, also known as the "poor men of Lyons." The movement, which in many ways anticipated the Protestant Reformation, began about 1173 and persisted despite the excommunication of Waldo in 1184.

3. John 4:24: "God is a Spirit: and they that worship him must worship him in spirit and in truth."

4. Blaise Pascal (1623–63), philosopher, mathematician, and scientist; Jules Michelet (1797–1874), historian; Alfred de Musset (1810–57), poet, playwright, and novelist; Alfred, comte de Vigny (1797–1863), poet and playwright; Victor Hugo (1802–85), writer.

5. Alfred de Musset, *La Nuit de mai* (1835).

6. Alfred, Comte de Vigny, *Le Cor* (1825).

7. one of his sisters: probably Adeline Pellissier herself.

8. The professor of botany at Wellesley was probably Clara Cummings (1855–1906), who summered in Franconia Notch.

9. Mr. A——: Edmund Kimball Alden (1858–1938), who taught at Packer Collegiate Institute in New York.

10. his cousin, G. P.: Georges Pellissier (1852–1918), literary critic.

11. Émile Erckmann and Alexandre Chatrian, *Madame Thérèse; or, the Volunteers of '92* (New York: Scribner's Sons, 1868).

INDEX

ISBN 1-58544-210-0